HEDGE OF THORNS

KNOCKALOE CAMP 1915-1919

PAT KELLY

Originally Published by The Manx Experience
10 Tromode Close, Douglas, Isle of Man
Printed by The Alden Press, Oxford

First published in Australia 2019
This edition published 2019
Copyright © Pat Kelly 2019
Cover design, typesetting: WorkingType (www.workingtype.com.au)

The right of Pat Kelly to be identified as the Author of the Work has been asserted in accordance with the Copyright, Designs and Patents Act 1988.

The Author of this book accepts all responsibility for the contents and absolves any other person or persons involved in its production from any responsibility or liability where the contents are concerned.

All rights reserved. No part of this publication may be reproduced, stored in a retrieval system, or transmitted, in any form or by any means without the prior written permission of the publisher, nor be otherwise circulated in any form of binding or cover other than that in which it is published and without a similar condition being imposed on the subsequent purchaser.

Kelly, Pat
Hedge of Thorns
ISBN: 978-0-6486817-6-2
pp308

ABOUT THE AUTHOR

The author was born in Scotland a year before World War II started, but swears she didn't cause it ...

In January 1968 she arrived in Australia as a 'Ten Pound Tourist' with her, then, husband and four children.

After the breakup of her marriage after twenty-five years the author was contacted by a man named Mike Kelly, whom she had known in her teens and had had no contact with for nearly thirty years. Mike's marriage having broken up around the same time as the author's. On learning she was 'on the loose', he obtained her phone number by courtesy of his mother — International telephone enquiries — and the author's mother, so rang to see if she was okay.

One thing led to another, they were married in 1988 and returned to the Isle of Man to start a new life. On Mike's retirement, five years later, they followed the summers and spent half their lives in Australia and the other half in the Isle of Man.

In their months on the island each year, they ran a daffodil and plant nursery and were well known throughout the island for their roadside stall, where they sold their daffodils and plants.

As age caught up with them, they realised it was time to settle somewhere permanently. Being the warmer country, Australia won, and they moved there in 2014, to live in a retirement village in Lakes Entrance — one of the prettiest spots in Australia.

This, they both feel, will suit them until they climb in their boxes (but not for a long time yet) and move on to higher places.

BY THE SAME AUTHOR

Shadow of the Wheel

The mighty water-wheel at Laxey mines in the Isle of Man has been set in motion. In its great shadow, Sarah and Patrick have fallen in love. It is a love that must be kept secret, for Patrick is Irish. Sarah's mother — Judith — has lost her mind and blames an Irishman for her husband being imprisoned 'across the water' in Liverpool, where she can never visit him.

The two young lovers desperately desire to wed and be together, but Judith's increasing madness, which began when she lost some of her childher to a savage disease and deepened on her husband's incarceration, proved too strong a pull.

Sarah's deep loyalty to her mother also stands between the lovers, indeed life itself thwarts their every effort to find a way toward their happiness.

Patrick's friend — Robert — is going to Australia to make his fortune mining for gold and has asked Patrick to accompany him. With no other option and seemingly with the cards stacked against them, Patrick and Sarah are both heartbroken.

Knowing that her mother will never recover from her illness and will always need her support, Sarah tells Patrick he must go with Robert to make a life for himself without her, and to forget her, and the love they share.

Smugglers Urchins

Smugglers Urchins is a tale of hardship, suffering, courage and, most of all, love. It is the story of two young children, born into the poverty-stricken years of the Isle of Man when drunkenness and smuggling were rife. Two children who were imprisoned for the heinous crime of stealing a scrap food to keep themselves alive.

Daniel, worldly-wise, who has had to fend for himself for most of his ten years. Unwanted from birth, abandoned and unloved, he has had the strength to develop into a caring young man, mature for his age.

Eight-year-old Isabella, who had been forced to flee from home to escape being sold into prostitution by a depraved mother. Small for her age, She is frail and unable to look after herself.

Released from jail in Castle rushen in midwinter, with no home to go to, the children team up in a heart rending battle for survival. As they slither rapidly into further trouble and disaster looms, it is only their involvement with a smuggling family that save them from deportation to the Americas.

This book is dedicated to the memory of my dearest friend, my late mother-in-law, Lou Kelly, whose story this is.

ACKNOWLEDGEMENTS

I would like to thank the late, and very kind, Frank Quayle for giving me several interesting pictures of Patrick and the camp at Knockaloe, when I was writing this book very many years ago.

Also, the Manx Museum for putting up with me hanging around asking endless questions. I was a complete newcomer to research and didn't really know what I was doing. The staff showed me great patience and were kind enough to allow me to use several terrific photographs which added greatly to the book.

To my beloved Lou Kelly for trusting me enough to tell me her wonderful story and to her son, Mike, my husband, for all the assistance he so lovingly gave me.

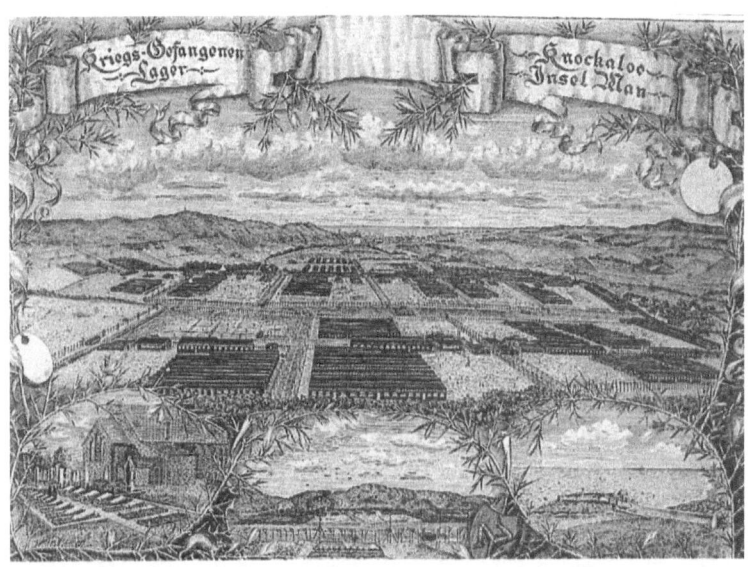

Pen drawing of the camp at Knockaloe that was done by one of the internees and given to Voirrey (Lou Kelly). It still hangs on the author's wall.

Patrick village in 1915 before the camp was built on the fields of Knockaloe farm on the left of the picture. The house at right centre, believed to be the old vicarage, was where Voirrey was brought up. Washing can be seen drying on the thorn bushes and it was one of Voirrey's duties to shake out the earwigs before bringing it in. (picture supplied by Frank Quayle)

A view of Peel Harbour in the early part of the twentieth century, showing one of the herring carts.
(picture supplied by Manx National Heritage)

Voirrey (Lou Kelly) in the arms of her mother, Sage Eleanor Quirk at her Christening. Sage Eleanor was one of eleven children of the Moore family whose connections with Patrick went back many generations.

In those days Patrick had its own pub which was run by Josiah Clarke, licensed victualler. Known to the locals as 'The Manchester' it is now a private dwelling at the Junction of the Patrick Road with the Peel to Dalby Road. (Picture supplied by Frank Quayle)

An early photograph showing the first compounds, each of which was self-contained and could accommodate up to 1000 men. (Picture supplied by Manx National Heritage)

One of the camp orchestras posing in front of the wooden accommodation huts. (picture supplied by Manx National Heritage)

Two drawings by an internee showing one of the compounds and sleeping accommodation in one of the huts. (Picture supplied by Frank Quayle)

Prisoners queueing for rations outside one of the cookhouses.
(Picture supplied by Manx National Heritage)

The camp bakery produced thousands of loaves each day.
(Picture supplied by Manx National Heritage)

One of the huts in each of the compounds was used as a recreation room for the playing of draughts, chess etc.
(Picture by Manx National Heritage)

The 'Ben-my-Chree', the pride of the Steam Packet fleet, was converted to carry seaplanes, one of which torpedo and sank a Turkish ship in August 1915. It was the first successful engagement of its kind in naval history. Two years later the 'Ben' was sunk by Turkish guns positioned on the island of Castellorizio. It was a sad loss to the Manx, but fortunately, all 250 crew, including Voirrey's uncle Edward, were able to reach the safety of the shore. (Picture supplied by Manx National Heritage)

The entrance to Knockaloe camp showing 'Caledonia' of the Isle of Man Railway, which hauled stores and coal along the one and a half mile purpose-built line from Peel.
(Picture supplied by Manx National Heritage)

News in 1917 that the paddle steamer 'Mona's Queen' had rammed and sunk a U boat in the English Channel brought great rejoicing to those back home on the island. The 'Mona's Queen' was employed throughout the war ferrying troops to and from France.
(Picture supplied by Manx National Heritage)

H compound had its own craft room where many fine pieces of
artwork were produced, some of which still survive. A speciality
was carving in bone, supplied from the kitchen
(Picture supplied by Manx National Heritage)

Saint Patrick's Churchyard, showing some of the graves in which
over 200 of the prisoners were buried during the war years. Later,
the bodies were removed, many being returned to their homelands.
(picture supplied by Frank Quayle)

On the left of this photograph is Lou (Voirrey) with her best friend, Nan Lace (nee Bridson) while attending Hereford College in 1927. They had both attended the Eastern Secondary School in Park Road, Douglas.

INTRODUCTION

Situated in the northern Irish Sea is an idyllic little paradise called the Isle of Man. With a length of 33 miles and a breadth of less than 12, it covers an area of roughly 227 square miles. At the outbreak of the 'Great War' in August 1914 the population of the island was only 46,000.

Although self-governed, and determinately independent of the United Kingdom, during the course of the Great War, 8261 Manxmen and women answered Lord Kitchener's famous 'Call to Arms'. This represented over a sixth of the Island's entire population and 82.3 per cent of its males of military age.

By the time 'the War to end all Wars' was over, 1165 Manxman had lost their lives and 1169 had been either injured or taken prisoner.

Once war has been declared the British government was faced with the problem of interning 'enemy aliens'. These were people residing in the British Isles some of them since childhood but whose country of origin was at war with Britain. It took very little time for British officialdom to decide the Isle of man would make the perfect, secure location.

Only days after the declaration of war a deputation from the Home Office in London arrived on the island to discuss the possibility of immediately housing many thousands of alien internees.

A site which quickly presented itself was Cunningham's Holiday Camp for young men in Douglas. Most of the young holidaymakers and many of the staff had vacated it to volunteer to fight for their country, so it stood conveniently empty.

With amazing speed, barbed wire fences and powerful electric lights were erected around the perimeter to secure the camp. On the 22nd September, only 7 weeks after the declaration of war, the first 200 prisoners took up residence.

By mid-November 1914 the camp held over 3300 prisoners, was vastly overcrowded and trouble was brewing. On the 19th day of the month five prisoners were shot dead during a riot over poor, foul food and bad living conditions.

The riot and the great number of prisoners, mainly Germans, Austrians and Turks, continually arriving on the island made it imperative that a site should be found, as quickly as possible, for a second internment camp. Another deputation arrived from the Home Office and decided that a large farm, Knockaloe, on the west coast of the island would be most suitable. This farm, nestled alongside the tiny village of Patrick, was chosen because of its proximity to the city of Peel, a busy herring fishing port. Peel's good-sized harbour was to be very convenient for the delivery by sea of freight and essential supplies for the camp.

Later a railway line was laid from the camp to join the Douglas to Peel line, making deliveries of supplies in prisoners even more easy.

Initially, it was intended the camp at Knockaloe should house 5000 prisoners, but this number was soon exceeded and by the time the war was over there were over 24,000 men in the camp, plus the guards and their families.

Over 200 prisoners died at the Knockaloe camp and were buried in Patrick churchyard.

After the war only 16% of the prisoners were repatriated, the

INTRODUCTION

rest being returned to their country of origin. Many of these men had left these countries as small children, Some had been born in Britain and many had British wives who refused to accompany them to strange, alien lands. So marriages and families were destroyed.

The Poignant story that follows is a factual account of the way of the Great War and the internment camp at Knockaloe affected one sensitive young resident of Patrick and her family. It is a heartwarming tale of love and happiness, hardship, fear and heartbreak. Every story is true, told to me in detail by that same little girl, many years later, when she was in her 80s.

CHAPTER 1

Voirrey excitedly clinked the pennies in her pinafore pocket.

It had been a good day — the best she could remember. Five charabancs had come that day, filled with holiday-makers to the Isle of Man from 'across' the Irish Sea.

With animal instinct, the children seemed to sense when one of these horse-drawn roundabouts was near. Like a swarm of locusts, they gathered, waiting excitedly. Eldest of the group, Stanley Clucas, started running toward the corner and, as one, the rest of the mob set off on his heels.

'I heard it first!' Stanley shouted as the first of the huge Clydesdales appeared around the corner.

The children descended on the charabanc filled with holidaymakers, surrounding it, jostling for position, hands outstretched as they smiled hopefully at the passengers. As they so often did, the folks on board, mainly from Lancashire, seeing the shabby, poor children, threw out a few pennies.

Bodies merged into a noisy heap, arms and legs flying, to eventually divide out into separate beings. Some were smiling and triumphant, others bloodied and tearful.

Voirrey picked herself up from the bottom of the heap. 'You hit me!' she accused Stanley.

· CHAPTER 1 ·

'Sorry! Didn't know! Didn't mean to! You shouldn't ha' got in the way.'

'"Twas your elbow!' Voirrey drew her sleeve across her mouth to wipe away the river of blood from her nose. 'I got another penny though!'

Stanley shrugged. 'I don't care. I got three already!'

Voirrey glanced into her pocket. Better not tell him she had four! Good to know she could beat big Stanley at his favourite game! Spitting out the blood that was creeping into the corner of her mouth, she tenderly caressed the four pennies. Think of the sweets she would be able to buy! Settling to wait for the next charabanc, listening for the metallic clink of hooves, she eagerly watched the corner. Before another arrived, she saw Edward trudging wearily around the bend.

Heart leaping, blonde curls flying, boots clattering on the stony lane, she raced to greet him. Launching herself at him, almost bowling him over, she cried, 'Uncle Edward! You're home! I didn't know you was comin' home today! I'm glad! I've missed you!'

Edward grabbed her up in his arms and swung her around, high above the road.

Pressing her face against his coarse, greasy gansey, she wrinkled her nose. 'You smell o' fish!' she announced in disgust.

Edward laughed, ruffling her curls as he gently unlocked her thin little arms. 'Well, I *am* a fisherman, you know!'

Seeing the smeared blood, his face softened, his grey eyes concerned. Gently cupping her face in his hands, he asked, 'Whatever has happened to you?'

'We was catching pennies and Stanley Clucas banged me wi' his elbow.' Seeing Edward's sudden anger, she added hastily, 'It was an accident! He didn't mean it!'

Edward shook his head and dumped her back on her feet. 'What a tomboy!' he muttered.

Voirrey clung tightly to his hand, scared to let go lest he vanished again. Reaching the gate she did finally release her hold of him and broke into a run, bursting through the front door shouting excitedly, 'Mammy! Granny! Look who's here!'

A scuffling from the kitchen brought two women to the doorway. 'Quiet, child!' the older one said disapprovingly. 'Young ladies *don't run!*'

'Or shout!' the younger one added. 'Whatever is all the excitement about? And what *has* happened to your face?'

'Oh, but Mammy, Granny!'

At that moment Edward appeared behind Voirrey and the two women started to fuss. A cup of thick, black tea was poured from the pot which stood, simmering constantly, on the hob.

'Was the fishin' good, Uncle Edward? Has all the fleet come in? Tell about it all. Did you have any storms?' Voirrey rattled out a constant stream of questions all afternoon. Excited at having her favourite uncle home so unexpectedly, she hardly gave him time to reply.

Later, hearing the rattle of her father's bike on the path, Voirrey rushed outside. 'Daddy! Daddy, Uncle Edward's home!' she blurted, grabbing her father's hand to drag him indoors.

'Priddas an' herrin' for tea,' Granny announced, lifting the pot from the hob. 'If I'd known in time you was comin' home, Edward, I'd ha' made broth instead.'

Edward smiled. 'Herrin' is fine, Mammy.'

Picking a piece of the herring and potato, Voirrey popped it in her mouth, sucking the juice from her fingers. *I wish it had been broth*, she thought, licking her lips at the memory of her grandmother's thick, Manx broth.

· CHAPTER 1 ·

Hearing her father ask, 'Is the whole fleet home?' Voirrey's thoughts focused on the conversation around the table.

'No, John, just a few of us came in this mornin.'

'Is the fishin' good?' Her grandfather picked up the questioning. 'When do you go back out?'

'Yes, the fishin's good, but I'm not goin' out again. I will be leavin' on Sunday, though!' Edward scanned the faces around the table, awaiting a reaction.

'Not goin' fishin'? Where are you goin' then?' Granny was the first to break the silence.

'I'm goin' in the Royal Navy! When we docked at Peel this mornin' there were a notice callin' reservists to enlist in case the war comes.'

There was a momentary hush, broken only by the ponderous ticking of the grandfather clock, carrying through from the parlour.

'The Royal Navy? The war?' John questioned.

'Aye.' Edward nodded excitedly.

'Has the war started? Are you really goin'?' Margaret looked shaken.

'No. It's not come yet, but they think it soon will. I signed this mornin' an' we leave on Sunday.'

'We?'

'Yes, Daa, many of the reservists have signed.'

Suddenly there was babble of noise as everyone spoke at once. Voirrey, looking from one face to another, could not make any sense of it.

John slapped Edward's back enthusiastically. 'The Royal Navy, indeed! Great! Great!' He cried loudly.

Daa shook his hand, his face fair glowing. 'I'm proud o' you, son. Very proud! I wish I was young enough to be goin' wi' you.'

Even Margaret seemed excited, hugging her brother tightly, laughing and chattering with the men.

'What about the fishin'? How will we manage without your money? Sunday is only three days away!' All eyes turned on Eleanor, who was flushed, bristling with anger.

'The country is more important than the fishin'. Jack says he'll get some young lad to help out to the season's end. If there is a war we'll have the Germans well beaten before next season.'

'The country? What country? England's not *our* country!' Eleanor snapped.

'King George is our king too! England is *his* country. I *am* goin' an' there's nothing you can say will stop me!' Edward turned defiant eyes on his mother.

There was to be no more argument. Edward had his mind made up and he was well endowed with typical Manx stubbornness.

Voirrey curled on her grandfather's lap after tea, snuggling close as he smoked his pipe. 'Daa — what is war?'

Henry drew his head back, smiling down at her. 'Bless you, child,' he said gently, 'you don't need to know that. You're too young to understand about war.'

'I'm not, Daa! I'm nearly ten!' Voirrey replied vehemently, sitting up straight. 'I want to know! Why is Uncle Edward going away? When will he be back?'

'I don't know a lot about it, lass. The Germans ha' bin threatenin' the countries round about an' it looks as though they're all goin' to fight. That is all war is — a big fight!'

'Is England near Germany, then?'

'No, but if they get through France they will only be across the water from England. About as close as Liverpool is to our Island. There likely won't be a war, but if there is we shall have them defeated and silenced in just months.'

· CHAPTER 1 ·

'Then Uncle Edward will come home?'

'Yes. Then Edward will return.'

Satisfied, Voirrey left the parlour, sneaking out of the house and up into the village.

'My Uncle Edward's goin' in the Royal Navy to fight the Germans when the war comes,' she proudly boasted. 'He's goin' to be a hero.'

Stanley Clucas, on the corner with a group of the older village children, looked down his nose disdainfully. Shrugging nonchalantly he said, 'Well if the war does come — I'm joinin' the army!'

The other children sniggered derisively.

'Bet you won't! You'd be too scared!' Voirrey sniped, before running off home.

'Would not!' Stanley's angry word followed her.

Later the three men went off to the pub to celebrate Edward's enlistment.

Voirrey, lying awake, heard them, very late, whispering and trying to subdue laughter as they tiptoed upstairs.

The following days flew by in a plethora of excitement. So many villagers called to shake Edward's hand that Voirrey, in the end, was certain every soul in Patrick had passed through their door.

'I wish all these people would stop comin', Mammy!' she confessed to Margaret. 'I have had no time to be with Uncle Edward since he came home from the fishin'.'

'There will be plenty of time after the war, child,' Margaret comforted.

Voirrey was skipping near the gate on Saturday afternoon when Joseph Callow came to call. 'Is your Uncle Edward home?' he asked.

'Aye. I'll fetch him.' Dropping her skipping-rope, she ran indoors. 'Uncle Edward, Mr Callow's here.'

'Joseph Callow? The herrin' man?'

'He says he wants you.'

With a puzzled shrug, Edward stepped outside. 'Afternoon Joseph.'

'Edward.' Joseph nodded respectfully. 'Heard you was goin' to the war.'

'Aye. If there is one.'

'Goin' t'morra?'

Edward nodded.

'On the railway?'

'Aye. We'll get the train to Douglas from St. John's.'

'Family all goin' too, are they?'

Edward nodded. 'They want to come to the harbour to see me off, then they'll have a day in town .'

'I come to say I'll gi' you all a ride to the station in the cart.'

Voirrey, standing beside Edward, screwed her face up and crying, 'Oh — the cart stinks o' rotten herrin'! I don't want to ride in that!'

Edward turned on her. 'Mind your manners, girl!' Then to the crestfallen herring man, 'Thank you, Joseph, we would all appreciate a ride.'

Joseph brightened instantly. 'I'll see you in the mornin' then, lad. 'Tis a brave adventure you're takin'. Were it not for my bad leg I'd go wi' you.' So saying, he turned and limped, more heavily than usual, off toward his cart.

Edward strolled toward the kitchen, Voirrey close on his tail. Chuckling, he said, 'Poor Joseph was fair draggin' his leg when he left. What happened to it, does anyone know?'

'I heard a horse kicked him an' broke it, but that was afore

• CHAPTER 1 •

he came to these parts,' Henry said. Laughing, he added, 'He only limps when he remembers.'

Sunday dawned, overcast, but dry. Voirrey's waking thought was of her uncle and the trip to Douglas. Sundays, normally, were taken up with Sunday school in the morning, followed by church with her mother, grandmother and whichever of the menfolk could be persuaded to accompany them. After dinner, it was back to Sunday school, then the second church service for the day. By the time tea was finished it was almost bed-time and the day was gone. It was all really quite boring and sometimes Voirrey felt it must be much more fun to be a sinner.

'Take the cows up Barnell, to pasture in the lhergy, as soon as you finish,' John said, as she sat down for breakfast.

'Oh, Daddy, must I?' Voirrey gazed up at him, her eyes pleading. Eleanor glared across the table, dividing the look between her son-in-law and his daughter.

'They must be put to the meadow,' John instructed quietly. Voirrey knew better than to argue further. It had been her job, come hail, sleet or shine for years now.

Once she had eaten, she jumped from the table and was halfway to the door when her grandmother caught the shoulder of her pinafore. 'Did you not forget something child?' she demanded sternly.

'Yes,' Voirrey whispered, nodding.

'Back to the table then!'

The girl crept back shamefacedly, settling gingerly on the edge of her chair. 'Please, may I leave the table?' she asked meekly.

John nodded and winked.

Voirrey left hurriedly, closing the door a little too noisily. Opening the cattle-shed door, she chased the three cows outside.

'C'mon, Dog!' she said to the eagerly waiting collie.

The animals seemed particularly tardy that morning, desiring to nibble every blade of grass along the roadside. 'Make them go faster, Dog,' Voirrey pleaded. 'I want to get back an' spend some time wi' Uncle Edward before it's time for him to leave.'

The dog, ever eager to please, gently nipped Brownie's heel. Satisfied with the result, he repeated it with Blackie and Whitey, who retaliated by kicking him and cutting his lip. While she continued to graze, the other two trotted up the road, with Dog bounding happily in pursuit.

Exasperated, Voirrey picked up a stick, giving Whitey a sharp, stinging slap on the rump. The cow turned to look, in hurt amazement then, seeing the stick raised again, bolted after her stablemates and the dog.

Voirrey, overjoyed at the pace she had activated, dropped the stick, picked up her skirts and raced after the four animals.

The mile journey to Barnell lhergy and back was made in too short a time that morning. As the girl and dog exploded, gasping for breath, through the door into the kitchen, Eleanor swung around, startled, from the table.

'Whatever are you thinking of, child? Young ladies *don't run*! Get that dog out o' here! You surely can not have taken the cows all the way to the lhergy so quickly?'

Voirrey shoo-ed the dog from the kitchen. 'The cows *are* in the field, Granny.'

'I hope you didn't make them run?'

'No! Well — that is — !'

Eleanor glared suspiciously.

· CHAPTER 1 ·

'Something startled them an' they bolted. Dog an' I had to run to keep up!' Voirrey lied.

Eleanor snorted. 'Startled is it? No doubt your dog an' your stick! Well, I hope you haven't put them off milkin'. Here, butter this bread an' I'll make some scallion an' cress butties for your uncle for on the steamer.'

Voirey took the butter crock from the larder, spread it on the thick slices of bonnag, then slipped into the parlour to snuggle onto Edward's lap.

'I'll miss you, young 'un!' Tightening his arms around her, he kissed her forehead.

Oh — and how Voirrey would miss him! He had been, always, her best friend and oft' times fellow conspirator. Yes, life would be so empty without him, as it always was when he was away at the fishing.

Beside the chair lay Edward's battered, fishy-smelling, canvas bag, into which he had tossed his few bits of clothing that morning. He had confessed to Voirrey that he found it a little frightening, packing to go with — how many — probably hundreds of men, mostly strangers. Liverpool was all right, he said, he had been there before, but from there they had to go by train to a place called Devonport to be trained for the Royal Navy.

Where then? What would happen after that? Time would tell. Undoubtedly it was an exciting adventure.

One by one, as it came near time to leave, the villagers arrived to say farewell. The parlour filled and people overflowed into the kitchen, all talking loudly, all at once and all laughing too loudly. All the while, Voirrey clung firmly to Edward's arm. There would be time enough to let go, she thought, when he had to board the steamer.

'I have a word to say!' A commanding voice boomed above the

hubbub. Voirrey looked up, to see Caesar Quine, the policeman, framed in the doorway.

Slowly a silence descended on the gathering. 'Say your piece, Caesar,' Henry invited.

'I have just received word,' the policeman said solemnly, 'that the Germans declared war on Russia yesterday, the 1st of August. It seems almost certain, now, that Britain will be at war quite soon!'

For a long while, the cottage seemed in the grip of stunned silence. Then suddenly there was a babble of excited sound, rising rapidly to a noisy crescendo.

Voirrey felt her heart about to break and bit hard into her lip to stop it trembling.

CHAPTER 2

Waiting afterwards for Joseph Callow to arrive, Voirrey could sense a new tension in the gathering. Voices were quieter, there were long, awful, strained silences, then everyone would talk together.

'Herrin'! Get your fresh herrin'!' came the sudden cry from outside.

Relieved and with the tension broken, Edward jumped, laughing, to his feet. 'Here's Joseph now. Fresh herrin' indeed!'

Laughing, everyone spilled out into the front garden.

Spying Joseph, dressed more smartly than she had ever seen him, Voirrey paused then ran up the path. 'Is that really you Mr Callow? And whatever have you done with Ned?' This last as she spotted the horse with grubby, tattered ribbons tangled in his mane.

Joseph straightened his skinny little body to its full height, puffing his chest proudly. 'Had to do things right, lass. Gotta give young Edward a good send-off. I washed Ned las' night. Give him a good brush up this mornin' I did. Even borrowed a necktie — see!' He self-consciously flicked the end of the ragged, stained tie wound untidily around his scrawny neck. 'Even spent half the night scrubbin' the cart so it wouldn't smell o' the herrin'!' Joseph glared meaningfully at Voirrey, who giggled and blushed.

Edward, remembering his smelly bag, spluttered, suppressing laughter.

'You might well have done wi' a shave too!' Eleanor interjected tartly.

Joseph deflated like a pricked balloon. Head hanging, he shuffled his feet, studying the shabby, unpolished boots. 'Sorry, Missus. Didn't have 'nuff time.'

Edward climbed on the front of the cart with Joseph, while the other four grown-ups crowded into the back.

'May I sit by you, Uncle Edward?' Voirrey pleaded.

With a smile and a nod, Edward leant to lift her bodily. Contented, she squeezed between the two men, pressing hard against Edward.

Joseph sat, tall and proud, driving his little cart through the village of Patrick. Every man, woman and child, it seemed to Voirrey, lined the roadside to cheer them on their way.

The train, when it arrived at St John's, was already crowded, with standing room only.

'Perhaps we should have gone to Peel,' Margaret said, surveying the multitude waiting to board.

With difficulty, they pushed their way into the carriage, crowding the earlier occupants to the other side. Two young men stood to give their seats to Margaret and Eleanor, while Voirrey, declining to sit on her mother's lap, clung tightly to Edward in the swaying train.

'Oh, Mammy, look at all these people!' Voirrey was wide-eyed as she alighted in Douglas. The whole town seemed a seething mass of bodies.

'I have heard,' Henry declared, 'That this summer there are more visitors to the island than ever before and all the boarding houses are completely filled!'

'They must all be at this end of town, then,' said Edward

CHAPTER 2

grimly. 'Hold tight, girlie, else you'll get lost!' He thrust his way through the crowd with Voirrey clinging desperately to his large hand.

A barrier was across the harbour and a policeman halted them there. Edward showed his papers and they were all permitted onto the dock.

Voirrey clung to Edward with both hands, her fingers so tightly intertwined with his that her knuckles gleamed white. Gazing around distractedly, she was awed by the noise, the babble of conversation. Mothers, fathers, sisters and brothers, children, huddled together in a variety of moods and postures.

There was a strange atmosphere. An uncanny mixture of excitement, fear, happiness and misery. Wide-eyed, Voirrey studied the milling throng. There were all sorts, mostly poor, shabbily dressed village people like herself. But there were also a few more smartly dressed.

Peering through a break in the crowd, Voirrey could see a huge queue of people, brightly dressed in their best holiday clothes, waiting to board the steamer. It seemed that all the visitors wished to leave the Island.

The huge ship towered over them. To see the very top of its bulk, Voirrey had to tilt her head right back, almost overbalancing. 'What a big boat!' she whispered, her voice unheard amongst the surrounding cacophony. 'At Peel Harbour, you have to look *down* into the boats.'

Suddenly the fishing boats she had always thought large shrank into insignificance.

In too short a time Edward was called to join a group of young men a small distance away. After cordial handshakes with Henry and John, a quick kiss for his mother and sister, Edward bent to pick Voirrey up, holding her close.

'Think of me, little one, pray for me always an' stay happy.

The war will be over very soon, then I'll be home again.' Placing her gently to the ground, he ruffled her fair curls, then with a quick smile, he was gone.

'Edward!' A man among the recruits called and Edward, his face lighting with a smile, waved and joined him.

'Was that not Edwin Quilliam's lad?' Henry asked.

'Aye. Ernest.' Eleanor affirmed.

In minutes the band of men were marched on to the steamer and, for a while, were lost to view.

Voirrey stood on Victoria Pier, just one small drop in the ocean of humanity assembled. Only the families of the volunteers, who were mainly fishermen or employees of the Isle of Man Steam Packet Company, had been allowed onto the dock. But there were many of those.

'How many lads are goin'?' Henry inquired of a nearby policeman.

'Close on two hundred, I heard. Come in by train wi' their kin from every corner of the island this mornin'. Douglas has never seen the likes!' He stared past them at the endless sea of heads.

'It is a heroes' farewell, all right! It would be good to be wi' them.' John's voice bore a trace of envy.

Voirrey looked up at her father and shuddered, clutching his coat. It was more than she could bear even to see her uncle go! But not her father! He could not leave her. Surely he wouldn't think of leaving too?

'There's Edward!' Margaret cried.

The men on board crowded to the rail as the hawsers were being cast off, waving wildly to their loved ones.

The stalwart engines grumbled deep in the bowels and the ship moved slowly astern. The water churned and boiled, throwing up a salty spray between the ship and the quay, the gap widening as the growling giant edged away.

· CHAPTER 2 ·

Voirrey stretched up her arms and John lifted her to his shoulders. 'Uncle Edward!' She screamed, feeling hot tears coursing on her cheeks. A knot of panic tightened high in her chest.

Edward heard her, his eyes sought her, then, face lighting, he smiled, waved and blew her a kiss as the steamer began to carry him away.

The huge crowd, as the ferry slowly pulled away, raised endless cheers and sang Manx songs and hymns.

The steamer moved slowly astern, turning gradually until she came between the watching thousands and the Tower of Refuge in the bay. For an age she appeared to stand still, her bows pointed toward England, then with a sudden, belching emission of acrid black smoke, which spread and drifted away like a thunderhead, she began to surge forward. The sea behind her bubbled furiously as her propellors bit the ocean in a forward thrust. Bows pulling high, she steamed south-east and was quickly lost from view behind the breakwater.

Not one soul moved to leave the harbourside until the last portion of the stern had disappeared.

Voirrey stared disconsolately after it, refusing to leave the quay until the boat was out of sight. There was an awful emptiness, like a gaping hole in her chest, as though her heart had been taken out.

'Come, child, we shall walk on the promenade.' Eleanor, sharing Voirrey's melancholia, was in one of her rarely seen moments of gentleness.

Voirrey took a final, yearning look toward the empty sea, sighed and took her grandmother's outstretched hand.

In the warmth of the afternoon sun, they strolled the length of the promenade, working their way slowly through the milling throngs. Voirrey gazed around in awe. Never before had she seen people in such great numbers. Even the horse-trams, when they passed, were overflowing — with passengers lined all along the foot-boards.

Passing the Palace Theatre, Voirrey saw the name Mignon Gloria Nevada and felt the sudden sting of tears. She remembered so clearly how Edward's eyes had glowed, his voice quietly reverent as he had told her of his visit to the theatre to watch Miss Nevada perform.

'She's packin' the theatre twice a day!' He had said, enraptured.

A huge placard outside the Derby Castle Theatre announced to the milling throngs that the famous Florrie F.ord was appearing therein, for their entertainment, to be followed by the world-renowned comedian, Wilkie Bard. All just names to Voirrey, but somehow they seemed magical. John paused to buy an ice-cream for Voirrey as they passed a vendor.

'If you smile, love, you may have this. Then we'll ride the horse-tram back to the station.'

Voirrey forced a watery grin and received her prize. An ice-cream, a tram ride *and* she had missed Sunday school and church. Life wasn't completely bad after all! It was turning out to be a passably pleasant day in spite of everything.

Sitting at the front, between her father and the driver, Voirrey thrilled to the sight of the huge horse, muscles rippling as he towed the crowded tram along the rails. The clopping of the great hooves was calming — almost hypnotic.

"Twere a big day on the docks,' the driver offered.

'Aye.' John agreed. 'All the lads off on their big adventure.'

'Many o' the holidaymakers I've heard talkin' to-day will soon be following them back across. They want to get into the war before 'tis all over an' they miss it. Could mean hard times ahead for the Island.'

'Folks will still need holidays,' John assured him, 'An' the war will be finished before next summer.'

CHAPTER 2

Rain was beating heavily down when they alighted at St Johns, making the long walk an unpleasant affair. Within the first few minutes, water had soaked through Voirrey's bonnet, chilling her head and running down her neck. Clutching the front of her collars together, she tried to stop it getting in, but soon she could feel the damp spreading through her chemise. After a while her feet were so wet she stopped trying to dodge puddles, sloshing straight through them in her haste to reach home.

Voirrey tripped in a pot-hole, sprawling full length in the mire. Swiftly, John lifted the muddy, weeping child and, swinging her to his shoulders, carried her the remaining distance.

Sticks were pushed hurriedly into the fireplace and bellows applied to fan the smouldering embers into a warming blaze. Everyone rushed to change into dry clothes and Voirrey's grazed knees were tended.

Later, eating a large bowl of hot broth, cosy and secure near the fire, Voirrey watched the lightning rip the night sky and listened to the rumble of thunder and the wind lashing frenziedly at every nook and crack.

The drumming of rain on the roof that night was her lullaby, though sleep was elusive.

CHAPTER 3

The following days passed in a haze of rumour and speculation, with Caesar Quine and the Isle of Man Times usually the more accurate informants.

Caesar strutted through the village on the morning of the 5th August, announcing excitedly to all he met that 'The war has really started!' Proudly he added, 'We declared war on the Germans!'

'We?' Henry questioned.

'Well! England! But we're in it wi' 'em!'

'Why, though? I thought it was the Germans makin' all the mischief.'

'I heard the Germans was goin' to invade some little country what couldn't take care o' itself. Belgium, I think was the name. So we jumped in to help.'

'I see.' Henry nodded approvingly. 'That would seem the right thing to do. It looks like our boys will get something worthwhile to do then, doesn't it?'

'I heard most of the visitors is goin' home. Fast as the steamers can take 'em across. Most of the men want to get into the war an' have a go at the Germans afore 'tis finished.'

'Aye,' nodded Henry, 'but 'tis goin' to be terrible hard for the landladies.'

CHAPTER 3

'Was aimin' to be the best season ever for 'em.' Caesar agreed. 'More holidaymakers was booked than ever before, but there's not many comin' now.'

Caesar wandered off toward the pub on the corner, looking for other bodies to hear his news.

Henry thoughtfully watched him go. Leaning his elbows on the gate, he pondered what would come next. Britain declaring war, indeed!

Pleasant August days drifted slowly through, and all talk in Patrick seemed to be of the war. Grown-ups discussed it animatedly whenever they met and the children caught the fever. Marbles became musket balls and suddenly skipping ropes were for tying up the enemy!

Three large posters went up in the village, on the police-house wall, the shop and the pub, calling on all young Manxmen to 'Heed the Call to Arms.' Recruiting drives were organized in every parish in the Island.

War, it seemed, was an exciting game.

Caesar, ever a reliable source of information, kept his villagers well up to date with events. Of the two thousand eight hundred men, he said, who had been camping under canvas at Cunningham's Holiday Camp for young men in Douglas, over two thousand had left the island to enlist, and so not miss all the fun, immediately that war was declared. Close behind them had gone over three-quarters of the camp staff, leaving the place almost deserted.

'There's a recruiting office opened in Douglas,' Caesar confided to Henry, John and Joseph, as they leant on the wall in a balmy summer sunset. 'A Major Hamilton's in charge an' each day there are queues out the door an' down the street, o' men wantin' to sign on an' take the King's shillin'.'

'The steamers are leavin' each day, full to bustin' wi' our

young men. I don't know who's the most excited — the men or their womenfolk. Heard tell a huge crowd from the Manx Society met the first boatload at Liverpool pierhead. When the ship was dockin' they were wavin' Union Jacks an' a Steam Packet Company flag 'cos it bore our *Three Legs o' Man*. Then they sang our Manx anthem an' 'Ramsey Town' an' 'Ellan Vannin'. The ordinary passengers was held aboard while our Manx soldiers was marched off ahead an' straight to the railway station.'

'It would ha' bin a proud moment,' Henry puffed slowly on his pipe.

Voirrey sat on the wall beside her father, imagining what it would be like. All those people — waiting there just to see you. Just to let you feel their pride and to wish you well.

'I wish I could go to the war, Daddy!'

The four men stopped their conversation, laughing. 'War's for men, love!' Henry spoke gently, seeing her confusion.

'Nellie Kinrade says she's goin.'

'Nellie's nearly twenty — an' she's a nurse.'

'When I grow up I'll be a nurse! Then I can go to the war!'

'The war will be finished long before you're old enough anyway. It will be over before Christmas!' Caesar said.

Voirrey slumped. If only she had been born ten years sooner!

'The crowd followed our boys to the train,' Caesar continued his story. 'The soldiers could see folks they knew, but they weren't allowed to greet their friends. They waved and the crowd cheered and cheered while following the soldiers to watch them entrain.'

'If I were younger I'd go wi' 'em,' Henry stated, looking searchingly at John.

'They won't sign you on over forty-one,' quoted Caesar. 'Though lots lie about their age.'

CHAPTER 3

'I wouldn't be believed, I'm afraid,' said Henry laughingly, and Voirrey had to agree.

'They wouldn't take me 'cos o' my leg!' Joseph turned, limping dramatically to his cart, where Ned stood absently nibbling the hedgerows.

'Is his leg really such a bother?' Caesar, frowning, watched Joseph drag himself painfully onto the cart.

'Only when it suits him.' Henry shook his head, smiling.

It was the following evening, as they settled themselves at the table, John cleared his throat. 'I have news to tell.'

Eleanor heaved the black pot from the hob, banging it on the table. The dishes jumped and danced noisily for a moment. All eyes focussed expectantly on John who, without a word, laid a newspaper, open, on the table.

Eleanor dropped the ladle in the pot. 'You know Daa an' me can't read!' She glared at John.

Voirrey stared, wide-eyed, at the large words in the full-page advertisement. 'It says, *Your country needs you — General Service for three years, or until the war is con - con ..... !*' Pointing to the last word, she asked, 'What does this say, Daddy?'

'Concluded!' John studied the faces around the table. 'I've bin thinkin' about what the Lord Bishop preached on Sunday. Do you all remember it?'

Voirrey remembered clearly. How could she ever forget standing, shivering, on Douglas Head, while the Lord Bishop of Mann delivered his address, his loud voice reverberating, encompassing the huge crowd.

'There are worse things than war,' he had boomed. 'To refuse to carry out obligations to our enemies. Any man not prepared to shoulder a musket for his King and Country is not worthy to be called a man!'

Voirrey had been startled by such vehemence from a man of the church.

It must have made its impression, though, she realised, because as they passed by the market place while returning to the station, a pacifist speaker had been trying to address the crowd. Such was the wrath of the people that they had threatened to throw him into the harbour.

John's voice continued, interrupting Voirrey's reverie. 'I have given it a lot of thought, and I have no choice, but to volunteer to go to the war!'

A deathly hush descended on the family. The ladle in Eleanor's hand hung motionless above the pot of herrings and potatoes. 'You too?'.

'Yes, Mammy. Me too! I *must* go. It is my duty!'

Eleanor nodded mutely. In her heart, she had known it must come. First her youngest son, now her daughter's husband. It was the child she worried for most. Too young, she must be, to understand why two people she cared so much about must leave. While the others fussed, shook hands, chattered excitedly, Eleanor quietly spooned the food into dishes.

The world was going to change. It would never be the same again! 'You'll soon be back to school will you?'

Voirrey looked up at her grandmother, seeing the understanding and pain in her eyes. Nodding, she agreed, 'Aye. Monday week.'

'That's good.' Eleanor smiled approvingly. 'I wish we could ha' gone to school, your Daa an' me. We could ha' learned to read an' talk right.'

'I'll teach you to read.' Voirrey was eager to hold onto this warm moment with her grandmother. It helped to push the war away. 'I'll teach you both!'

CHAPTER 3

'Bless you, child, we're too old now. It would ha' been nice, though. You must work hard. Get the best that life can give you.'

'I will!' Voirrey nodded enthusiastically for she loved learning.

'I'm goin' to Douglas t'morra' to sign on,' John said resolutely. Eleanor sighed and shook her head.

Voirrey slept little. For endless hours she stood by the window in the sloping roof of her attic bedroom, her mind bursting. 'Thank you, God,' she said fervently, 'For making Daa too old to go to war.'

In the morning John, like a child to a picnic, set off for Douglas. His heart was singing with the excitement of it.

Too upset to say goodbye, Voirrey had called Dog and run off early to take the cows to the lhergy up Barnell. From the top of the lane, she saw her father in the distance, striding vigorously toward St John's and her young heart felt as if it was tearing apart.

Trailing disconsolately home, she dragged her feet in the ridge of wet grass between the cart ruts, kicking the occasional stone. Dog, sensing her melancholy, trailed behind, head drooping, tail clamped tightly between his legs. Now and again he pushed his wet nose in her palm, to have it swatted irritably.

Caesar and Henry were propping up the gate when she arrived back. 'You must be proud o' the boy.'

'Aye.' Henry grew several inches.

'I hear young Stanley Clucas has gone to fight!'

'Surely he'd be too young?'

'Aye. Only sixteen. But his Mammy went wi' him an said he was eighteen.'

'Can you do that?'

Caesar shrugged. 'Well, they did it! He's joined!'

'Isn't it agin the law?'

'Aye. But he's her boy. If he wants it an' she wants it 'tis none o' my business. 'Tis between them an' the army!'

Henry drew another lungful of tobacco smoke. 'Aye.'

Voirrey went indoors. 'There's goin' to be no men left in the village — 'cept old ones!' she grumbled.

Eleanor looked up. 'We must pray it doesn't last long. Come, peel the priddas, lass.'

Voirrey took a knife and absently set about the potatoes.

'Peel them thinner!' Eleanor commanded. 'When Joseph comes we'll get some kippers for a change.'

John returned late in the afternoon, the spring gone from his step. 'I signed!'

'Why the long face, then?' Asked Henry.

'Well, I signed for the Isle of Man Volunteers because I felt I'd best like to serve with a Manx company. Then they said I wouldn't be posted overseas. I'll ha' to stay on the Island to guard the war signal stations and the telegraph cable at Port Cornaa. Then they are setting up a prisoner of war camp at Cunningham's Holiday Camp in Douglas. I'll ha' to help guard the prisoners.'

Henry and Margaret tried to hide their disappointment, while Eleanor bowed her head to conceal her smile.

Voirrey caught and comprehended her grandmother's expression. Leaping to her feet, she ran to her father. Locking her skinny arms around him she asked, 'Does that mean you won't be going away?'

'Aye, child.' John sighed and stroked the golden curls.

'Good!' Voirrey snuggled closer.

'I want to fight for my country. Not to guard rabble. I tried to tell them, but they wouldn't listen.'

In spite of his early misgivings, John settled comfortably to his military duties. On the 22nd September, as a raw recruit, he arrived home aglow after his most exciting duty to date.

· CHAPTER 3 ·

Wide-eyed, Voirrey listened at his knee after tea. 'We were sent to the pier,' he related, 'an' wi' bayonets fixed, we escorted the first 200 aliens to the camp!'

'What's aliens an' bayonets?' Eleanor's query only just beat Voirrey's.

'Aliens are the enemy an' bayonets are short swords we clip on the end o' our guns,' John explained patiently before continuing, 'We marched the prisoners down the gangplank an' all along the sea-front to the holiday camp. All the people still in Douglas lined the sides of the streets to watch us pass. You wouldn't know the camp. There are new buildings put up as guardhouses. All around are high barbed-wire fences and bright electric lights.'

'Electric lights? What're electric lights?' Voirrey frowned, puzzled.

'You don't light 'em wi' a match — just press a switch an' the light comes on!'

Voirrey studied the oil-lamp flickering on the table. 'How does it work?'

All eyes were on John. Dumbfounded, he shrugged. 'Don't know! Makes a bright light though. All around, they are. Light up the camp just like daytime, so the prisoners can't escape. An' the rain doesn't put them out!'

It was all beyond Voirrey's understanding.

One wet night, early in November, John was very late home looking downhearted and weary. 'There nearly was trouble at the camp today,' he told Henry over a pint of jough.

Henry took a deep swig of the ale, smacking his lips in appreciation. 'Aye?'

'After the rain all day many of the tents were awash. The prisoners refused to return to them. Colonel Madoc, the Camp

Commandant, was called to bring them to reason. This he did, permittin' the men from the worst affected tents to sleep in the dinin'-room. There was much grumblin', but in the end, the prisoners gave in wi'out a fight.'

'You could be less safe than you know,' Henry ventured.

John laughed. 'I think not. They aren't fightin' men. The trouble is there are too many confined in too small an area. There are already over 3000 prisoners there, an more comin' in all the time.'

'Aren't they captured soldiers, Daddy?'

'Bless you, no! They're Germans, mostly — an' some Austrians — who've been livin' in England, some since they were childer. Many are married to British girls an' have families. The Government of England says they have to be kept locked away so they can't spy for Germany. Some o' them are quite wealthy an' have been privileged to buy themselves the luxury of a private tent or hut an' a servant to care for them.'

Voirrey's eyes widened. It sounded a strange war indeed.

Helping her grandfather to chop sticks, two weeks or so later, Voirrey heard his sharp intake of breath. Turning to follow his look, she saw her father by the door, pallid and trembling. His face, half-hidden by a bandage, was a mass of angry weals.

'Whatever has befallen?' Henry whispered hoarsely.

Voirrey moved slowly to her father, afraid to touch, yet wishing to comfort.

'There was a riot at the camp .' John spoke slowly, his lips swollen and pain-racked. 'The prisoners said there was weevils in the food an' they refused to eat. Then they broke everythin' up an' threw at us all they could lay their hands upon. We were covered in soup and jam. They were about to charge us when shootin' started. There are five men dead!'

Henry shook his head sadly. 'Manxmen?'

CHAPTER 3

'No! All prisoners. Germans. But people, just the same. Men wi' families somewhere.'

Suddenly, to Voirrey, the war seemed a far more serious matter! Without warning, it had arrived on the island. 'Do you know it's nearly Christmas?' she asked abruptly.

The two men stared, startled.

'Christmas?'

'Yes! You said the war wouldn't last long. Everyone said so. Said it would be over by Christmas. But it isn't goin' to be, is it? Christmas is only another month away. Will the war be finished before then?' Voirrey 's voice was catching in her throat, sobbing, angry and tears stung her eyes.

John shook his head sadly. 'I don't think so, love.'

'But you promised! When Uncle Edward went away — you promised! You all did!' Turning, she ran indoors and upstairs, throwing herself, weeping bitterly, onto her bed. 'They promised!' she sobbed into her pillow. 'They lied to me! They all lied!'

CHAPTER 4

The first bogie came just after school started.

Voirrey heard the ponderous clump of the big shires' hooves. Leaning forward, craning her neck, she watched them straining up the hill, turning up the track to Knockaloe Farm. Lathered with sweat, huge muscles bulging, shimmering, they dragged the heavily laden wagon away from her up the incline.

'Voirrey Kelly! Will you pay attention girl!'

Startled, Voirrey flicked her gaze to her teacher and blushed guiltily. 'Sorry, Mistress Quayle. I was just watchin'!'

'Well kindly watch the blackboard instead of the goings-on across the road.'

'Yes, miss.'

Mabel Kinrade sniggered and was rewarded with one of Sage Quayle's iciest glares.

Four more bogies were hauled up Knockaloe's track that day, watched covertly by many of the school's inmates. Two carried planks of wood, one bricks, and one held what seemed to Voirrey to be railway sleepers. Once or twice, she noticed, Sage had positioned herself where she could watch both her pupils and the activity across the road.

None of the children took in much of what Sage tried to teach them that day.

· CHAPTER 4 ·

After school, the children all lingered at the roadside, eager not to miss any of the activity.

The farm track and one of the fields seemed alive with men, all busily employed.

Voirrey stood near Caesar Quine, wondering if she dared ask what he knew.

'What goes, Caesar?' Joseph Callow saved her the bother as he pulled Ned to a halt beside the policeman.

Voirrey moved to the other side of Caesar to get upwind of the herring cart.

'Afternoon Joseph. I hear tell they're puttin' war prisoners out here. England's sendin' a lot more across and there aren't room for them in Douglas. The ones there've bin revoltin' I heard.'

'Daddy said five of them got shot!'

The two men looked down, seeing the girl for the first time. Caesar frowned at her, not liking to be upstaged in his storytelling,

Joseph stood watching the activities for a few moments. 'They be sendin' a lot o' men here then?'

Caesar nodded. 'Aye. Five thousand I heard!

Joseph brightened suddenly 'Five thousand!' he squirmed excitedly. 'They'll be wantin' a lot o' herrin' then!' With a click of his tongue and flap of the reins, he set Ned trotting along the road. As they moved away he gleefully rubbed his skeletal hands, making mental notes of his future riches.

Caesar shook his head, saying to the crisp night air, 'Silly old fool! Doesn't he realise that for that number o' men they'll get their herrin' straight from the boats?'

Voirrey skipped home, eager to impart her news.

'There's five thousand prisoners comin' to Patrick!' She yelled, bursting into the kitchen.

Eleanor and Margaret froze mid chores. 'Young ladies *don't run!*' Eleanor said severely.

'Or shout!' Margaret added. Curiosity got the better of her. 'What was that about prisoners?'

'A whole lot o' bricks an' lumber was brought to Knockaloe on bogies an' lots o' men are workin' there. Mr Quine says England's sendin' five thousand prisoners here.'

'Prisoners? On Knockaloe?' Eleanor was thoughtful. 'I don't think I like the sound o' that. All those desperate men, not one hundred yards away!'

John, that evening, confirmed their fears. 'I heard there was to be a new camp on the west of the island. So 'tis to be here is it?'

'So I hear,' Henry confirmed. 'The lass came home full o' it this afternoon. Said she saw it all from the school. Bogies full o' wood an' all sorts.'

'I don't like the idea o' it at all.' Eleanor grumbled.

'Could be good for the village, Mammy. Go on, Daa!' John was on the edge of his seat, leaning forward eagerly.

'Well, I wasn't sure if Voirrey was exaggeratin'. I thought maybe the fairies'd got to her head.'

Voirrey drew herself up, glaring indignantly.

'So I went up to look for mysel'. Sure 'nuff there's piles o' that wire — what's it called — wi' spikes on!'

'Barbed wire?'

'Aye.'

'Caesar says they're puttin' five thousand Germans there. Five thousand!'

John whistled softly. 'Like a whole big town on our doorstep!'

'Where'll they put 'em? There aren't room for all them folk in them few lherghies!'

'Most o' the folk in Patrick were up there lookin' — an' a few strangers besides!'

CHAPTER 4

'I think I'll take a stroll up there after tea an' have a look.'

'Can I come?' Voirrey pleaded.

'Aye, lass.'

They all went! In fact, most of the village went! No one was prepared to believe anything other than the evidence of their own eyes. All this going on — right under their noses — in their own tiny village!

Everyone was there; from babes in arms to the very oldest; they stood huddled in little groups, surveying the fields of Knockaloe, all certain that five thousand bodies could not possibly be housed there.

Heads shook and the conversation was in whispers. Almost like a funeral.

Eleanor shook her head, tutting. 'I don't like it. Not one little bit, I don't. All those prisoners — in our village! What will become of us all?'

'It'll be good for the Island, Mammy.' John was now more enthusiastic than ever.

'How can our Island possibly benefit from havin' all these Germans here? An' so close to us too!' Margaret was incredulous.

'Look at all the work it'll bring for our men. All the work that will need to be done in the buildin' o' the camp. The materials to be made. Clothing! Food! Industry! All those — an' more we haven't thought about yet.'

'No good'll come o' this!' Caesar said mournfully as he strutted to join them. 'There's not enough food for *us*. How will all these thousands be fed?' He nodded toward the field.

'They'll ha' to send it across,' John suggested.

'An' what if the Germans sink all the supply ships? What then?' Caesar asked darkly.

'They won't do that in case there's some o' their own folk aboard,' John dismissed him airily.

Caesar wandered off, muttering obstinately, 'No good'll come o'it I tell you.'

As daylight failed and the evening grew chilly, the huddles of villagers dispersed. In ones and twos, the folk drifted homeward, talking excitedly all the while, many shaking their heads. A township of five thousand in their lhergies was beyond imagination.

In the weeks that followed, there was an ever-present current of excitement, with little else talked about in the district. Even young children stood in awe-stricken clusters, watching the progress of the buildings.

The camp grew rapidly, providing a terrible distraction in the schoolhouse across the road. Sage Quayle fought a losing battle for the pupils' attention.

Almost by magic, word spread from one end of the Island to the other, that there was much work to be found in Patrick.

Strangers arrived in droves, walking swiftly to give themselves the appearance of being good, hard workers. Crofters from miles around, trying to eke a paltry living from the land, left their wives to care for the crofts while they moved to Patrick to earn a better living than they had ever known before.

Men slept beneath the stars. Others slept huddled together in semi-constructed huts. The luckiest begged lodgings with the villagers.

Catherine Gelling, in the corner shop, rubbed her hands in glee and often expressed the wish that there was no rationing.

One morning a knock came on the door. Voirrey, lingering behind Eleanor in the darkness of the hallway, saw four men huddled outside. One, obviously elected spokesman, was prodded forward.

CHAPTER 4

Clearing his throat, he started uncomfortably. 'Mornin' Missus.'

'Mornin'.' Eleanor eyed him suspiciously.

'Edgar Clague. From Port Erin.' He extended a grubby hand. Frowning, distaste puckering her lips, Eleanor touched his fingertips.

'We's come to work at the prison camp an' we was wonderin' if you ha' a spare room we could bed in?'

Eleanor studied them doubtfully. Shaking her head slightly, she opened her mouth to refuse.

'Please, Missus. We'll pay well.'

Eleanor shut her mouth quickly and her head stilled. 'Come inside an' we'll talk it over.'

'Come into my parlour,' thought Voirrey, amused at the vision of her grandmother, ready to pounce and trap these men in her web.

'I have no spare beds, but you could sleep on the parlour floor.'

Voirrey smiled secretively, well pleased at her accuracy.

'Very kind o' you, Missus. We'll make do. Much better'n sleepin' under a hedge.'

Voirrey was thrilled to have the men there, *all* the way from Port Erin. Though she saw little of them, the fact that they were from so far away — it must be fully 13 miles — made them fascinating and mysterious. They seemed to work all the hours God gave. Right into the night too! There appeared to be a desperate hurry to have this camp built.

Every morning hundreds of prisoners arrived, brought from Douglas to Peel by train. Marched the mile and a half from Peel to Knockaloe between guards with fixed bayonets. All day, they worked beside Manxmen, then in the evening were returned to Douglas.

Huge mountains of cinders arrived daily, and an army of

men worked, in perpetual motion, it seemed, to lay it on the clay soil to form roads.

All the while there could be heard the constant sounds of sawing and hammering.

Curious villagers, those who had not found employment in the Knockaloe lhergies, were ever-present in their clusters, watching as huts sprang up, like mushrooms, from the ground.

Deep holes were being dug everywhere — around the perimeter and all across the farm, dividing it into squares. Into these went posts, some high for fences and some even higher, to which huge lights were fitted.

High barbed wire fences sprouted all around. When this was completed and sufficient huts built, the working prisoners and a division of guards and civilian staff took up residence.

The villagers of Patrick, from the youngest to the oldest, kept a very interested eye on it all. Magically the huts multiplied. Daily, large groups of prisoners were marched from Peel railway station to take up residence. Once there they became, willing or not, construction workers.

Teams of shire horses came and went, testing their huge muscles to their limits with the weight of the building materials loaded on their bogies.

It seemed a magical world to Voirrey's young eyes. At night, from the skylight window in her attic bedroom, she could see the sky illuminated with the brightness of the electric floodlights. They were magic too! Lights without a wick, which just suddenly came on. Steady and unflickering in the breeze. Even when a storm blew and rain poured down, the lights refused to falter or dim.

The glow they put in her bedroom was brighter than the candle Margaret used to light her daughter's path to bed, then took away. Quite quickly Voirrey found her room to be bright enough for reading, so often she crept off to school in the morning, well-read — but heavy-eyed and yawning.

'They're goin' to build a railway line here now!' Caesar told an excited audience one day.

'What for?'

'So's easier to bring stuff out from Peel, I s'pose!'

Sleepers and rails were laid down the Knockaloe track, across the road, behind the church and all the way to join the St Johns to Peel line.

People came from all parts of the island to watch, in wonderment, as the work progressed and the new railway took shape.

After that most of the supplies came directly by train from the vessels docking in Peel Harbour. The huge shire horses rarely came now, much to Voirrey's disappointment. Most of the new prisoners also arrived by train, so that only a few *trusties*, who were taken out daily on exercise marches, were seen outside the compound.

Gradually the villagers became accustomed to the town that was growing rapidly in their midst. The excitement died a little and the children settled to their lessons again.

'There is a chance I soon might get to fight for our King,' John announced one evening.

'How so?' Henry was immediately alert — interested. Excited even! He had taken it almost as a personal affront that John had been kept on the Island.

'The 1st Manx Service Company is to be formed. I have asked to join it. We will be trained for combat and attached to one of the expeditionary forces.'

Voirrey sat at her window late into that night. Heart heavy, her thoughts were of Edward, so long gone. And now her father, so excited about leaving his family and going to war! A tear ran down her cheek and she swiped it away.

Opening the skylight a crack, she could hear music. Beautiful music, as though there was an orchestra in the garden. A magical, invisible orchestra, playing strong, gentle music for her.

In the brilliance which lit her garret, she became a famous singing star. Perhaps like Florrie Ford, whom Uncle Edward had been so taken with. No! More! She was a beautiful princess, bedecked in priceless jewels.

No, the orchestra was *not* in the garden. Princess Voirrey sat enthroned in her Golden Palace while the musicians — her musicians — the best in all the world, played just for her, in the courtyard.

Hearing her parents come to their room, just below hers, Voirrey was drawn, reluctantly, back to reality. Straining to hear every note of the pleasurable, silvery music, she heard her parents' voices droning into the night.

They both sound so happy and excited, she thought. *I wish Daddy wasn't going to go.* Her grandmother felt the same, she knew.

The music finally quietened, Voirrey, turned her back to the skylight and drifted to sleep, to dream of fairy princesses in crystal palaces.

The days, such few days as she had left with her father, flew exceedingly fast and Voirrey's heart became increasingly heavy with every day that passed. Two of the three men she loved most in all the world were going to be missing from her life. And for how long? How many Christmasses might pass before she had them back?

John sailed from Douglas on the 9th March, just four short days after the 1st Manx Service Company had been formed.

'We are going to train with the 16th Battalion King's

CHAPTER 4

Liverpool Regiment,' he announced proudly. 'Then we'll be off overseas to rout those Germans an' do our share to finish this war!'

The day, to Voirrey, seemed much the same as the day Edward had left, though colder and wetter. The skies, she thought, were weeping the tears she was fighting to hold back.

Joseph Callow offered the use of his cart to St. John's again, but forgot to scrub it and to polish Ned. It seemed the men going off to war were no longer heroes! The novelty was long gone!

This time there were three men going, including young Stanley Clucas. He held himself tall and tried to look much like the man he would undoubtedly soon become.

If he lived long enough!

The cart was crowded with all the families — and smelly. It seemed to Voirrey there were people bristling out from all over the herring cart — like quills on a hedgehog. Poor Ned struggled, and most of the passengers had to alight and walk when they came to the slightest upward slope.

Waiting on the pierhead for the rest of the Company to assemble, John lifted Voirrey, holding her tightly to him. 'Be a good girlie for your mother, won't you?'

Voirrey nodded mutely, the power of speech having deserted her. Tears nipped the corners of her eyes and she nervously fingered the brass shoulder badge, the Three Legs emblem enclosed in a circle. 'What's this?'

'It's a special badge only the Manx Company can wear.' John replied quietly, proudly. "Tis unique — peculiar to us.'

There was no mass of holidaymakers that grey March day, but half the population of the Island were on the quay to bid the heroes farewell. As the ship drew away Voirrey heard the strains of the Manx National Anthem from the soldiers aboard.

In a faltering voice and sobbing, she took up the refrain. In moments all the vast crowd had joined in and, as the steamer cleared the harbour-mouth Douglas resounded to wave after wave of cheering.

In the emptiness that followed, Voirrey found herself locked in her grandmother's arms. 'Don't fret, child, he'll soon be back,' the old lady whispered shakily.

Voirrey bit on her lip, her top teeth chattering against it. Gulping, she nodded and gave her grandmother a watery smile.

The crowd drifted slowly away. Groups lingered, talking in high pitched, excited tones, of the fun the lads would have in sending the Germans back where they belonged. The older men, some envious, others frustrated, the women excited — for their husbands were heroes.

CHAPTER 5

'I thought we might go for some flithers this mornin,' Henry ruffled his granddaughter's hair.

Voirrey looked up, a flurry of excitement rippling in her chest. She loved going out with her grandfather.

'Oh, yes please. Where shall we go, Daa?'

'Traie Cabbag, perhaps. We should find some there.'

'You must take the cows to the lhergy first,' Eleanor quickly reminded her.

'Yes Granny. I'll put my boots on.' Jumping to her feet, Voirrey ran upstairs. Quickly pulling on her boots, she undertook the arduous task of lacing all the buttons. This done, she rushed down, two steps at a time, arriving, breathless, in the kitchen.

Racing outside she threw open the cow-shed door, sending it crashing against the stone wall.

The cows kicked and sidled at her boisterous arrival, then settled and sauntered lazily from the shed, nibbling at anything green enough to look appetising. Voirrey slapped Brownie's snout as she set about Henry's favourite pink rose bush.

Seeing Whitey chewing the edge of her grandmother's best bloomers, where they lay drying on the thorn bush, she raised a leg, in a most unladylike manner, delivering a swift, sharp kick to the cow's rump. Startled, Whitey shot off across the newly planted vegetable bed like a frightened rabbit.

Dog, enjoying all this unexpected action, danced around, barking furiously.

'Voirrey!' Eleanor glared from the kitchen window. 'If you don't learn to behave right the fairies'll get you!'

The fairies! She'd forgotten about them! The dreaded fairies who, she was forever being told, watched her day and night and at some time would punish her for her sins. Sobered, the girl rounded up the wayward cows and threw the knickers, reasonably undamaged, back onto the thorn bush.

At the top of Barnell, Voirrey shooed the cows into the lhergy. While she fastened the gate Dog suddenly barked wildly, bounded across the path and through the hedge. Racing off up the glen, in pursuit of a rabbit, he disappeared round the bend beyond the tholtans.

'Dog!' Voirrey called. No response. 'Come back here, Dog!' Not even a bark in the distance.

'If you don't come out of there the fairies'll get you!' Her voice grew shriller. The glen was full of fairies. Granny kept telling her. That's why she must never go there. Still, Dog was silent!

Nervously Voirrey climbed the glen gate. Apprehension fluttering her heart, she crept toward the corner, staying as far across the pathway from the row of tholtans as she could manage. She knew it was in these ruined cottages the fairies lived. Miss Quayle had told the class once that no Manx cottage was ever knocked down when it became uninhabited. Always they were left standing for the fairies to occupy. Were you to disobey this, then the fairies would take vengeance!

Voirrey could feel them watching her! Hundreds of little eyes peering at her through glassless windows, cracks in doors, from chimney pots, behind trees, leaves, stones. They were everywhere! Watching! Waiting! Planning what? Voirrey shuddered. Long, cold fingers of fear clutched her tummy.

'Dog! Please come back, Dog!' she called timidly, unnerved by the awesome quietude of the place.

The undergrowth rustled close behind Voirrey's foot. Hand clutched to her mouth and muffling a scream, she whirled and glimpsed a movement, but fleetingly. Something tiny! It *had* to be a fairy! But it had disappeared into the bushes. '*It was trying to come close enough to get me,*' she told herself, trembling violently.

Suddenly Dog hove into view, tearing down the glen, tail between his legs, ears flattened to his head. Whining, he shot through the hole in the hedge, straight past his young mistress and down the lane toward home.

Her terror complete, Voirrey scurried in his wake, fairly throwing herself over the five-barred gate, catching and tearing the hem of her skirt.

As fast as her legs would carry her, she fled home, throwing herself through the back door and slamming it behind her. Leaning her back against it, she stood, wide-eyed, breathless and trembling like autumn leaves in a storm.

Eleanor whirled. 'Young ladies *don't* ---! Noticing her granddaughter's dishevelled state and the wild terror in her eyes, her voice trailed. 'Good heavens, child, whatever has happened?'

Voirrey rushed to the protection of the old lady's arms, all the while looking fearfully over her shoulder.

'They nearly got us!' The girl was sobbing — near hysteria.

Henry and Margaret, having heard the commotion, arrived in the kitchen together. Still trembling, Voirrey related the tale of the rabbit, the dog and the fairy who crept up behind and almost got her. The story, by some means, grew in the telling!

'Fairies indeed! Pah!' Henry snorted. 'That's you two silly women fillin' the child's head wi' nonsense!'

Concerned for the girl, the two women ignored his caustic comment.

'How many times have you been told not to go in the glen?' Margaret started to chastise, but her father's thunderous look silenced her. 'Change your dress so I can stitch it. Then you can go out with Daa,' she finished lamely.

'We'll take your father's bicycle. If you sit on the bar an' hold this we should do alright.' Henry pushed a metal pail into Voirrey's hand, some minutes later when they were ready to leave.

After a struggle and a few aborted starts, the pair wobbled off toward the main road. Voirrey sat uncomfortably on the crossbar, clinging to her grandfather with one hand and the pail with the other.

Eleanor and Margaret, watching from the gate, shook their heads.

Rounding the corner by the shop, Henry almost collided with Caesar.

'Mornin' Henry. What's you about?' the policeman asked glumly.

Henry braked, almost tipping Voirrey into the road. 'Just takin' the girlie to get some flithers.'

'Oh, aye.' Caesar nodded approvingly. 'I'm tryin' to keep an eye on as much of that there camp as I can!' He craned to get a better view.

Voirrey's eyes followed his scowl to the barbed wire. 'They got guards for that, I thought,' Henry frowned.

'Aye. But since they sent our volunteers to the war they got old men from Across to guard the prisoners. The Royal Defence Corps, they call them. Men like us what's too old to go an' fight! I don't trust 'em! Don't think they're no good!'

'Is there any news o' the war?'

CHAPTER 5

'Aye. Enemy submarines ha' laid mines all over the Irish Sea an' many ships ha' bin sunk. Yesterday. No! The day before, March the 13th, it was, H.M.S. Bayano was sunk half-way between the Island an' the Mull o' Galloway. A lot o' the bodies ha' bin washed up on our beaches.'

Voirrey shuddered, growing rapidly less keen to go looking for shellfish on the beach.

A large group of men marched down the lane from Knockaloe. Flanked by their khaki-clad guards, they turned right into the road, marching briskly past the three villagers on the corner, they disappeared, singing, toward the south.

'An' that's another thing,' Caesar said with increasing vehemence.

Henry raised an inquisitive eyebrow.

'Why don't they keep them inside the camp to exercise? Takin' two hundred men out on the open road, indeed! With old men for guards!' Caesar spat contemptuously.

'They didn't look so old to me,' Henry ventured.

'Old men!' Caesar insisted vehemently. 'Too old an' slow to catch the prisoners if they run off!'

'Isn't that why they have guns? So they don't have to chase after them?'

'Can't shoot! Bet they can't!'

Realising he was fighting a losing battle, Henry withdrew from the fray. 'Must go, then, Caesar.' With a quick wave, they wobbled on their way.

'What if the prisoners do escape, Daa?'

'Why would they? Where would they go? There's no way off the Island. That's why England's sendin' them all here!'

As they cycled past the camp many of the prisoners stood, staring wistfully through the wire. Some appeared lost in a world of their own, others smiled, waved and some even called a greeting.

Voirrey waved back.

'You must ignore them!' Henry said sharply.

'But why? Some of them seem so nice — so friendly.'

'They are the enemy!'

Nearing the Traie Cabbag track, the twosome met up with the troop of prisoners, with their ageing guards, now returning to the camp.

The narrowness of the road forced Henry to stop and pull his bicycle onto the verge to allow them passage.

Voirrey watched in fascination, the strange assortment of prisoners. Scanning the faces as they passed, expecting them to look like villains, she found herself almost disappointed that they were just like ordinary men. Suddenly she saw one man, in particular, and her heart faltered, then leapt with excitement. He reminded her greatly of her father and she felt strangely drawn to him. As he drew level she leaned forward to see him better. Catching her eye, he smiled and winked — as her father so often did. Voirrey thrilled, grinning in return and felt her grandfather's gentle cuff to the back of her head.

The ride on the crossbar down the rough track to the beach was an agonising affair. She never would have believed a person's body could suffer so much pain or so many bruises. Keeping hold of the pail all the way had been no more than a reflex action. Something to cling to.

Henry soon found a rock with some flithers clinging to it. With his trusty penknife and a rock to hammer it, he quickly set about chipping the black shells from the rocks.

Voirrey crept beside him, moving from boulder to boulder, picking the flithers from the sand, dropping them into the pail. In no time there was nearly a bucket-full.

Henry pulled his pipe and tobacco pouch from his pocket

and settled himself on a rock. 'I'll just have a quick puff, then we'll go home.'

Voirrey nodded absently. 'Maybe I can find some crabs.'

'Aye.' Henry's face lit up. He hadn't tasted crabs for quite some time. 'They would make a welcome change.'

Turning over large rocks and humming one of the tunes she had heard from the camp, Voirrey moved off along the beach. Scrambling around rocks, studiously searching every pool, she prodded and poked a stick into every crevice, hoping it would emerge with a crab clinging to it.

Having found two or three smallish ones, she took them to her grandfather and went in search of more.

Rounding a headland, she noticed a large dark hump on the shingle a little way off. Thinking it a seal, she cautiously drew closer.

The man lay on his back, one leg twisted grotesquely under him. His hands were stiffened in claws, desperately grasping to hold on to the life he had lost. Huge, staring eyes bulged from an obscenely bloated, blackened face.

Voirrey felt her insides clamping up as her stomach turned a million somersaults. Her heart was a lead lump in her throat, constricting, choking, faltering. Everything rushed round in ever speeding circles and someone was screaming. Far away, loudly at first, then fading, making her head hurt. The sea, the sky and the cliffs merged, whirling crazily, then all went mercifully black and the feeling of sickness was gone.

Voirrey didn't remember much of the journey home. Henry half walked, half carried her and she could remember her feet dragging, stumbling. All the time she was crying. Then the blackness would come again to numb her mind. He had got her home, then had gone back for the bike and the pail of precious shellfish. There were nights to follow when sleep was accompanied by the nightmare of the ghoul on the beach. Voirrey spent uncountable hours by her window, warming in the glow from the camp's light, trying to eradicate the awful memory. Always there were voices and she didn't feel quite so alone. She could hear people laughing, singing, shouting sometimes. It was the music and singing which fired her imagination most.

The spotlights too. The magical glow which permeated every corner of her room with life and warmth. With the music and song, they carried her on silken wings of fantasy away from the real, cruel world and into a kinder one. A world beyond the lightened, reflective clouds, where she was no longer a poor girl. Where she still had her father and uncle Edward and could have anything she desired — even meat *every* Sunday!

When the music stopped and the voices faded, Voirrey went to bed, to sleep fitfully and dream unwelcome dreams.

Two days, she was allowed, to recover from her shock, then Margaret insisted that she must return to school.

'Daa?' she ventured at breakfast, pushing her porridge around her bowl.

'Aye, lass?'

'Who was that man? The man who died on the beach.'

'Hush, child, don't think about him. You don't need to know. Put it from your mind.'

'I want to know, Daa,' she pleaded tearfully.

'He was just a man,' Henry sighed and frowned.

'The girl has a right to know. He was from a boat what was sunk,' Eleanor interceded.

'Did the Germans do it?'

'Aye.'

Walking to school, Voirrey stopped to look at the men

· CHAPTER 5 ·

behind the barbed wire. Suddenly she saw them in a different light. Somehow they were now more sinister and evil!

A prisoner among a group saw her, smiled and waved. For a moment there was a thrill of recognition, of her father, then the awful reality that he was *not* her father, he was a German!

Shaken and frightened, Voirrey poked out her tongue, spun on her heel and ran to school.

Some new children were in the yard, all strangers of differing ages, clustered together, clinging to their mothers' hands. Voirrey studied them curiously until the bell rang to call them into class.

'We have some new childer from Across starting with us today.' Sage Quayle herded the group of new youngsters from the corner where they were hovering nervously. 'Their fathers are in the Royal Defence Corps who have come to guard the prisoners. They will be living at the camp and attending this school for the duration of the war. I'm sure you will all make them very welcome.'

Voirrey covertly studied the newcomers. They looked all right — most of them anyway. One girl, about her own age, had the longest, darkest hair Voirrey had ever seen, and huge brown eyes as velvety as Brownie's.

'Would you all please find a desk,' Sage invited.

Voirrey smiled at the new girl, signalling her to the empty desk next to hers. Moving gracefully, the girl slipped into the seat.

'My name's Voirrey Kelly.'

'Mine is Lily Beckinsale.'

'Settle down now, children. Let us all say the Lord's prayer, then we shall do our times tables.'

Voirrey, nosey as ever, had to wait impatiently until playtime to find out any more.

'Do you live in the prison camp?'

'Yes. Daddy is an officer in the Defence Corps. He came over here two weeks ago, but Mummy and I have only been here three days.'

'Do you like it here? On the Island?'

'I haven't really seen it. Only the camp. And on the train from Douglas. I was sea-sick on the boat coming over.'

'Weren't you scared? Mr Quine — he's the policeman — says the Germans keep sinking ships with boats that sail under water.'

'Submarines,' Lily corrected airily.

'What?' Voirrey frowned.

'Submarines. That's what they call the underwater boats.'

'Oh! Well, weren't you scared?'

'No. Daddy says the enemy never sink the Steam Packet ferries because all the German prisoners come here on them an' they don't want to kill their own people.'

'Oh, I see,' Voirrey nodded, unsure whether that might be true. 'What age are you?'

'Ten. I had my birthday last month.'

'I'll be ten soon. In two weeks. On the first day of April,' said Voirrey proudly. How nice it was that her new friend was the right age.

From Lily, Voirrey was able to learn much about the affairs of the prisoners. Proud to be in the know, keen to stay in the limelight, and be accepted, Lily was happy to impart her knowledge and, perhaps, exaggerations.

Voirrey ran all the way home from school at dinner time, bounding into the kitchen like a spring lamb. 'I've got a nice new friend!' She announced breathlessly.

Eleanor, punishing a shirt on the scrubbing board, gave her a withering look. Detaching a lather-laden arm from the sink, she wagged a finger. 'Young ladies *don't run!*' she said wearily.

CHAPTER 5

Voirrey shuffled her feet, studying a scuffed toe-cap. 'Sorry, Granny. But a new girl started today an' she lives in the camp. She told me about the prisoners.'

'Take the wet clothes out an' spread them to dry, please.' Eleanor returned to her attack on the washing.

Sighing, Voirrey did as she was bid, impatiently spreading the dripping articles on the thorn bush. She had all this exciting information, but no one willing to listen to it.

At the table, with the grown-ups now a captive audience, she tried again. 'Lily says there's lots of famous people in the camp,' She mumbled past a mouthful of soda bread and butter.

'Don't talk with your mouth full!' Margaret tutted. 'Who's Lily?'

'There's lots of singers an' musicians!' Voirrey ignored her mother. Leaning both elbows on the home-made, scrubbed wooden table, she propped her chin in her hands. Her boot started a rhythmic drumming against the planks that formed a shelf under the table.

Margaret gave her a piercing look, then frowned. 'Who is Lily? I haven't heard of her before.'

'She's my new friend. She lives in the camp.'

'Is she a prisoner?' Eleanor was puzzled.

'No, her Daddy is a guard. The prisoners are all practisin' to have a concert.'

'Is that what we hear at night?'

'Aye. They're goin' to put on shows. Lily says there are famous artists an' sculptors an' all sorts too.'

'Indeed?' This Lily sounds interestin'.'

Having, at last, gained the attention she had been seeking, Voirrey was placated. Even bringing the cattle from the lhergy that afternoon seemed much less of a chore than usual. During her wanderings, she imagined herself to be proudly conducting the world's greatest orchestra. Glowing in the glare of the footlights, she took bow after bow as the vast audience called for endless encores.

Dog whimpered and kept a wary distance as she strutted haughtily. In final despair, he herded the cattle, unaided.

Voirrey daydreamed her boot into the steaming mess Blackie had just dumped unceremoniously and unseen, in the lane before her. Slipping, she landed heavily on her lost dignity in the cowpat and came quickly back to earth.

'Oh, you horrid cow! Ugh!' Voirrey tried to towel the muck from her boots and skirt with handfuls of grass but lost the battle.

As a punishment, when she got home, she was ordered to bring in the washing, then break up the flither shells for the hens.

The washing, she regarded as a dangerous chore. Long before it was ever dry every earwig in the district had taken up residence. Voirrey gingerly plucked each article from the thorn bush, shaking it vigorously. Whenever one of the little brown insects dropped out she would squeal in terror and stamp on it.

Later, sitting on a stool (she had started on the ground, but Eleanor had scolded her, saying it was too cold) with the bucket of black flither shells beside her and a small hammer, she smashed the shells.

'Daa, why do I have to do this?' she grumbled.

'Because you were naughty.'

'But why do the shells have to be broken up?'

'For the hens.'

Voirrey shook her head in puzzlement. 'But why do the hens want broken shells?'

'Makes 'em lay better eggs.'

'How?'

· CHAPTER 5 ·

Henry scratched his head and thought for a moment. 'Blowed if I know. It just does.'

When the music, the songs and the laughter began that evening, Voirrey opened her window wide to allow it unbridled entry, then huddled under the blankets to escape the chill which came with it.

Every shadow in the room rose and danced to the music. A handsome prince drifted through the window, whirling her through steps she had seen in a film Edward had once taken her to see in the picture house. Still dancing, she floated to sleep.

'Mammy, can Lily come to tea tomorrow?'
'Lily? To-morrow?' Margaret asked vaguely. Then remembering it would be Voirrey's birthday, she nodded. 'Yes. Bring her straight home after school.'
'I'll make broth an' a fruit puddin'.' Eleanor volunteered.
Voirrey rushed downstairs in the morning and, for once, was not scolded for running. On the table, the little brown paper parcel waited. Fervently tugging the string away, the girl paused, wishing to savour the moment. The grown-ups watched, eager not to miss her reaction. Slowly, wanting to make the anticipation last, she opened the paper, laying it flat on the table.
'Oh, they're so pretty.' One by one she picked up the dolls clothes her mother had so painstakingly stitched. Fingering each one, she held it to her cheek. Each one was a memory, made from clothes Voirrey had long ago outgrown. Under them were some boiled sweeties and a red rubber ball. A note read, 'from Mammy, Daddy, Granny, Daa and Uncle Edward.'
'Thank you. Thank you so much,' she whispered, gazing lovingly at the three anxious faces. Tears nipped the corners of

her eyes for she knew how much work and love had gone into every stitch.

Voirrey and Lily hurried down the school steps that night, impatient to be home. They had plans to play ball.

Some prisoners smiled and waved. Voirrey lowered her head, hurrying past, while Lily almost ran behind.

'I hate those Germans,' Voirrey said vehemently.

'Not all of them are Germans,' Lily said airily. 'A lot of them are Austrians. Some of them are quite nice. I talk to them sometimes. When no one 's looking! I'm not supposed to, though.'

'Why do you?' Voirrey couldn't imagine why anyone would want to talk to the enemy.

'They 're interesting. And nice. I learn things from them.'

'I don 't think they're nice. I found a body once — a man. Last month, it was. All black an' swelled up. It was three times the size it should be an' its eyes had popped right out an' was hangin' down on its cheeks. An' all its hair was fallin' off an' its hands was like witches claws tryin' to grab me. There was crabs an' gibbins comin' out o' its ears and eye-holes,' Voirrey exaggerated.

Lily's face was grey, eyes wide in undisguised horror. 'What happened to him?'

'The Germans did it! Sinked his boat an' drowned him!'

Lily shuddered. 'The Germans?'

Voirrey nodded enthusiastically. 'Aye.'

Margaret was waiting at the door when they got home, a warm smile lighting her face. 'Welcome, Lily, 'tis nice to meet you at last. Voirrey has told us so much about you.'

'It's a pleasure to meet you.' Lily dropped a quick curtsy. Drinking in the surroundings, her soft, dark eyes widened. Never

· CHAPTER 5 ·

in her life had she seen such drab poverty. Yet the home had an air of warmth and love. Later she was to tell her parents, 'It was dark inside, lit only by one wick of a dim, flickering oil lamp. The wallpaper in the parlour has bright red roses, but at the bottom, because the house is so damp, it is all dark and green and peeling. The kitchen was comfortable because there were sticks to fire the stove and on the hob was a huge black cooking pot.'

When it was time to eat, a bowl with a fruit pudding wrapped in cloth was taken from the pot of soup, where it had been steaming, then the soup was served. It was Manx broth, very thick and it had a slight sweetness from the pudding. Afterwards, we had the pudding with thick, fresh cream. It was all very nice. They were all very nice. They have cows for their own milk, butter and cream and hens for fresh eggs. And do you know, they don't have knives and forks, but eat everything with their fingers or a spoon.'

'Did they not have electric lights, dear?' asked her mother.

'No. Just small oil lamps, or candles. They just burn one wick of the lamp during the week but two on Sundays. Voirrey has her bedroom in the attic and the lights from the camp make it very bright. I was a bit scared, though, because they flickering lamps made strange shadows. I kept hearing funny noises and Voirrey said it was mice.'

'Mice!' Emily pulled a face, shuddering. Yes, she had found more than her fair share of those here. 'I expect it's because we're in the country, dear. Mice and hedgehogs.'

'Voirrey has a pet hedgehog! Well — sort of. She holds bits of food for it sometimes and it eats them from her hand.'

Emily, having lived all her life in Manchester, found this quite horrifying.

CHAPTER 6

'Where you bound for, Henry?' Caesar Quine hailed them as Henry and Voirrey set off for the train.

'Jus' takin ' the girl to Douglas, Caesar. See if we can dig some gibbins.'

Caesar licked his lips, thinking he wouldn't mind a few fried sand eels himself.

'If you have any spare I'll buy them. Terrible business — that ship — weren't it?'

'What's this?'

'Germans sunk another ship. Lucy something. Off Ireland somewhere. Five days ago 'twere, 7th May they say. One o' them torpedo things done it. More folks dead than alive. Mostly Americans, I hear, though some o' the crew was Manx.'

'Bad that!' Henry shook his head and sighed.

'Aye.' The men glared at the fellows behind the barbed wire. Voirrey, following their gaze, caught the eye of the prisoner, who, looking so much like her father, smiled, waved and winked. The girl drew breath to poke her tongue, but couldn't. Not to him. He was, for some reason, a little special.

'Fishin' boat from Peel, the Wanderer, was the first boat there. They saw the Lucy — whatever sink, about three miles off an' made straight for't. Were the only boat there an' picked

· CHAPTER 6 ·

up 160 folks, many as they could take, an' had two boatloads in tow afore the patrol boats showed up. Some had no clothes, so the crew had to give 'em their spares. They say there was many young babies among 'em.'

Voirrey felt ill. The demons were killing young babies now! With sudden sick anger, she stuck her tongue out at the smiling prisoner, then turned her back.

A sunny afternoon spent digging for gibbins on Douglas beach put the disaster to the back of her mind. The people who had drowned were only in a story, not real people she tried to convince herself. No one would kill babies!

As they strolled through Douglas later, Henry with the canvas bag of eels slung over his shoulder, Voirrey saw a newspaper placard and stopped to read it.

'Oh, no! That's awful!!' She blanched and put a trembling hand to her lips.

'What is it, love? Read it to me.'

Voirrey took a deep breath to steady herself. 'It says the great liner, Lusitania, pride o' Cunard's Atlantic Fleet, was torpedoed by a German submarine an' sank within minutes. It says about 1200 souls, men, women an' children were lost. Many more would have perished, had it not been for the courage of the seven-man crew from the Peel fishin' boat, Wanderer. It says they bravely sailed into the teeth o' the enemy, riskin' their own lives, to save the passengers.'

A sound of many marching feet caused Henry to look up. Approaching rapidly down Bucks Road, overseen by a handful of elderly guards, were a number of prisoners. Henry grabbed Voirrey's arm and hurried her down the road.

'We've sunk a British ship!' an excited voice proclaimed.

Suddenly a great noise started up behind them, with cheering and shouting.

Glancing fearfully over her shoulder, Voirrey saw the prisoners gathered around the placards. The doddering guards made futile attempts to bring into line their two hundred charges, whom it seemed had gone mad. Roaring with laughter, they jumped up and down, clung to each other in joy, danced and threw their hats and tin mugs in the air.

Henry pushed Voirrey into a shop doorway, placing his bulk between her and the danger. Peeping round from behind him, she saw the guards scuttling around like little rats, waving their muskets in an impotent threat. Still out of control, the mob moved down toward the station, sparing hardly a glance for the old man and the child trembling behind him in the doorway.

A cable car rumbled up Bucks Road toward them and, seeing the rioting prisoners, ground, grumbling, straight past the queue of people who waited at the roadside to board.

The abandoned would be, passengers moved back against the wall of the building, looking in dismay at the disappearing cable car.

Henry let the prisoners go well out of sight before he stepped from the doorway. Voirrey followed, clinging tightly to his hand.

'They were awful men, Daa,' she said tremulously.

'No need to be frightened, child, they're gone now. Come — I'll buy you an ice cream.'

Voirrey stepped timidly, dragging her feet behind her grandfather. How dreadful those men had been. So excited about babies dying!

The skies cried for those babies that night, and all else who had needlessly died. It started when the train was half-way to St John's. First a cluster of huge droplets. Gathering power on the strengthening wind, it became a blustering deluge, rocking the train. Then God made his anger known. Hissing, seething streamers of angry light snaked from the sky. The world trembled with the voice of His wrath!

Leaving the train at St John's, Voirrey and Henry huddled in the lee of the station until the storm abated slightly.

'Come, child,' Henry said, during a quieter moment. 'Let's hurry.'

Clinging to his hand, trailing slightly, Voirrey had to run on the rough, slippery road to keep up with his long stride. When breathing finally became too painful, and she had a stitch in her side, she had to beg him to slow down.

'Sorry, girlie, I forgot your short legs.' Henry slackened his pace slightly.

A sudden bolt of lightning exploded in a giant beech tree above. Branches shattered and flew with sparks falling all around them. The crown of the tree flared like a bonfire. The accompanying violent gunshot crack of thunder launched Voirrey, screaming, into her grandfather's arms.

'Hush now, love. Don't be afeared,' Henry said comfortingly while he prayed the girl would not feel the tremor in his body. He had known many a night like this at sea, but never with a child in his care.

The fire in the tree-top sizzled for a moment in the rain, then died. Blackness, more impenetrable than ever, enveloped them.

Water flowed like a river, through Voirrey's clothing, saturating even her camisole and bloomers. Adding to her misery, her boots filled with water and with each step she took she fought to lift a vast weight. Dragging her feet through the runnels in the rough road, she stumbled behind the speeding Henry, tripping frequently.

A drumming, whooshing messenger from Satan rushed suddenly out of the blackness, missing Voirrey by the merest fraction and showering her with mud. Squealing, she leapt away, hawthorns and brambles tearing her face and hands as she tumbled into a ditch.

'Whoa, boy! Whoa now!' The devil's chariot halted a little way past. Footsteps sloshed and splashed back toward them. 'You all right there?'

'Is that you, Joseph?' Henry asked as he caught Voirrey's elbow to help her from the ditch.

'Aye. Oh, 'tis you, Henry, Voirrey. Sorry! Didn't see you till t'late. Do you hurt? You like a ride home?'

'Aye. Please. You're about on a bad day.'

'The herrin' has got to be sold no matter what the weather. Anyhows they don't mind getting wet.'

Henry helped Voirrey into the cart, where she gratefully huddled, shivering, between the two men. Ned delivered them home at a brisk canter.

No handsome princes in ice castles came to visit her that dreadful night.

Instead, the camp floodlights conspired with the flashes and crashes of God's wrath to allow the dreaded fairies to haunt her room. Even with her eyes screwed tightly shut she could see the little creatures flitting tormentingly in the shady corners of her room. What little sleep she managed was fitful and uneasy.

'I hope you don't mind me just calling in like this,' asked Emily Beckinsale, 'But Lily has told us so much about you that I almost feel that I know you. I'm Lily's mother. Voirrey's friend,' She added in answer to Margaret's unspoken question.

'Oh! It's nice to meet you. Do please come in.'

Margaret ushered Emily into the parlour. 'It's nice to meet at last. You have a lovely, well-mannered daughter.'

Emily smiled, bowing her head in appreciation.

Discussing their daughters soon overcame their initial

strangeness. Quickly, the two women were chatting like old friends.

I'm pleased Lily has made such a good friendship with Voirrey. We were a touch concerned about bringing her away, but Percy did not wish to leave us in Manchester.'

'It has been good for Voirrey, too. She was very upset when my brother, Edward, went in the navy, then devastated when her father left too.'

'She must miss them terribly. Lucky she still has her grandfather.'

Eleanor, who had been hovering in the hallway, curious to know who the stranger was, had a flash of inspiration. She poked her head around the door, smiling questioningly at the visitor. 'Would you care for a cup of tea?'

'Thank you. That would be very pleasant.'

'I'll help you, Mammy. Will you excuse me please?' Margaret smiled questioningly at her guest.

Left alone, Emily, studied the room, her feelings paralleling her daughter's. It was a nice room, echoing the family's warm friendliness. Adorning the walls the paper, with its large bright flowers smiled down cheerfully, almost overruling the black and green mildew which encroached on the lower edges. At either end of the mantle-shelf stood an ornate brass oil lantern, between which stood several family photographs. One was of Voirrey between her parents, and another of her gazing lovingly up at a striking young man in a fisherman's oiled wool gansey and knitted hat. The dresser displayed the finest china, obviously an heirloom handed down through several generations.

The well-scrubbed slate floor, which had allowed the damp to rise and stain the walls, had two faded, well worn, hand made rugs as its only decoration.

Margaret appeared in the doorway, slightly flustered. 'I

— we — were wonderin' if you would care to take tea in the kitchen where 'tis warmer? Or do you prefer to stay here?'

Emily arose. 'The kitchen would be very nice.' Instinctively she liked this family and yearned to become a friend, not to be held at a distance and entertained, as a visitor, in the front parlour. Far from home and cast amongst strangers in the camp, she was keen to be accepted in the village. The country kitchen held endless fascination for the city woman. Wide-eyed, she took in the shelves full of gleaming jars, homegrown herbs hanging to dry, scenting the kitchen deliciously. When the larder door was opened, to fetch a tin of bonnag, she saw rows of preserves and jams; bottles of wild fruits, painstakingly picked the previous autumn — when the war was young!

In a tiny vase on the window sill, a bunch of pink campions and golden buttercups smiled gaily in a shaft of sunlight, whilst a serene haze of bluebells adorned the scrubbed wooden table.

Pleased to have lured their guest into her kitchen, Eleanor poured three cups of strong, black tea from the eternally simmering pot beside the hob. 'Are you liking the Island?'

'It is a most beautiful island. I have lived, always, in a city and never have I seen so much brilliant colour,' Emily replied with unaffected enthusiasm. 'The variety and profusion of wildflowers in the woods and laneside verges is truly wonderful. And the hedges of hawthorn and fuchsia are exquisite.'

'Do you not find it a poor place after your city?' asked Margaret. She felt drawn to this friendly woman, but also slightly in awe of her. Never had she seen such beautiful clothes, neatly designed, and in such pleasant colours, too.

'I find it very different!' Emily nodded. 'Before I came I was sure I would hate it. But it seems to have a sort of magic about it that captivates. Who could dislike such a place? Wherever you go there is the calming sound of running water laughing gently in the runnels, wind whispering amongst the leaves. I recently walked over the Creggans with Lily and found a spring of clear, cold, sweet water gurgling there.'

'Oh, there is a spring much nearer. Not one hundred yards from here. Just yonder!' Eleanor gestured vaguely. 'We get our drinking water from there and store it here.' With that, she gestured toward a row of large, stone crocks on the floor.

Do you not have a pump?' Emily was startled.

Eleanor smiled, shaking her head. 'Bless you, no. No pump.'

Studying the row of crocks, Emily asked, 'Do you have water in all these pots?'

Eleanor shook her head. 'Only in the one. Another has water from the stream at the end o' the garden. We use that only for washing 'cos it has dirt in it. The third and fourth have herrin'. We buy them in the season an' store them in salt to see us through the winter. An' we salt as much stockfish as we can get an' hang it to dry for out of season.

Emily, looking to where the strings of fish hung outside the window, nodded knowingly. Far be it from her to admit she had been wondering about them! She had a lot to learn about the way of life in her new homeland.

'Then in the larder,' Eleanor continued, 'We keep a crock wi' a few inches o' water an' a bit o' butter. For catchin' the mice, you know.'

'Mice?' Emily echoed blankly. 'How?'

'Well, they can't get up from the outside so they jumps in from the shelf above to get the butter. Once they're in they can't climb up the slippery sides of the crock to get out. So they drowns — you see?'

Emily shuddered. Perhaps it was an explanation she could have better done without!

'In the end crock are eggs,' Eleanor continued, undaunted by her visitor's horrified expression. 'We have twelve hens an' the extra eggs in summer we preserve for when they're not layin'. We make all our own butter too an' keep it on a slate tile on the pantry shelf to keep it cool.'

'You seem so very well organised,' Emily said admiringly.

'Nothin' can be wasted,' Margaret told her without embarrassment. 'We have little money. Especially since Edward an' John went to the war.'

'It must be very difficult for you.' Emily made sympathetic noises.

'Do tell us about the camp,' Margaret deftly switched the subject. 'Are you not frightened living so near those desperate men?'

Emily's laugh was warm and tinkling. 'They are not such desperate people really. We feel in no danger. And we are not much nearer to them than you are. There is the same barbed wire between us. Do you know, most of them have not been in the war, nor want to be. They are just men of alien nationalities, who were living in Britain. Some of them are even naturalized.'

There followed a discussion of the meaning of naturalization and Emily stayed for most of the afternoon, leaving only when the girls were due to finish school.

In the weeks to follow, friendships formed and flourished between the children, and also among the women. Other ladies took to visiting Eleanor and Margaret. Someone — no one could remember who — suggested they should sell cups of tea from the cottage, to help bolster their meagre finances. Soon many of the guards' wives were whiling away their afternoons in the friendly atmosphere of the Quilliam's cottage. It drew them together, like one large family, helping to alleviate their homesickness. If anyone noticed the shabbiness and the mildewed walls, no one cared. It provided an amiable refuge from the camp's wooden huts.

CHAPTER 6

The growth of their circle of friends produced many fringe benefits for Voirrey and her family. As well as the extra pennies the cups of tea, sandwiches and bonnag earned, the camp ladies often brought little tit-bits of food. On occasion, a morsel of fresh meat, usually only enough for one. The family would take turns to enjoy this special treat, with Voirrey being given more turns, she noticed, than the grown-ups. Still, it wasn't her place to argue with the grown-ups about that, was it?

Small paper twists full of tea, dried peas, beans and rice swelled their range of diet.

Voirrey and Lily became almost inseparable. Often they laughed at their reactions when first they dined at the other's home. Lily's shock at having to eat with her fingers. Voirrey's confusion when faced with a knife and fork for the first time. She had turned them over wonderingly, watched how her hosts held theirs and furtively attempted to emulate them. The utensils, she found very difficult to handle. Noticing her dilemma, Emily had smiled kindly and suggested she might prefer to use her fingers. With true Manx stubbornness, Voirrey had determined she would master the art. And so she did!

'Why don't we have knives an' forks?' she asked her grandmother that night.

Eleanor was startled. Frowning, she said, 'We cannot afford the likes. What do you think God gave us fingers for?' she asked sharply.

'Lily's family use them!'

'Well, they's city folk. Posher'n us, they are. Don't go gettin' ideas above your station jus' 'cos you've made friends wi' a city girl!'

Voirrey had gone home filled with wonder after that first visit to the Beckinsales. The close proximity to the prisoners had been a little frightening at first. Then, at Lily's prompting, they had sneaked up to the wire, when they thought no one was looking and talked to one of the men who was standing nearby.

A guard had spotted them, shouted, and they had scuttled away, tumbling into the house, giggling, moments later.

'He seemed nice!' Voirrey was surprised.

'A lot of them are nice — but we're not supposed to talk to them because they're the enemy.'

By the time Percy came home, he had learned of the girls' trespass at the wire and scolded them firmly, though Voirrey thought she saw a twinkle of amusement in his eye.

CHAPTER 7

Through the early part of summer, Voirrey watched for the roundabouts of holidaymakers with their pennies. It became quickly apparent, to her bitter disappointment, that they would not come.

Caesar Quine brought forth the information that, as a consequence of the danger to shipping by mines and submarines, very few visitors dared venture across the sea. In addition, eleven of the Steam Packet Company's ships had been diverted to war duties, leaving only three to serve the Island.

'Almost the only travellers comin' over now,' Caesar said, 'Are people to visit the prisoners. If the visitors are enemy aliens they are only allowed to stay on the Island seven days an' may only pay three visits to the camp. Then they won't be allowed back onto the Island until three months have passed.'

'How'd the authorities keep track?' Henry asked, puzzled.

'Well, when they arrive they has to register 'emselves at the police station in Douglas. Then if they wants to travel more'n five miles — like to come out here – they has to get a permit.'

'Lily says some o' the prisoners have English wives an' children!' Voirrey piped up. 'What happens to them?'

'In some cases, if they gets approval, they can come an' live on the Island an' visit their husbands once in each fortnight.

Others can get a permit to stay on the Island a month. They may visit wi' their menfolk on three occasions in that time.'

'It must be very difficult for women wi' young children,' said Margaret thoughtfully.

Caesar threw her a quizzical look. 'No harder than for a woman, left here with her man at war. And all this is causin' terrible hardship for the landladies. With no holidaymakers comin' they have not the money t' pay their rents. With no rents being received the owners cannot pay their mortgages — or even the interest on them!'

'Aye, Charles the painter tells me he is owed a lot from the boarding houses, but they cannot pay,' Henry said.

Caesar nodded his agreement. 'A lot of tradesmen cannot collect their debts, but the wolf has been kept from the door for many by the work the government has given them in the buildin' o' the prison camps. But mark my words well, Henry, this war will be the ruination of many on the Island!'

Henry nodded absently. Grim-faced, he reflected on how hard his family were struggling, with John and Edward both gone.

As summer drew toward a close Voirrey and Lily roamed the hills together. Enjoying showing off her island, Voirrey took her friend to places she knew she was forbidden to go.

One Saturday Lily came early and went with Voirrey to take the cows to the lhergy. She had never been so close to a cow before and considered this a brave new adventure.

Responding to Lily's excitement, Voirrey suggested a visit to the sea.

'I'd rather go up there. It looks nice amongst the trees.' Lily was half-way over the gate, looking up Barnell glen.

Panicking, Voirrey cried, 'No! Not up there! We can't go there!'

'Why not?' Lily was startled by her friend's reaction.

CHAPTER 7

'Because its---! I'm not allowed!
'Why not?'
"Cos!'
"Cos what?'
"Cos Mammy an' Granny say I mustn't.'
Lily's lip curled slightly. 'They won't know.'
Voirrey paused thoughtfully. 'It's dangerous!' she confided in hushed tones.
Lily's eyes widened. 'Dangerous?' She threw a wary glance up the lane. 'Why? What's up there?'
Hesitantly Voirrey whispered, 'Fairies! Bad fairies!'
'Fairies!?' Lily snorted derisively. 'You surely don't believe in fairies?'
Stung, Voirrey turned away. 'There are *so* fairies! Mammy an' Granny say that if I'm naughty they'll get me!'
Lily giggled, climbing one more rung up the gate. 'Well, *I'm* going!'
Voirrey clutched at her arm. 'No! Please don't go! They *are* there!'
'No one believes in fairies!' Lily pulled her arm free.
'I saw some!' Voirrey cried. 'It — they tried to get me, but I got away. They live in those tholtans!' She gestured to the row of ruined cottages.
Lily studied the ruins thoughtfully. 'You actually saw some?' She stepped down.
Voirrey nodded. 'I know a quick way to the sea from here. It's safer to go there.'
Lifting their skirts above the wet grass, the girls trudged across the fields.
Dog, refusing to be sent home, romped with them.
Crossing the road, they scrambled up the Creggans, their feet sinking in the wet, marshy ground. At the spring, they

stopped to drink, sitting for a while to study the camp, set out like a map at their feet.

'Look how it's all in neat squares.' Voirrey was awed at the enormity of it. It looked so much bigger from above.

'Yes. Daddy says it is all divided into compounds. Each one is surrounded by barbed wire and holds one thousand men.'

'Why are they kept separate?'

'Daddy says they are less likely to riot and break out if they are kept in small numbers. Each compound has its own kitchen and the cooks are prisoners.'

Voirrey pulled a face.

'They have very good cooks,' Lily assured her. 'Some of them were chefs in big, posh hotels and restaurants in London and other cities. There are all sorts of people there, like singers, musicians and artists. They have formed whole orchestras and often hold concerts.'

'That must be the music I hear at night.' Voirrey said.

'Yes. And see that?' Lily pointed toward the centre of the camp. 'Those are courts where the prisoners may play tennis.'

Voirrey gazed around her, enjoying the beauty of the scene. To her right, just beyond the camp, was Patrick village. The church, with even the gravestones showing, was visible in the clarity of the day. And the schoolhouse. She could even see her three cows, far off in the lhergy.

A train ground wearily past the church, across the road and up the new line, trailing a puffy haze of thick, black smoke. Clanking to a halt, it disgorged a collection of distracted prisoners and noisy, bustling guards.

They were held in the cindered square for a time while an officer – Lily said he was the Camp Commandant — addressed them. Finally, they were herded, like sheep, to a group of huts, where they disappeared from view.

CHAPTER 7

'Let's go on.'

At their first move, Dog leapt to his feet, bounding ahead of them. Over the top of the Creggans, they went, and down the hill toward the clifftops.

Suddenly Dog squealed. From the distance the girls could see him throwing himself around, then he disappeared.

Panic-stricken, Voirrey raced over the rough ground, Lily close behind. Dog's high pitched squeals of terror led them quickly to where a piece of twisted wire, attached to a wooden peg, stretched over the cliff.

Dog hung over the cliff, suspended by one leg, on the end of the wire! Sickened, Voirrey said tearfully, 'He's caught in a loob! We'll have to pull him up.' Grabbing the wire, she leaned back against it. Dog howled more loudly.

Lily, lying on her stomach, looking over, cried, 'Oh stop, Voirrey! The wire is going to cut his leg off!'

Voirrey lay beside her, sobbing bitterly, watching Dog hang there, his struggles gradually weakening.

'I must save him,' she sniffed. 'Lie behind me an' hold my legs while I try to reach him.'

Voirrey wriggled her shoulders past the cliff-edge, reaching down frantically.

'Just a few more inches!' She squirmed a little further down.

'You'll fall!' Lily squealed, her eyes rolling in terror.

'I won't. I've got to save him.'

Lily wriggled forward a little, digging her toes into the heather, tightening her grip on her friend.

Voirrey pushed herself down until her body, from the waist up, hung over the cliff face.

Below her, jagged rocks reached ominously upward, the sea thrashing over them, like some great monster trying to suck her into its awful, foaming mouth. Hypnotized, she stared down, her left hand absently fumbling in Dog's direction.

A rock slid out from under her, spinning, hurtling, to shatter on the rocks far below and she felt her heart thundering against her ribs. Feeling herself slipping forward, Voirrey screamed.

'Voirrey!' Lily panicked. Her grip tightened and she felt her fingernails cut into Voirrey's leg. Her toes dug deeper into the ground above. Opening her eyes, Voirrey saw Dog was now within reach. He had stopped struggling now and hung limply. Heart cringing at the awful reality of the danger, she reached tentatively, getting a grip on Dog's tail. Twisting him round slightly, she managed to catch the leg with the wire, taking some of his weight from it.

A few stones broke away, bouncing and clattering to the sea below, but Voirrey maintained her grip and inch by inch the two girls writhed backwards up the slope. A lifetime later Voirrey had dragged her whole body to safety and lay prone, Dog still hanging over the cliff, suspended by his tail and leg.

'Let go of me an' help to pull Dog up!' she pleaded.

Lily crept down, nervously eyeing the crumbling cliff edge all the while until she could stretch out beside her friend. Reaching blindly, she caught the scruff of Dog's neck and together they managed to haul him to safety. Trembling, Voirrey gently removed the offending wire. Dog lay motionless.

'Is he dead?' Tears pricked Lily's eyes as she gnawed at her bottom lip.

Voirrey shook her head. 'No. He's still breathin'. We'd better get him home. Don't tell anyone it happened at the cliff.'

'I won't!' Lily vowed, wide-eyed. The fuss the grown-ups would make then would be unbearable!

Taking turns to carry the heavy collie, the girls stumbled tearfully home. Following the shortest route, close to the

· CHAPTER 7 ·

barbed wire, they had to wade through thick, cloying marshland. Immersed in misery, they failed to notice several prisoners watching concernedly.

CHAPTER 8

Sage Quayle rapped her cane on the desk. 'Pay attention now children. I have something of importance to tell you.' Instantly the buzz of chatter and laughter stopped. As one, the class turned to the front, all eyes expectantly on their teacher.

'Some prisoners will be coming to build a stage in the empty classroom, so that we may perform plays and concerts there.'

There was a gasp, followed by whispering, shuffling and scraping as the children discussed the news.

'These men,' Sage continued, after another loud crack with her cane, 'Will be moving around the schoolyard. They will be accompanied by guards at all times. It is absolutely forbidden for them to enter into conversation with you children. If any of them should speak to you, you must ignore him. Is that clear?'

The children, in one voice, said, 'Yes, Miss Quayle!'

Shortly afterwards a bogie, laden with planks of wood, pulled up by the school gate. Voirrey watched, enthralled, while a gang of prisoners carried the wood, to pile it against the wall.

Sensing her gaze, one of the men looked up, smiled and winked. Voirrey's heart lurched as a memory of her father was stirred. She had seen this man before, she remembered. Yes, the day she had found the body on the beach. Since then too!

CHAPTER 8

Several times she had noticed him watching wistfully from behind the wire. Always watching! And quick to smile when he caught her eye. Voirrey found herself eagerly watching his movements, subconsciously willing him to look at her again.

Dragging her thoughts back to the classroom, she found Sage watching her irritably.

'Now you have kindly honoured us with your attention again, Voirrey, perhaps you would be good enough to read the next paragraph?'

'Yes Miss.' Voirrey stood up, book in hand. What next paragraph? Which was the last paragraph that had been read? Panicking, she stared blindly at the book, trying to effect a realistic-sounding fit of coughing. From the adjoining room, she could hear the monotonous drone of the little children reciting their arithmetic tables.

The clock on the wall ticked ominously, while Sage beat a tattoo on the desk with her fingernails.

Lily tugged Voirrey's dress under the desk, surreptitiously pointing to her reader. Voirrey glanced down, hurriedly turned two pages and started to read.

'Thank you Voirrey. Pay attention in future. And *you*, miss,' Sage fixed Lily with her iciest glare, 'Leave her to sort out her own troubles in future!'

Lily kept her head bowed, wriggled uncomfortably and studiously examined her finger-nails.

At playtime Voirrey and Lily ventured close to the spare classroom, hoping for a peep through the window.

'You keep watchin' while I try to look in.'

'You'll be caught! Then we'll both get into trouble!' Lily hissed desperately. Nonetheless, she stood with her back to the wall, watching warily.

Voirrey stood on tip-toe, peering eagerly through the window.

'What can you see?'

'Not much. 'Tis awful dark inside.'

A prisoner — *the* prisoner — came out and, seeing the girls, stopped, smiling at them.

Voirrey, startled at his nearness, took two quick backward steps, treading on Lily's foot.

He smiled again. 'I won't harm you. I have a daughter about your age.' His voice, Voirrey noticed, was without an accent. 'Did your dog recover?'

'How do---?' her brow creased.

'I saw you carrying it.'

'He recovered well, thank you. He will always limp, Daa says.'

'Keep away from those children!' Suddenly a guard was behind the prisoner, hitting him about the shoulders with his rifle butt, pushing him away.

Voirrey caught a sudden breath, then with an angry sob she leapt at the guard, grabbing his arm. 'Don't hurt him! He wasn't doin' no harm.'

The man pushed her roughly away. 'You children stay well away! You must never speak to these prisoners. They're bad men. Now get out of here!'

From behind him, the prisoner smiled and winked, his green eyes shining warmly.

Voirrey sensed a presence before she stepped through the kitchen door that afternoon. Just an aura. A feeling. Nothing tangible. Heart jolting unsteadily, she burst through the doorway, seeing him immediately, standing with his feet planted firmly — as though to steady the heaving deck — in front of the range.

'Uncle Edward!' Voirrey hurtled across the room, throwing her arms around him.

CHAPTER 8

Catching her, he swung her in the air, studying her while he held her aloft. Unruly golden curls flopped wildly down around her face.

'My — how you've grown!' Edward lowered her, holding her close against him.

'Is the war over? Are you home to stay? Will Daddy soon be home, too?'

Edward's face fell and he shook his head sadly. 'Hush, little one. No, I fear the war still has a long way to go. I have only three days leave, so can only be here for two. I don't know when your Daddy might come home. If his regiment is sent overseas he may be allowed leave to come home first.'

'It's been so long,' she protested angrily. 'You promised me it would be over in just a few months!'

'I know, love,' his voice was gentle. 'It looks as if it might last much longer than we thought.'

Voirrey and Lily — who fell in love with Edward on sight — selfishly took up the greater part of his evenings. The grown-ups, they both agreed, had him during the day while they were at school. Where'er he went they followed, Voirrey clinging to one hand.

Lily, bashful, but infatuated, would slip her hand tentatively into his other. Dog would hobble painfully but happily determined, behind the trio.

For hours they strolled in the hills, browning now as the bracken and heather donned their Autumn coats.

'Have you killed any men, Uncle Edward?'

'Not that I've seen, but the planes from my ship sank an enemy ship with torpedoes. Men died, so I suppose that makes me partly responsible.'

'Is the war really exciting?' Lily's brown eyes shone with more devotion than Dog's.

'Exciting? I'm not sure if that is the right word. Frightening, yes! We live in fear! In our bunks at night, we know not when we might collide with a mine. Or when a submarine will send a torpedo into the ship's bowels. We sleep only lightly, fearing a sudden explosion, an unexpected gush of icy water and the dreaded list which will take us plummeting to the ocean bed!'

Voirrey shuddered. To have to live, constantly, with such fear was unimaginable!

Climbing to the top of the Creggans, they sat down to regain their breath, gazing out over the ever-growing spread of the camp. Tiny people, like swarms of bees, buzzed around the wired encampment. One group marched briskly, exercising under the orders and eagle eyes of the guards. Some played tennis in the autumn sunshine, others played football, while many just strolled in solitary thoughtfulness.

Even from that distance, Voirrey thought she could recognise *the* prisoner, staring longingly toward the east.

'What ship are you on, Mr Quilliam?' Lily asked, gazing up at him through a mist of love.

Edward, drawn from his reverie, smiled down at Lily. 'I do wish you would just call me Edward. The Ben-my-Chree is my ship. It is fitted to carry aeroplanes.'

'Which ship did you sink?'

'"Twere the planes sank it — with torpedoes. A Turkish ship, an' they hit two more. That was at Gallipoli. We were the last British ship to leave after they evacuated Gallipoli. Soon after, the Southland was sunk an' we picked up over 800 souls. The lifeboats and rafts was overcrowded,' he told a distant hill. 'Some o' them poor men was in a dreadful mess, wi' burns an' cuts an' blood everywhere. Folks wi' limbs tore off. Screamin'! Some beggin' to live. Other pleadin' to be helped to die. Dreadful! Dreadful!'

CHAPTER 8

Voirrey, seeing the tear in his eye and the tremor on his lip, pressed close against him.

Lily sat silent. Stunned.

"Tis not what we thought it would be. Not at all like it!' Edward whispered.

'It must be awful,' Lily muttered, shuddering. 'To have so much pain.'

'Aye. There are no words to describe the suffering I have seen.'

Dog spotted a rabbit and with a wild yapping, bounded in pursuit, with his strange new gait.

The sombre moment was gone and Edward returned to the present. Pointing to a hillside beyond the camp, he asked, 'What's that yonder?'

Voirrey followed the direction of his finger, squinting against the low evening sun.

'It looks like The Legs O' Man!'

'It is!' Lily aired her knowledge. 'The prisoners pegged out the Three Legs on the whole of that field and put on manure to make the grass grow greener inside the pattern.'

Walking home in the twilight, they heard, music starting in the camp, sounding as if from a heavenly orchestra.

When Voirrey returned from school the following day, Edward was gone — off back to sea. Two broken hearts were left on the Island, the girls having to adjust, wondering, at times, if he had ever really been there at all.

Voirrey gazed dreamily through the window. A sudden break in the black cloud directed a shaft of sunlight through the giant sycamore, standing tall and proud at the bottom corner of the schoolyard beside the gate. It fluttered its leaves in appreciation of the welcome warmth.

A movement through the hedge caught Vorrey's eye and, as she watched, a small cluster of men turned in through the gateway, shuffling toward the schoolhouse. Flanked by three disinterested guards in khaki uniforms, they halted close to the window where she sat.

As had become his habit, *the* prisoner looked up, his eyes holding Voirrey's, then he smiled broadly and winked.

Catching the look, one of the guards stepped forward quickly and viciously prodded his bayonet into the prisoner's ribs.

Voirrey gasped, feeling the pain of the sharp weapon. In terror, she watched as the man stumbled, rounding on the guard with his fist raised. Swiftly the rifle was raised and aimed, the men locked eyes challengingly. Then, as though resigned, the prisoner sighed, lowered his eyes and his body sagged.

'Get back into line!' The guard snarled. 'Next time I'll shoot!'

Voirrey shivered, feeling the sting of tears. He was so like Daddy. His smile. The way he winked. Everything! She would hate anyone to treat her father like that. It must be awful to be a prisoner of war. To be trapped on this little island so far away from your own people, your family, with armed guards watching you all the time.

With a crack like gunfire, the cane crashed onto the desk close to Voirrey's hand. Startled, she jerked around, focussing, finally on Sage Quayle who, face flushed, was glaring angrily at her.

'Pay attention, girl! I've spoken to you three times!'

'S-s-sorry, Miss.' Voirrey stammered miserably. 'I thought the guard was goin' to shoot one o' the prisoners.'

'Germans!' Sage spat the word. 'Better if they shot them all!'

Subdued laughter rippled in the classroom and Voirrey, eyes still fixed fearfully on her teacher, sensed, rather than saw, the other children turned in their seats, watching.

Sage Quayle's eyes flickered around the shabby room, her hot glare briefly touching each child in turn. Shuffling uncomfortably, each one moved to face the front.

· CHAPTER 8 ·

Almost gently, Sage said, 'Try to concentrate, child. Remember it is men like those your father is away fighting.'

Voirrey nodded mutely, her eyes filling with tears. It seemed such a long time since she had seen her father. *This* man, she was sure, was nothing like the soldiers her father was fighting. Surely *they* would all have uniforms and guns?

A sharp knock on the door heralded the arrival of one of the guards. 'Excuse me, Ma-am, but we are ready to start work on the stage again if it is convenient.'

Sage frowned and sighed. 'Very well, but tell the men to be as quiet as possible. Some of the children seem to have trouble keeping their minds on their lessons, without all that hammering to distract them!' She looked pointedly at Voirrey, who blushed wildly. The guard nodded, touched his cap and backed out, pulling the door shut behind him.

From the corner of her eye, Voirrey saw the group of men drift towards the empty schoolroom.

'Now, children, I think it is time we got on with some spelling,' Sage said decisively.

A hand went up at the front of the room. 'Please miss?'

'Yes, Thomas?'

'Please Miss, my Mammy an' Daddy says it's not right havin' the likes o' them desperate Germans around us children.'

'Well, you see, Thomas, they are not all Germans. There are Austrians and Turks amongst them. They are *not* desperate men. Only the most trustworthy are permitted to leave the camp and they are well guarded, as you can see, so you children are in no danger.'

Voirrey leaned her left elbow on the desk, propping her forehead in her hand. While ostensibly studying her books, she covertly watched the movements outside.

How much things had changed, she thought, since the prisoners had come. Such a small, poor country village before, Patrick had, overnight almost, become a huge, bright, noisy wooden city.

Voirrey clearly remembered the first of the prisoners arriving. Marching smartly up the road guarded, then, by the young men of the Volunteer Corps. Now *they* had gone to war — her father with them — and many of the present guards were quite old.

The stage in the spare classroom was coming on quite well, Sage had told the class.

There were hopes it might be finished in time to be used for the Christmas concert. To do it full justice the children were practising hard, determined to perform their best concert ever.

The golden autumn leaves fell, piling high in the lanes, leaving the trees stark, black skeletons. Nights drew in until it was dusk when school ended.

In the dark Voirrey fetched the cows from the field. Dog limped bravely along always, devoted as ever and no less keen to help.

'Well, my lass,' Henry said after tea one night. 'There's a beautiful moon. Would you like to come wi' me to gather some wood?'

Voirrey jumped eagerly to her feet. 'Yes, let's.'

She loved these times, roaming the woods and country lanes in the dark with her grandfather. In spite of the intense cold of the evening air, there was great warmth in the closeness they shared as they scoured the hedge-rows together.

Wood of all sizes, from tiny twigs, for kindling, to stout branches, found its way into the canvas sheet they carried between them. Coal was scarce, Voirrey knew because it had to come from Across and the Germans were sinking the colliery

CHAPTER 8

ships. A large stockpile of timber must be collected to fuel their fires through winter.

Voirrey enjoyed the crunch of her boots on the crisp, frosted grass and iced puddles. Hand in Henry's hand, she watched, fascinated, the little snow-puff clouds which hung before their faces whenever they breathed.

'Daa. Why can you see your breath white in the winter?'

Henry frowned, shrugging. *How should he know?* 'Look at them hills!' He changed the subject.

Voirrey's eyes followed his pointing finger. Gasping, she gazed up at the hills, looking as if a light shone from within them. Still clad in the previous night's snow they shone a luminescent blue in the moonlight, gleaming against the dark sky.

"Tis a beautiful island in any weather,' Henry said thoughtfully. 'In the springtime, you got the primroses an' bluebells in the woods' an' riverbanks. An' there's birdsong all around. New buds on the trees. Marsh marigolds an' bogbeans in the Curraghs. Summer 'tis fuchsias, wild cherries an' hawthorn in the hedges. Trout in the streams an' the smell o' wild garlic before the rain. Autumn's got the gold an' red. Blankets o' leaves underfoot. Streams run faster. An' in Winter we got this!' His arm swept airily — encompassing all.

Voirrey nodded. 'An' in winter we got Christmas.'

Last Christmas seemed so long ago when she had been upset because the war was not already over. Another year had gone! Still, the war went on! A tear pricked her eye and she sighed.

The cold permeated her boots — dampness from the logs her gloves, and as her toes and fingers turned painfully numb, the evening became a little less beautiful.

On her plea, they hurried over the lhergy, stopping momentarily to gaze in awe at the camp lights below them in the distance, sparkling like a million stars, blazing the pathway to a dream.

CHAPTER 9

Voirrey and Lily were skipping in the lane, just two days before Christmas Eve, when Joseph's cart approached at a fast rate. Squinting into the low winter sun, Voirrey could see, three figures.

'Whoa, boy!' Joseph leaned back on the reins as the cart drew to the gate.

Voirrey's heart lurched, then leapt, thundering with excitement. 'Daddy!' she squealed. 'Daddy you're home. I didn't know you was comin'! No one told me!' Speeding forward, she tugged impatiently at his coat tail, almost pulling him off balance as he climbed down from the cart.

'Many thanks, Joseph.'

'That's a'right. Lucky I was passin' the station jus' after the train come in.' With a quick wave and a click of his tongue, Joseph galvanized Ned into action and they trotted off to deliver their other passenger home.

Voirrey gazed after the cart, clinging joyfully to John. 'Are you an' Stanley Clucas home to stay? '

Lily was hanging shyly in the background.

'No. Just for a few days. Is this your friend you've written so much about?' John smiled at Lily, who shuffled self-consciously.

'Yes. This is Lily.'

'Hello, Lily.'

With a flutter of her long lashes, the girl blushed, whispering, 'Good afternoon, Mr Kelly.'

Tugging at John's hand, Voirrey hurried him to the door. 'Mammy! Granny! Daddy's home!' She yelled, dashing inside.

'Well, this looks like being a jollier Christmas than we'd expected,' Henry enthused, drawing a lungful of smoke from his smelly pipe. 'The girl misses you real bad, John.'

Voirrey snuggled deeper into John's lap. Lulled with the gentle warmth of her father's love, together with Granny's herring pie and bun loaf, she listened contentedly to the grown-up's conversation.

'So, you really believe you're goin' to be sent to the fightin' now?' Henry was asking.

'Aye. That's why they've sent us all home for Christmas. We've been on stand-by a long time now, just trainin' an' itchin' to get over an' do our share of the fighting. We're beginnin' to feel all there is to the war is runnin' bayonets into bags o' straw.'

'Caesar Quayle says there's a lot o' men dyin' over in the war,' Margaret broke in earnestly. 'An' Edward says it too.

'There's allus a lot dies in war,' Eleanor said fearfully.

'Our lads'll be a'right, woman!' Henry scowled at his wife.

'Well it's good you got home for Christmas.' Margaret settled on John's chair arm, gently stroking Voirrey's hair. 'She frets real bad sometimes for you an' Edward.'

Voirrey felt John's arms tighten around her, and his kiss, like a whisper, on the top of her head.

'We've got somethin' special for Christmas dinner!' Eleanor skilfully moved the topic away from the war. 'There's a tin o'

CHAPTER 9

corned beef one o' the camp ladies brought a time ago. We bin savin' it for a special day.'

'Corned beef indeed!' John sounded impressed. He felt no need to spoil their surprise by telling her the army gave it to him often.

At the mention of food, Voirrey was quickly wide awake again. 'Can we have some honey sponge, too, please?'

'We can, that.'

'Lily says Manx honey is nicer than English.'

'Aye. 'Tis.'

'Why is it?'

'Well, we ha' special bees, y' see,' Henry started. 'We show our bees respec' an' let 'em know they're special. When the head of the household dies. we must always tell the bees, 'cos it's important they know. An' did you know that if a bee flies indoors it brings good luck wi' it? An' on the ol' Christmas Eve, what used to be January 4th, the bees can be heard hummin' loudly in memory o' the birth o' Jesus Christ. An' 'tis because we pay them such respec' they make us nicer honey.'

Voirrey thought she would never see a bee in quite the same light again. A whirlwind of noisy excitement rushed the hours away until Christmas Eve.

John strolled the lhergies and lanes hand in hand with Voirrey, absorbing the beauty of his island in winter and wondered, aloud on occasions, how long it would be before he saw it again.

Voirrey tagged along everywhere with him, drinking up every moment she could manage to share his company. Proudly she aired her knowledge about the affairs of the camp, pointing out the field where the prisoners had made the Legs of Man in a brighter green.

On Christmas Eve she begged one of her grandfather's largest stockings, hanging it, in hope, from the mantel.

John lit her way up the creaking stairway to bed. His hand laid softly against the back of her waist, he pushed her gently.

Voirrey was confusedly excited. Keen to go to bed, to bring the morning faster, yet reluctant to leave her father. Wide awake, though tired. Eager to sleep yet scared lest when she awoke the contents of the stocking should disappoint her.

John dowsed the candle immediately they entered her room.

'My word. 'tis brighter than daylight in here!' Crossing the room, he gazed, in wonder, through the sloping window.

'It's always like this now,' Voirrey said, her eyes aglow. 'Ever since the camp came. Things they call floodlights so they can see if the prisoners try to go through the wire at night. And the music they play always is so lovely, Daddy. Listen! Every night there's beautiful music.'

John tucked her into bed, sitting on the edge to listen for a while. It was indeed beautiful music. Obviously, they were skilled musicians. Some of the tunes he recognised — others not. There were several carols and many voices singing in harmony.

'Lily says they have many of those orchestras. Sometimes I dream I am a famous dancer. Dancing in places all around the world, in front of hundreds of people. Kings an' queens sometimes. Then the music stops an' I wake up an' I'm still here. The war is still on an' you an' Uncle Edward are still gone.'

'We won't be gone much longer. The war must end quite soon. When I get over there those Germans will know they're beaten an' surrender. Hold onto your dreams, love. We must all have our dreams. When you have one — keep it. Keep it forever an' work to make it come true.'

Holding her father's hand, Voirrey fell asleep to the refrain of *'Silent Night'*, sung in a Germanic tongue.

When she opened her eyes the sky was still black, but her

· CHAPTER 9 ·

room was lit like the stage of the Gaiety Theatre in Douglas. The house was still and quiet, save for the groaning of the wind around the eaves, and the rhythmic clicking of a loose roof slate. An occasional eerie creaking gave evidence the closet door had come unlatched.

Voirrey sat up, wriggling out from under the blankets. Shivering at the cold of her feet on the bare boards, she slipped on her coat and tip-toed to the door. Turning the handle slowly, she edged the door open, to minimise its squeaking. As she crept down the stairway, she counted each step.

Holding tightly to the rail, she stepped over the sixth — the one that always complained most loudly.

When she had safely negotiated the stairs without any voice shouting at her to go back to bed, she rushed into the kitchen, heart thundering with anticipation.

It was there! The stocking still hung where she had left it, but not as flat as before. Standing on a stool, she unhooked the curtain that was no more than a square of linen hung on two nails above the window.

Slowly, wishing to savour every moment, she dug her hand into the stocking. In the dim light that filtered through the tree-tops from the camp, she found, first a knitted doll. Further investigation produced a sugar mouse, an apple, a pear, eight boiled sweeties and twelve hazelnuts.

Huddling close up against the range to absorb its last lingering warmth, she lovingly turned the articles over in her hands, fingering them gently, inspecting each one intimately.

The sugar mouse was special, the most beautiful creature she could ever remember. He sparkled like snow on the hills on a sunny day. His little pink eyes gleamed in the half-light and Voirrey could almost swear he twitched his whiskers and string tail.

The doll, soft and warm, had been knitted and stitched with such care. She could feel the love which had been worked into every stitch.

Laying the treasures gently on her nightdress, she gathered up the hem and stole back upstairs. The sixth step from the top groaned noisily under her weight and she heard a dull murmur of voices from her parents' room, but no one called out.

Safely back in her room, where the light was better, she laid all the riches on the dresser top. Unwrapping one of the sweeties, she slipped it slowly into her mouth. Being careful not to bite, she sucked gently to make it last. Lining everything up, she gazed lovingly at them for a while. Suddenly, aware of how unbearably cold it was, she picked up the doll and slipped, shivering, into bed. In no time she was sound asleep, the precious new doll wrapped cosily in her arms.

Christmas Day passed in a flurry of cooking, eating, dish washing, laughter, warmth and, most of all, love.

Voirrey found herself often looking from one to the other of her parents. Moments when she caught them gazing, each into the eyes of the other, love and longing openly displayed.

'If only Daddy didn't have to go away,' she thought, *'Everythin' would be perfect. Perhaps by the time Christmas is over the war will be ended, then he won't have to go.'*

Voirrey found the corned beef — adeptly made into a pie to stretch it further — quite the nicest meat she had ever tasted.

Granny's honey sponge, made only on special occasions came, as ever, straight from heaven.

After dinner they went walking, Voirrey, Margaret and John. It was such a beautiful, clear bright day, with only a few puffy white clouds to break the blue sky, they felt they could not stay indoors. Wrapping up well, for there was a sharp frost, they

· CHAPTER 9 ·

stepped out along the crunchy lane up Barnell. At the top, John turned left toward the glen.

'It should be a pleasant walk through here to-day.' He started to unlatch the gate.

'No! No! Voirrey cried, pulling back. 'Not there!'

''Tis all right.'

'No! The fairies are there! They'll get us!'

John threw Margaret an irritated look. 'You an' your mother must stop fillin' the girl's head wi' nonsense.' he muttered. Then more loudly, 'There are no fairies.'

'There are! They live in the tholtans! I saw one!'

John shook his head, smiling. 'Then walk between us an' you'll be safe. They won't dare to harm one of the King's soldiers.'

Trembling, Voirrey moved to the middle, clinging tightly to her parents' hands. As they passed the ruined cottages, she pressed hard against John, her frightened eyes constantly seeking, searching for movements amongst the shadows. She didn't see any fairies, but she could sense them looking, creeping from tree to tree, watching — waiting. Her heart stammered violently, and she could feel her mother shaking too.

Beyond the corner, with the tholtans out of sight behind them, Voirrey relaxed enough to enjoy the beauty around her. Huge sycamore and horse chestnut trees, like giant sentinels placed there to guard the glen, dotted the woodlands their path passed through.

A robin watched from the branches of a blackthorn bush, his feathers puffed against the raw cold. A chattering pair of blue-tits clung on a hawthorn bush, contentedly pecking its berries.

Down to their left, a tinkling stream laughed its way downwards. And further on they came to a reservoir, its gentle waters guarded by a crisp, black crust of ice.

'I never knew this was here.' Voirrey spoke in awe, her words hanging before her mouth in white vapour puffs.

'It such a peaceful haven.' John said quietly.

'It would be a good place to skate — if I had skates.' Voirrey eyed the ice longingly.

'Don't you ever come here by yourself!' Margaret anticipated danger. ''Tis not a safe place to be!' She glanced around nervously, sensing an unfriendly presence.

'I won't!' Voirrey, remembering the fairies, was more than willing to concur.

They leaned, for a while, on the gate above the reservoir, drinking in the solitude and quietness, broken only by the bird-sounds in the clear winter air.

After tea, they roasted chestnuts John had brought with him from 'Across'. Having laid them on the coal shovel, they held them over the wood embers in the parlour fireplace. The nuts crackled and popped and jumped until their hard skins split open and they were cooked.

Voirrey's eyes popped with them, in anticipation of the treat ahead, starting slightly whenever a nut jumped on the shovel. The ecstasy, when finally she tasted the first, was well worth the waiting.

When the nuts were all gone and Voirrey well filled with more than her share, they all sat silently in the flickering warmth from the fire. Strains of a gentle overture drifted from the camp, lending to their pleasure at just being together.

Later, snuggled into bed, her arms around her hot water bottle and John's kiss still warm on her cheek, Voirrey drifted away on the wings of the prisoners' music. Tonight, she was a famous skater, gliding on the ice of Barnell reservoir. But it wasn't in the glen now, with the dreadful fairies all around. It

CHAPTER 9

was in the garden of a spectacular, glittering ice palace, with thousands of brightly dressed ladies and gentlemen applauding vigorously.

It had been the happiest day Voirrey could ever remember.

Suddenly, painfully, John was gone again, back to Birkenhead, to the 3rd Cheshire Regiment, with whom his Company had been training.

Joseph and Ned arrived to take them to St John's, with Stanley Clucas; all signs of boyishness now gone; already aboard. John had asked that the family not go right to Douglas to farewell him, to which they agreed with reluctance.

Waving forlornly as the train pulled out of the station, Voirrey had an unbearably leaden-hearted feeling of loss and foreboding.

CHAPTER 10

The long, cold damp days dragged wearily into months. It was the most miserable winter Voirrey could remember.

A letter came from John early in January, dated on the 2nd day of that month, telling them excitedly that at last, he was to get into the war. The 1st Manx Service Company, he related, were to leave the 3rd Cheshire Regiment on the following day, to embark on a journey to Salonika, in Greece. All the men were joyful that finally, they were to make a real contribution to the war effort.

The Knockaloe internees, who had managed to get the stage well enough advanced for the children to hold their nativity play, came back after Christmas to complete the work.

Struggling to overcome her loneliness after her father's departure, Voirrey found that watching the prisoners was a welcome distraction. She found herself searching for *the* prisoner, longing for him to come into sight. When he did she could not take her eyes away from him. There was a certain, unspoken empathy between them. It was nothing she could explain, but he seemed to fill a void. When he was there her father did not seem so far away.

When the stage was finally finished and the men no longer came to the school, there was a feeling almost of bereavement.

CHAPTER 10

As the snowdrops died and the crocuses began to fade, Spring was ushered in by the primroses, daffodils and the eternal Manx gorse in hedgerows and banks. The island turned golden and the sun began to give a little heat. It warmed, slightly, the spirits of the island's peoples, whom the war had left struggling and grieving.

Some had gained and grown rich through the work the internee camps had brought. But many were bankrupt — or otherwise suffering. The families of the men who had gone to the war were penniless and hungry. Early excitement about the war was gone and reality had closed in to crush them.

Women had become widows! Children were orphaned! Sons and brothers were dead, lost on some foreign shore. The excitement of having what they had regarded as a hero in the family had long since gone.

Occasionally — not often, because neither Edward nor John was fond of writing — a letter would arrive.

A short note to Henry and Eleanor, which Voirrey or Margaret had to read to them, brought the information that Edward was still on the Ben-my-Chree and on his way out to the waters off Turkey and Greece.

'John writes,' Margaret read aloud the less private parts, 'That he did, indeed sail from Liverpool docks on a ship named the S.S Olympic, on the 3rd day of January. They sailed through the Mediterranean and Aegean Seas, disembarking at a Greek island named Limnos. From there they travelled by cargo ship to a place called Salonika. After they landed, they were marched, in the most awful heat, almost ten miles to join the 2nd Cheshire Regiment.'

'All these strange foreign names,' Henry grumbled. 'Don't tell us where John is, do they?'

'I'll show you!' Voirrey scuttled upstairs, returning quickly with her school atlas. In no time she had found Limnos. Quickly afterwards she also located Salonika. The grown-ups gathered round to study it, but maps were an unknown entity to them and they could not make much sense out of it. It was just drawings on paper and it certainly went nowhere near telling them where John was.

'Does Daddy say anything else?' Voirrey asked, frustrated.

'Let's see.' Margaret took up the letter. 'Yes. He writes that in the beginning the 2nd Cheshires, being a regular battalion, had just recently arrived from France, where they'd had a rough time with a lot of fighting. They thought our lads were a bunch of amateurs, for we had never fought. Anyway, a trench line had to be dug, about ten miles from the town. That was where our Manxmen showed their worth. For among them were so many masons, joiners and miners, who knew how to blast, that the trenches were soon made. Now, John says, the Cheshires have a great deal of respect for them an' they get on well together.'

"Tis good they're settled well together,' Henry said, nodding his head approvingly.

'I don't think it's good,' Voirrey thought moodily, 'I want him home with us!'

On Lily's birthday, she rushed down early, bursting with excitement, to show Voirrey the new (second-hand) bicycle she had been given. 'Daddy bought it from a lady who's going to nurse the injured soldiers,' she explained.

Voirrey gazed in awe. It truly was quite beautiful. Black and shiny, with wheels which shone like silver.

'I wish I could ride a bike,' she sighed. 'Will you teach me, please?' Her blue eyes pleaded, but after a momentary hesitation, Lily shook her head.

'No, you might fall off and break it.'

· CHAPTER 10 ·

Voirrey nodded, trying to hide her disappointment. Suddenly she brightened. 'Maybe Daa will teach me to ride Daddy's bike!'

''Tis a mite big for you, lass,' Henry furrowed his brow when she asked. 'You could find it hard to balance.'

Voirrey had just warmed his slippers and placed them on his feet, while he sat filling his pipe. Now she knelt with her elbows on his knees, face cupped, melting him with her eyes. 'Please? I won't be hurt.'

'Let me think about it for a while. Now run an' post the letter on the mantel for your Mammy.'

Standing, Voirrey picked it up. 'It's to Daddy, but it has no stamp!'

Henry gave her a ha'penny from his pocket. Wrap this in a bit o' paper and drop it in the box wi' the letter an' Amos the Postie'll see it right.'

Margaret walked with her to the door. 'Keep calling coo-ee, so I'll know you've not been snatched,' she instructed.

Made scared by the shadows the camp lights cast through the trees, Voirrey fair skeltered up the road, tripping and slipping on the tufts and rocks. She fancied she could see fairies in every shadow, awaiting their chance to pounce. Feeling more like screaming than shouting coo-ee, she pushed the letter and the ha'penny through the slit, heard them drop inside the box and ran home without ever stopping.

The following day Voirrey's cycling lessons began. Henry lowered the saddle as far as possible and her feet still only just reached the pedals. She took a few tumbles, but none too serious. The time she dived into a thicket of brambles and nettles was painful but, she felt, worthwhile when she finally managed to stay upright and pedal until she was too tired to go any further.

Now we can really travel around,' she told Lily excitedly. 'We can take a picnic an' I'll show you the whole of the island.'

In the excitement of their new-found freedom, Voirrey's eleventh birthday passed almost without notice. Her present though, a second-hand book of poems she had long desired, immediately became one of her most prized possessions.

In the early days, the girls explored near to home, Voirrey feeling important and keen to air her knowledge.

'Let's go to Traie Cabbag Bay an' see if we can find some flithers for tea.'

'What are flithers?'

Voirrey rolled her eyes at her friend's ignorance. 'Sort of fish with black shells. They're stuck on the rocks an' you have to knock 'em off. I'll show you where I found the dead man too.'

With a bucket each hanging on their handlebars the girls sped up the road and around the corner by the shop, each trying to see who could go the faster.

Caesar Quine was in his favourite spot, rocking from the balls of his feet to his heels. Eyes narrowed, he watched the stretch of high barbed wire, well prepared to foil any escape attempt.

Voirrey braked quickly, tipping her bike almost onto its front wheel.

Trying to avoid her, Lily almost fell off.

'Is there any more news of the war, Mister Quine?' Voirrey asked.

'Best news is there's a man, Samuel Norris, a journalist, has organized a union to fight for help for the landladies who've been ruined. They have no holidaymakers comin' but are still bein' made to pay one-third o' their rents to the property owners, an' the full amount o' the rates to the government. A meetin' was held las' week in the Villa Marina Hall an' a demand is to be sent to the Home Secretary for a Commission of Enquiry to be sent to the island. They also pledged for 'passive resistance' against full payment of las' year's rates.'

'I see,' said Voirrey, not seeing at all. 'We're goin' to look for flithers.' With a quick wave, she set off again.

Lily, having picked herself up and dusted herself down by then, hopped on her bicycle and pedalled wildly after her.

The prisoner, watching from behind the wire, smiled and waved.

Voirrey waved back and sped on her way.

The path to the beach was slippery and rough, giving the girls a hazardous ride, but having negotiated it safely, they set about searching the rocks for the little black shells.

Rounding a bend, they came to the spot where the body had been. Voirrey stopped, shuddering. She could almost see it there. Those awful, staring eyes! The bloated, purple face! Clutching at Lily's arm, she pulled her back a step.

'It was there!' she whispered, pointing a trembling finger toward Lily's feet.

'What was?'

'The dead man! He was where you're standing!'

Lily squealed, jumped backwards and stared at the pebbles as though they somehow offended.

Skirting apprehensively past the spot, the girls wandered around the coast, knocking the flithers from the rocks. With their buckets more than half-full, they pushed their bikes over the long path to the road.

'Race you home!' Voirrey shouted.

Arriving home, breathless, they grabbed the pails, dropped their bikes on the grass and dashed, giggling and sweaty, into the kitchen.

Eleanor, on her knees scrubbing the floor, lifted her head

to glare from one to the other. 'Young ladies,' she growled, 'Do *not* run!'

'Sorry, Granny.' Voirrey made a poor attempt at looking shamefaced. 'But see how many flithers we found.'

Eleanor was impressed but did not over-enthuse. 'Would you care to stay for tea an' taste some?' she asked Lily.

Lily rushed home to ask her mother, returning in double-quick time. 'Mummy said 'Yes',' she told them jubilantly.

'Next Saturday we'll go to St John's an' I'll show you Slieu Whallian.' Voirrey suggested, enjoying the new found freedom the bike had brought.

'Sloo who?'

'Whallian.'

'Who's Slieu Whallian?'

'Not who! What! Haven't you heard of it'

'No.' Lily shook her head and looked puzzled.

''Tis a steep hill where they used to roll the witches. If they thought someone was a witch they put 'em in a barrel wi' spikes on the inside, an' rolled 'em down the hill from top to bottom!'

'Then what?'

'Well, if they was still alive at the bottom that showed they was a witch,' Voirrey said darkly, 'So they killed 'em!'

'But what if they were already dead?'

'That proved they wasn't a witch — so they was allowed to have a proper Christian burial!'

Lily shuddered. 'Gosh — I'd like to see that!'

'We'll go there next Saturday then.'

'I wish we didn't have to go to Sunday school, then we could have gone tomorrow.'

'Mammy an' Granny wouldn't let me miss it. I have to go twice — an' to church twice every Sunday. 'Tis bedtime before I have a chance to see anything of the day.'

· CHAPTER 10 ·

'How awful!' Lily sympathised. 'Well on Saturday we'll go to Slieu Whallian.'

'There's one good thing about Sunday School. That's the picnic.'

'When's that?'

'Later this month. We go on a buggy to Glen Helen. 'Tis a long, long way. Miles. It takes so long to get there we only ha' time for a picnic an' a few games, then we ha' to come home again. It's the ride that's the really good part.'

Voirrey and Lily left straight after dinner on Saturday. It had been a dull week at school, so they were in high spirits at their release.

Pedalling furiously down the rutted road, they were quickly at St John's.

'Should we climb to the top?' Voirrey gazed up breathlessly to the crest of Slieu Whallian.

'It looks a bit steep!' Lily eyed it doubtfully. Being city-bred, she was rather less fit than Voirrey.

'There's a track all the way. C'mon.'

Awaiting no further argument, Voirrey leaned her bike on the hedge and started upward. Lily reluctantly followed, complaining mildly from time to time. Even she had to admit that the view from the top was too spectacular to have missed.

Lily turned a slow circle, thrilling at the peaceful beauty. Looking up to where fleecy clouds scudded across the sky she gasped, 'You feel as though you need only reach up a hand to grasp Heaven!'

Most of the island was laid out like a vivid oil painting. From this view point in the centre of the island she could see to the north, the mountain, Snaefell, towering like a brave sentinel, guarding her island. Southward stood South Barrule with, beyond it, on Bradda Head, Milner's Tower, looking down on Port Erin. Almost every hill of any note was in plain view, while below, clearly seen in all its length the Central Valley, stretching from Peel to Douglas, with the ribbon of road that cut the island in two.

'What is that tower on top of Peel Hill?' Lily asked. 'I've always wondered.'

'Corrin's Folly. 'Twas built by some fellow named Corrin, who wanted to be buried there. Don't know why, but I don't think he ever was.'

'Oh!' Lily shrugged. Looking straight down the steep hill, she asked, 'Did they really roll witches down here?'

'Oh yes! In barrels with huge, sharp spikes inside.'

Lily shuddered. 'How awful!'

Voirrey was looking in the opposite direction. 'Look over there. You can clearly see the camp. 'Tis like a whole wooden city. It grows every week. See the Three Legs on the hillside?'

Lily followed her gaze. 'Oh, yes, it's quite clear from here. There are some of the prisoners going back from work.'

'I think it's time *we* went home too.'

When they turned in at the gate Caesar was just arriving, wearing his most sombre expression. From the corner, he had seen Henry pottering in his garden. The news he had to impart was too important to be left, so the decision was made to leave his watching vigil outside the prison camp for a short while.

'Have you heard the awesome news?' He positioned himself comfortably on the gate.

'What news is that then?' Henry made a last futile attempt to draw smoke from his pipe, scowled at it, then, shoving the stubborn thing back in his pocket, he settled himself against the wall.

'I hear Lord Kitchener is dead! Drowned, they say!'

CHAPTER 10

Henry's eyebrows shot skywards. 'How so?'

'He was travellin' to Russia, they say, on a ship called Hampshire. It hit a mine near the Orkneys, in Scotland an' sank. Many died. They searched through the night, but no sign was found o' him.'

'That will have a sad effect on our fighting men, I think. When'd it happen?'

'Dunno for sure. Not long since. Maybe 'bout the fifth or sixth o' June.'

'Aye, sad! It was his pleas — Kitchener's I mean — among others, made John join up'

'Aye — an' many more wi' him. Funny thing, though, when the news o' it was taken to the officers in the camp some o' the prisoners seemed to know already. I reckon they have a spy somewhere! How's your Edward? What ship's he on now?'

'Last we heard he was still on the Ben-my-Chree. Hope he stays there — they got them air-planes to protect 'em.'

'Don't seem natural to me,' Caesar frowned. 'Men flying around in machines. How do they stay in the air?'

Henry shrugged and shook his head. 'Dunno!'

Voirrey woke early on the day of the Sunday School picnic. Rushing to dress, she sped down the narrow staircase.

'''Tis a nice day for it,' Eleanor said, glancing out of the small window to the blue sky beyond.

'I've made you some bread an' honey. An' there's an apple there too.' Margaret laid a paper package on the table.

Bolting down her porridge, Voirrey jumped to her feet. 'Can I go now, please?' she asked eagerly.

'Mercy, child, 'tis far too early. The bogie won't go for at least another half of an hour yet.'

'I know Granny, but I want to call for Lily.'

'Off wi' you then.' Eleanor smiled fondly at her.

'Have a nice day,' Margaret, standing in the doorway, returned Voirrey's brief wave.

The girls saw the bogie arriving just as they left Lily's doorway. As was usual, Lily had been slow to dress and Voirrey had waited, kicking her heels impatiently, for quite some minutes. With Emily calling instructions to their backs, they raced down the path, their skirts flying, panicking lest they should be left behind.

Two huge shire horses stood quietly waiting in their traces. Behind them stretched the long flat bogie, with its bales of hay for the children to sit on.

Voirrey gazed admiringly at the patient giants. How different they looked today, shined and beribboned, dressed in their polished harness, brasses gleaming.

'The horses look lovely today, Mr Cannell' she told the driver. 'You must have taken an awful lot o' trouble wi' them.'

"Tis nice you noticed, lass. They don't look like the same animals what plough the field, at all, do they? I think, they likes to get all fancied up, sometimes an' wear their best show harness.'

'No — they don't look at all the same when they're not all covered in mud an' sweat.' Voirrey agreed.

'You'd best get aboard now, lasses, else you won't get a decent seat.'

Voirrey and Lily scrambled up onto the bogie, quickly claiming the prime positions.

From doorways, paths and corners appeared children. All sizes and shapes of children. All dressed in their Sunday-best clothes and carrying their paper parcels of food, all giggling, excited and hurrying to join those who were already waiting. Together, jostling for position, they climbed onto the bogie, settling themselves on the straw.

· CHAPTER 10 ·

With everyone aboard, the driver shouted, 'Gid up, boys,' and flapped the reins against the flanks of the shires. Muscles bulging and skin twitching, they strained against the traces. The bogie started to move and with one voice, the children cheered. They waved excitedly to those grown-ups who had come to watch them away and lined the roadside.

Seeing *the* prisoner watching from close by, Voirrey's heart fluttered and leapt with excitement. Thrilling, she smiled and waved, glowing with the warm feeling, almost, that it was her father seeing her off.

He nodded, winked and smilingly waved back.

Passing the school, they waved to Caesar Quine, who raised a hand, but kept his eyes fixed steadfastly on the camp.

The bogie carried the children, singing discordantly all the way to St John's, thence to Ballacraine crossroads. As the gradient increased, the great horses strained to pull their heavy burden up the steep hill toward Glen Helen.

'Just before the war started,' Voirrey confided to Lily, 'Daddy brought me to the crossroads here to watch the Tourist Trophy motorcycle races. It was very exciting, but a wee bit too dangerous for my liking. They went so fast!'

'That would be good. I wonder if Daddy will take me some time.'

'Oh, they're not on now. The war stopped the races. The war has stopped a lot of good things!'

Lily nodded her agreement.

Eventually, the bogie turned into Glen Helen and stopped. The children tumbled off and disappeared into the undergrowth, girls to one side of the clearing, boys to the other, to commune with nature.

The horses were unharnessed and tethered to graze. The

children, when they had all reappeared, were made to sit quietly and eat their sandwiches.

Lily, regarding her corned beef sandwiches as dull and boring, was only too pleased to exchange them for Voirrey's honey.

'I don't feel like such childish things,' Voirrey muttered airily when a grown-up suggested games and races.

'Nor I!' agreed Lily.

'Let's sneak away then and go explorin'.'

Waiting until the grown-ups were all absorbed with pacing out a running track, they slipped quietly into the bushes, dodging quickly out of sight behind the trees.

Away from the clearing, it was dark and eerie. Down the slope toward the river, the children's distant voices faded into stillness and all to be heard was the chattering of water against the river banks. The remnants of that morning's mist wreathed in ghostly ribbons above the forest floor. Voirrey found herself treading uneasily.

'I don't much like this place,' Lily whispered nervously.

''Tis a good enough place. I come here often,' Voirrey lied.

A huge fallen tree lay across the river, from bank to bank, high above the water.

Arms extended, keeping each foot in a straight line with the other, Voirrey walked to the centre of the log. Seating herself carefully, she called, 'Come an' join me here. Don't be scared.'

Lily gazed uncertainly at the tree and the spuming white water far below and hesitated.

'Come on!' Voirrey egged. 'Don't be a scaredy-cat!'

Sighing resignedly, Lily placed first one timorous foot, then another, edging unsteadily out until she was able to lower herself thankfully at Voirrey's side.

'I don't like this place,' Lily repeated. The city girl in her

CHAPTER 10

found the dank bulk of the woodland threatening. Shadows in their depths were like crouched animals waiting to pounce.

Voirrey saw in them a different picture. Speckles of sunlight filtered between the leaves, throwing blotches of light upon the ground like golden coins.

Below the girls, the river water ran, roaring, with the speed of a millrace. It churned, frothing and eddying in its desperate rush between the treelined banks to reach the sea.

'If we fell in .....!' Lily looked down at the seething black and white water, shuddering.

'We got here without fallin' — we'll get back too! We'd best go back to the others anyway, else we'll get into trouble.'

Good! I don't like it here!'

Voirrey snorted derisively

Lily stood halfway up, her foot losing its grip on the wet moss of the tree bark. With a scream, she twisted, throwing herself face down across the log. Slowly she slid, her fingernails breaking as she attempted to dig them into the wood. The cold water seemed an evil demon, reaching up to devour her.

Voirrey's lunged forward and managed to get a grip on the back of her bodice, arresting her fall.

Pulling herself back to a sitting position, she sidled, sobbing to the bank.

A little less confident now, Voirrey followed in a similar fashion.

They brushed as much moss and muck from their skirts as possible and started back toward the rest of the party.

'A prisoner escaped yesterday, you know. From the work party at Ellerslie Farm,' Voirrey confided.

'Where's Ellerslie Farm?'

'Daddy says it's not so far from here.'

'What were they doing there?'

'Building a barn. Daddy says it is going to be the only two-storied cowshed on the island. Anyway, a prisoner ran away when the guard wasn't looking.'

There was an unnatural silence, with the only sound the river, snarling angrily at losing its prey. Even the birds were silent and still. There was none to be seen in the shadows of the wood.

'There's someone watching us!' Lily whispered tremulously.

'I feel it too! It might be fairies!' Voirrey was equally fearful. A dreadful thought took her. Clasping a trembling hand to her lips, she hissed, 'Oh, no!'

'What is it?'

'Perhaps it's a buggane! I wonder if it might have been him what tried to push you from the tree!'

Lily's eyes popped, a question forming on her lips.

At that moment a twig cracked, like the lashing of a whip in their ears and the girls started, fearfully looking ahead.

'Who's there?' Voirrey called shakily. No reply came. Her mouth unaccountable dry, she called out again. The two girls moved together, clinging to each other, trembling.

Heavy footsteps sounded, coming in their direction, and a sound of bushes being brushed aside.

Lily clutched at Voirrey's arm as they clung together, eyes bulging as they peered into the blackness. A scream was strangled at birth as a pony strolled out of the underbrush toward them.

Giggling in relief, the girls reached out to pet him. With a soft whickering, his head came reaching out to nuzzle them and he leaned against them. Mouthing Voirrey's golden hair with gentle lips, a flow of soft, grassy breath gusted from his nostrils.

'Isn't he beautiful?'

'Voirrey! Lily!' Suddenly the girls became aware of anxious voices and ran to meet them, calling in reply as they went.

· CHAPTER 10 ·

'Where have you been? We thought you were lost. It was very naughty of you to wander off!' Sage was boiling, her face scarlet and blotchy.

'We found a pony,' Voirrey offered lamely.

'And I slipped and nearly fell in the river,' added Lily.

Voirrey gave her a black look.

'Well, you should *not* have been near the river! What were you doing there anyway? Oh, never mind! Now you've made us late leaving. We should have been gone home long since. And look at the colour of you two! Goodness only knows what your mothers will say!'

Caesar Quine was leaning on the wall when Voirrey arrived home. 'Them guards is a funny lot!' He was telling Henry.

Voirrey hitched herself up on the wall to eavesdrop. 'How's that, Caesar?'

'Well, they call themselves the Royal Defence Corps, but they're all too old to fight. Some's *really* old!' His eyes widened as he said this. 'Wi' not havin' their families wi' 'em — a lot hasn't anyway — I reckon they gets lonely at night. They goes into Peel an' stays in the taverns until they gets thrown out an' they're too drunk to walk. They've got so bad now folks are callin' 'em the Reformed Drunken Corps!'

'I heard that' too, Henry agreed. 'Rumour says they have to send a patrol to Peel every night wi' a cart to bring 'em all home.'

'Aye. An' up at the Bungalow, on The Mountain, where they got some o' the prisoners kept 'tis even worse. The prisoners wander free an' them's the ones what brings the guards back when they get too drunk to walk!' Caesar looked thoughtfully up the road and shook his head. 'You mark my words, Henry, they'll break out o' there one night an' we'll all be murdered in our beds!'

'Lily says a prisoner got away from Ellerslie Farm yesterday,' Voirrey volunteered.

'Aye! I heard the guard went behind a wall to have a – um ---!' Caesar broke off, flustered, when he remembered the girl's presence. 'Well — you know!' He finished lamely. 'The fellow ran off when the guard's back was turned.'

'They shouldn't have 'em loose. They should keep 'em behind the barbed wire.' Henry shook his head in wonder at the stupidity of the authorities.

CHAPTER 11

Voirrey and Lily, leaning on their bicycles, waved to the passengers as the train passed them to pull into the station.

Watching it go, puffing balloons of black smoke as it disappeared into the distance, Lily asked, 'What shall we do now?'

'Let's ride on further toward Douglas.'

'Better not. Mummy said I must not go far.' Lily shook her head, but without much conviction.

'She wouldn't know unless we told her. I won't tell. There must be lots of interesting things we haven't seen yet!'

Lily, looking doubtful, shrugged her shoulders noncommittally.

'Well, I'm goin' on further. You can get away home if you're scared.'

'I am *not* scared!' Lily retorted hotly. 'Oh, all right,' she sighed finally. 'But don't you ever tell!'

They saw a long way further on, an old church without a roof. It stood alone in the centre of a field on their left.

'What a strange place. Let's look at it closer.' Lily still found the numerous Manx ruins fascinating.

Leaving their bikes by the road, they wandered up the

field together. Exploring around and in the roofless church, Voirrey felt uneasy. There was something bad about this church. Frightening, even! It gave her a bad feeling. Eyes were watching. She could feel them on her — like in the glen at Barnell!

'I wonder why it doesn't have a roof?' Lily asked. 'It's eerie here. I don't like it.'

Voirrey shuddered. 'Something happened here. I heard a story once — a long time ago — about a church with no roof. I can't remember, but I think it was something to do with a fairy.'

Lily looked around uneasily. It was not a safe place to be, she felt.

The girls returned hurriedly to their bikes and pedalled quickly away, looking fearfully over their shoulders until they had put quite some distance between themselves and the ruined church.

It took a few weeks before Voirrey found the courage to ask about the church. Only she, Lily and Eleanor were in the cottage at the time.

'Granny. We cycled, one day, to a church that had no roof. It had a bad feeling.'

Eleanor's head lifted swiftly, her eyes piercing. 'A church wi' no roof, you say?'

Voirrey nodded. 'Aye.'

'That must have been St Trinian's, in the Parish of Marown. You didn't go into it did you?'

Voirrey widened her eyes. 'Oh, no! Of course not! We were too frightened. What is the story of it, Granny?'

Eleanor threw her a suspicious look, then began her tale.

'It is said that very long ago, over eight hundred years, it was, an Irish chieftain — Brodar Marune by name — was short o' money. He was told the tale that Jarl Haco, the richest man in the Island, was a moneylender. Takin' all his family jewels

CHAPTER 11

— Irish diamonds — this Brodar Marune set sail straight away, landin' soon after at Peel.'

'Is that where the moneylender lived?'

'No. He lived in a fine castle at the foot of Greeba Mountain — near where you saw the church wi' no roof. When Brodar Marune arrived at the castle of Jarl Haco, he was made welcome. The Irishman left a small bag o' his jewels with Jarl Haco an' it was agreed that a servant would be sent to Brodar Marune's ship in Peel wi' the money, which would be exchanged for the rest o' the diamonds.'

'Could the master trust his servant not to run off with his money?' Lily was doubtful.

'Oh, yes, the servant could be trusted. To where would he have run on this small island anyway? 'Twas the Irishman what was not to be trusted, for he wanted both the diamonds an' the money. He plied the servant, a man named Quiggar, wi' a strong whisky-punch. Not bein' used to strong liquor, Quiggar soon fell into a drunken stupor, an' the Irishman had him carried ashore. Now, this Brodar Marune had been warned by some Manx fishermen that bugganes, witches, fairies an' other spirits may sneak aboard while his ship was in harbour.'

'Fairies again?' Lily murmured, wide-eyed. 'And what is a buggane?'

'He's a very mischievous fairy. Makes nothin' but trouble. Anyway, where was I?'

'You were tellin' us about the fishermen's warnin', Granny.'

'Oh yes! Well, the fishermen had said that before he left Manx shores he must light a fire and carry a blazin' torch throughout his ship, pushin' it into all dark corners to drive out the fairies. But, so hastily did the Irishman sail from the Island, for fear o' bein' caught, he forgot to heed the warnin'.

Unbeknown to him a buggane, who had crept on board, was sleepin' soundly under some ropes on the deck.'

'And he was taken with them to Ireland?' This insight into Manx history was much to Lily's liking.

'No! No! When the buggane awoke an' found he was well out toward Ireland, he called upon all his great powers to bring him back to the Isle of Man. Standin' at the bow o' the Irishman's ship, he blew with all his might, drivin' the vessel backwards to Peel.'

'Golly!' Lily was right forward on the very edge of her seat. Her breathing measured, she hung on every word.

'In the end, the strain was so great that the mast broke. It pierced the hull and water poured into the hold. This so excited the buggane he decided, for devilment, to sink the ship entirely. Blowing even harder, he drove the ship toward the rocks of Contrary Head, just beyond the prison camp there.'

'That's the headland you see from the clifftop,' Voirrey told Lily, airily waving her arm in vaguely the right direction.

'When were you on the cliffs?' Eleanor eyed her suspiciously.

'Please go on with the story, Mrs Quilliam.' Lily jumped in quickly to the rescue.

With a last questioning glance from one girl to the other, Eleanor continued. 'It happened that the Irishman carried wi' him a small leaden image of his blessed Saint Trinian. Beggin' the Saint to save him, he promised that if he lived he would return the Manxman's money an' build a church to St. Trinian on the Island.'

'And did he?'

Voirrey frowned, irritated at Lily's interruptions.

'After many prayers an' just as the vessel was about to be thrown onto the rocks, Saint Trinian appeared. Graspin' the buggane, he hurled him onto the cliff-top. In a desperate rage, the evil little fairy cried out that Saint Trinian would never have a church on Ellan Vannin.'

Lily gasped and sat up a little straighter. 'Ellan Vannin?'

'Isle of Man — stupid!' Voirrey said rudely.

Eleanor tutted, scowling at Voirrey. 'Mind your manners' she warned before continuing. 'Brodar Marune tried to make good his word an' the church was begun, but 'twas beset with ills. Rocks fell, without reason, to hurt the quarrymen who cut the stones for the church. The horses that pulled the stone carryin' bogies were forever goin' lame an' at night all that had been built the day before was knocked down.'

'But did they get it built?' Lily prompted impatiently.

Eleanor sighed. 'Saint Trinian advised that the church must be guarded day an' night an' a good fire kept blazin' to keep away all the fairies an' the likes. At last, the church was finished an' the Abbots readied to consecrate it. Alas, the night before, the guard fell asleep an' the fire went out. Seizin' his chance, the buggane rushed in an' threw down the roof.'

'Golly! So that's why the church has no roof!'

'Yes. That was the first time. But the Abbots refused to consecrate the church if it had no roof in place, so the Irishman returned to his homeland in anger.'

'And it still stands without a roof to this day,' Voirrey concluded.

'It stood for hundreds o' years like that, then a few efforts were made to finish it. Each time, on the eve of completion, the buggane would throw off the roof with a fiendish laugh. Then one brave man, Timothy the Tailor, determined to see the church finished, undertook to sit in it all night an' make a pair of britches.'

'Would that make the buggane leave the roof on?'

"Twas said by then if someone would stay all night an' work, the roof would be left on, but in the night the head of the buggane rose from the ground in front of Timothy, where he sat in the chancel. Three times he appeared to the tailor, each time rising further from the ground. Twice Timothy refused to look an' be frightened by him. He kept busy with his stitchin'. But the third time, just as the buggane spoke, Timothy sewed the final stitch, jumped to his feet an' fled from the church in terror. Laughing fiendishly, the buggane brought the roof crashin' down. No one, since then, has tried to put a roof on Saint Trinian's Church!'

Lily's cheeks glowed, her eyes sparkling with excitement. 'Golly! To think we were there and that awful old buggane was likely watching us!'

'We won't go there again!' Voirrey was quite adamant.

'No! An' you won't go near those cliffs again either!' Eleanor glared.

'Let's go to Foxdale an' I'll show you where the lead mines used to be,' Voirrey suggested when they were planning their next foray into the countryside.

'Foxdale? Are there foxes there?'

'No. Daa says there are no foxes on the Island. It used to be 'Forsdale'. That means the 'valley of the waterfall'. 'Tis a Viking name. But it jus' got changed to Foxdale somehow!'

Is there a waterfall?'

Voirrey nodded.

'Then let's go there. I would love to see it. Is it far?'

The road to Foxdale was rough and rutted, the hedges full of the season's first ripening blackberries. Voirrey saw them as she cycled past, taking note of where the best ones were. She would pick some soon and Granny or Mammy would make the blackberry pies she so loved.

· CHAPTER 11 ·

'Listen to it roar!' Lily gazed up at the waterfall, the city dweller in her held in awe by its unfettered power.

The surge of water leapt from the ledge above them, plunging to the depths of the smooth, deep pool below. Sunlight slanting down between the trees formed gentle, beauteous rainbows amongst the myriad droplets in the spray.

'Let's climb to the top.'

Lily looked up doubtfully. There were times when she wished her friend was a little less adventuresome. Though she had to admit Voirrey made interesting company.

'Come on! Then we'll look at some of the mines.'

Voirrey moved towards the side of the falls. With a shrug of surrender, Lily followed. Clutching at tree branches, roots and tufts of grass, they hauled themselves up the steep slope. The more agile of the two, Voirrey turned occasionally, arm hooked round a sapling, to catch the back of Lily's pinafore and help her up.

Standing, at last, amongst the brambles and nettles atop the waterfall, the friends looked down to it's plummeting depths far below.

Lily looked down at her clothing, sighing in dismay. 'Look at the mud and grass stains on my pinafore! And the tears at the hem! I kept catching it underfoot when I was climbing!'

Voirrey shook her head, smiling. 'When will you learn to lift your skirt from under your feet when you climb!'

'How can I lift my skirt when I need both hands to keep from falling?' Lily's voice was pitched high with righteous indignation. 'Why can we not just walk on paths like everyone else? Mummy will have the vapours when she sees me in this mess again!'

'Paths? How tame! There's no adventure to that. Everyone walks on paths! Come — let's find the mines.' Voirrey turned and stepped on briskly. Lily, as ever, followed meekly a couple of paces behind.

'Here's a mine-head!' The boarded adit was barely visible amongst the weeds. Voirrey started quickly down the overgrown track.

Lily trod more carefully.

A tiny creature, startled, froze momentarily, then scuttled into the undergrowth.

Lily squealed and jumped back a pace. 'Did you see that?'

'Yes .' Voirrey nodded nonchalantly.

'What was it?'

'Just a lizard.'

'Ugh! Looked horrible! Are they dangerous?'

'Harmless!' Voirrey replied disdainfully.

'Are there many around?'

'Oh, yes! Lots!' This was said with an evil smile as she peeped stealthily from behind lowered lids.

The mine was sturdily boarded up and, try as she would, Voirrey was unable to force any sort of an opening.

'Let's just leave this place.' Lily was backed up against the boards, watchful for any lizards which might plan to attack.

Voirrey acquiesced reluctantly. She would greatly have loved to find a way to explore. Two further mine shafts were equally obstinate and in the end, to Lily's delight and Voirrey's chagrin, the effort was abandoned.

Caesar Quine was there, still watching the camp when the girls arrived back in the village. He gave them a long, searching look and shook his head. 'You two'll be in trouble when you gets home!'

Voirrey braked, backed her bike up to Caesar. 'Why so?'

'Jus' look at the colour o' you! Where you bin? Looks like you

CHAPTER 11

bin in the midden!' He was stationed, not in his usual spot, but right on the corner opposite the tavern.

'Expectin' trouble, Mr Quine?'

'No. Jus' watchin' the goin's on there.' He nodded toward the house on the corner. It had stood empty for many months, but had been recently bought and was now a hive of activity.

'What's to do then?'

'Heard tell it was to be a chip shop,' Lily chipped in.

'Beg pardon?'

Lily gave a nonchalant shrug before she aired her city knowledge. 'They sell fried chips of potato. And usually, fish too.'

Voirrey sneaked through the back door, hoping to creep upstairs before any of the grown-ups should see her dishevelment, the soil and grass streaks on her pinafore, and the black boots, now brown with drying mud.

They were all in the kitchen. Mammy, Granny and Daa.

'I've never heard of this — what did you say they call it?' Eleanor frowned.

'Malaria, John calls it.'

At the mention of her father's name, Voirrey rushed to join them. 'Have you heard from Daddy?'

Hitherto unnoticed, Voirrey's voice startled the grown-ups. As one, three heads turned sharply and she became the centre of attention.

'Oh, Voirrey! Look at the mess of you again!' her mother said in despair.

'Sorry, Mammy — I tripped an' fell. Have you had a letter from Daddy?'

Margaret proffered the letter. This one contained nothing personal or that might have worried her daughter too much.

'My dearest family,' it began, *'I could never have believed such Hell would exist as this place I find myself in. It is such a hostile,*

burned country, with such heat as you could never imagine on our beautiful island.'

'We had a great deal of footslogging, which was a dreadful ordeal in such conditions. Our advance was slow, but we forced ourselves on, making our own roads as we went until we came to a place named Lozista, in the Struma Valley. It is no more than a swamp and must be the most unhealthy place in the world.'

'Oh! Poor Daddy!' Voirrey clutched a trembling hand to her cheek, flicking away an escaped tear.

'Many in our regiment have been struck down by a severe sickness called Malaria. It seems it is spread by mosquitos, which are like large midges, and we have not been given the nets we need to keep them off us while we sleep. This illness can take you quite suddenly and severely.

Young Stanley Clucas was marching beside me and in the next instant, he was on the ground. We thought he had been shot, but it was this Malaria that had taken him.'

'Our only hope now is that the Bulgars have it too!'

Voirrey turned the paper in her hand, sniffing down a sob as she read on.

'When most of our company, and the Cheshires, had gone down with the fever we were sent from the line, supposed to be for six weeks rest. Many of us also are suffering from the most awful, weeping Veldt sores, which will not heal. After only half that time, though, we were pulled back to fight the Bulgars at Jenekoi. Thanks be to God, we beat them!'

Blinded by tears, Voirrey was unable to read any further. Handing the letter back, she asked, 'Is Stanley dead?'

'Your father didn't say. He would have said if he was, I think.' 'Don't you say anything 'bout this to anyone, lest Stanley's Mammy hasn't heard yet!' Eleanor warned.

Voirrey nodded sadly. Poor Stanley. And poor Daddy!

CHAPTER 12

'Please, can I buy some chips, Mammy?' Voirrey had watched eagerly while the house at the corner was converted to a chip shop.

'No. I don't want you in there. 'Tis a bad place. Always full o' drunken guards. All coarse talk, not fit for a nice girl's ears.'

'Lily gets chips there sometimes an' she says they're real good.'

'I'll wager her Mammy or Daddy goes in the shop an' not her. They have more money to waste than us too.'

'Oh, please?' Voirrey begged, looking as appealing as she could manage.

Henry tapped his pipe out on the trivet and winked at his granddaughter. 'Come on, lass. I'll gi' you a penny an' take you there.'

'See you go into the shop by yourself Henry. Don't let the child in wi' you!' Eleanor scolded.

Henry sighed and rolled his eyes. 'I won't. Don't you be worrying An' I'll get a jug o' ale too,' He added as an afterthought.

'See you bring it back for my share. Don 't go drinkin' it all in the tavern wi' your cronies!' Eleanor glowered.

Henry uncurled himself from the chair. 'C'mon girlie.' He held out his hand.

Voirrey pulled her knitted hat down firmly around her ears

and turned her collar up against the frosty north wind. With one small hand curled snugly into her grandfather's large, rough warm one, she dug the other deep into her coat pocket. Trotting at Henry's side, she chattered excitedly about the treat to come.

Leaving Voirrey standing on the footpath, Henry went quickly into the crowded shop with its steamed windows.

The girl pressed her nose against the glass and gazed in longingly. Fascinated, she watched through the mist as greasy steam rose from the fryer in the corner. Pile after pile of golden chips were heaped onto newspapers, salted, vinegared and wrapped. Licking her lips, she pushed her hands deeper into her pockets and kicked her toes on the ground to keep her circulation flowing.

At last, after what seemed like a lifetime to her, Henry emerged amidst a cloud of steamy air. Voirrey felt the cosy blast of hot air as the door opened, then eagerly accepted the hot newspaper bundle he offered her.

'We'll jus' nip across to the tavern now an' get my jar o' jough.'

Tankard in hand, Henry ducked quickly through the doorway, leaving Voirrey outside. She dipped her fingers into the package, closing her eyes in ecstasy as she savoured the first hot chip.

'How is your dog?'

Voirrey turned sharply, her heart speeding with excitement when she saw *the* prisoner standing by the wire across the road.

'He's well, thank you. He limps a bit. Daa says he always will 'cos his muscles was cut bad.' Voirrey wandered toward him, drawn by this man who seemed so comfortingly familiar.

'I had a dog. A big brown fellow.' His eyes held a faraway look. 'And a little girl like you! How old are you?'

'I'll be twelve in April. On all fools' day.'

'Just one year older than my daughter.' The man smiled sadly.

'Does she look like me?'

'Perhaps just a little. Catherine is smaller and has darker hair. More like your young friend, but with your liveliness.'

'You look like my Daddy. He's gone, though. Fightin' in the war. So's my Uncle Edward.'

'I'm sorry.' He shuffled uncomfortably. Gazing along the length of the barbed wire, which now was all that separated them, he smiled grimly. Touching a finger to a spike, he said absently, 'This devil wire was described by its inventor as 'a strong thorny hedge."

Voirrey looked at it sadly. That's just what it looked like — A high hedge of thorns! *'It wasn't right,'* she thought crossly, *'for such a nice man to be trapped behind the vicious wire.'*

Suddenly a voice, loud in the still night air, shouted, 'Hey you! Get away from that wire! Right away! Right now or I'll shoot!'

Voirrey spun around, startled. Across the enclosure, a guard had his rifle pointed at the prisoner. With a terrified squeal, she ran across to the pub door, almost dropping the precious chips. She was still looking apprehensively towards the barbed fence when Henry emerged.

Slowly the pair strolled towards the cottage, Voirrey munching contentedly and Henry supping his ale. He halted outside the kitchen door.

'Peep in in an' check the coast's clear!' he whispered, his finger to his lips.

Voirrey frowned in puzzlement.

'Make sure your Granny aren't in the kitchen. I must fill the tankard before she sees it.'

Voirrey slid the door open quietly and poked her head around it. 'All's clear .' she whispered, giggling quietly.

Like thieves in the night, they stole into the kitchen, Henry filling the half-empty tankard from the drinking water crock. Pressing his forefinger to Voirrey's lips he whispered, 'Not a word to your grandmother, mind.'

Eleanor frowned after her first mouthful. 'I swear that landlord is watering his ale!'

Henry smiled meaningfully at Voirrey, winking as her father used to do. 'I expect it's the war,' he sighed.

Later Voirrey lay in bed listening to the music in her lighted bedroom. Her thoughts and dreams were of *the* prisoner, trapped behind the rifles, spotlights and the strong thorny hedge, pining for his daughter, as Voirrey yearned for her father.

Just before ten o'clock, the singing stopped and Voirrey, straining her ears, could hear the murmur of voices and occasional laughter as the prisoners returned to their huts. Then the last post was sounded on the bugle and she knew — because Lily had told her — that all the lights in the prisoners' wooden dwellings would be switched out.

The silence was uncanny, but in her mind, Voirrey could still hear the music as she drifted into sleep.

Henry tightened the nut on the bicycle wheel. 'That should be safe enough now, lass. Just be careful where you ride an' don't go over any more thorns.'

'Do you think Daddy'll want his bike back when he comes home?'

'I s'pose so. He'll need it to get to work.'

'Maybe I can get one too. Then we can go for rides together.'

Henry frowned doubtfully. 'Don't hope too much. They cost a lot o' money an' we don't really have none to spare.'

· CHAPTER 12 ·

Caesar sauntered in their direction. Propping half a buttock on the wall, he asked, 'Heard anything of John or young Edward?'

'Aye. Bits. Neither o' them's good to write often. Edward's still on the *'Ben'*. Seems to be cruisin' near the same area John's in. They send their planes to rout out the Turks an' the Bulgars what John's lot's fightin'. He says they sailed through the Suez Canal for a while an' their planes bombed the Arab's railways an' camps.'

'John says most o' the Manx Company's bin taken wi' disease. Most o' them's gone down wi' this malaria thing, an' some ha' something called black-water fever an' dysentery. There's less than two dozen o' them left to fight!'

'Aye. 'Tis bad, a'right. Mabel Clucas tells me young Stanley's real sick. Collapsed, he did, an' was in a field hospital for a long spell. They thought they had him cured an' sent him back into battle. Then he was took bad again. Now his Mammy says he's in hospital in some place called Malta. Looks like his war's bin fought!'

'Let's pray you're right an' they don't never send him back!'

The winter dragged on, long and hard. The New Year of 1917 blew in on the teeth of a blizzard. Scant news filtered through of the menfolk away fighting in the war.

Voirrey, aching for John and Edward, watched her mother and grandparents struggling to live with their fears. Many times she surprised her mother, looking longingly at a photograph of John, a tear in her eye.

Sometimes she would quietly wrap her arms around her mother and they would grieve together in silence. On other occasions she crept away, to leave Margaret to her private thoughts and fears and loneliness.

The frequent visitors from the camp helped to lighten the atmosphere, with their cheerful chatter and laughter over their cups of tea. There was always some gossip to be told and listened to.

'You know Evelyn McLaren?' Emily asked the group one day.

They all nodded, except for Margaret, who frowningly shook her head.

'Yes, you do,' Emily told her quickly. 'The one with the red hair and the hooked nose. She always complains about her tea being too strong!' 'Well, she was caught in a very compromising position last week with one of the guards.'

Everyone gasped, expressing their disgust.

'I always said that one was no better than she should be!' Eleanor was tight-lipped. 'Too full o' herself by far.'

'He's a married man, too! The one who was caught with her!' One of the other ladies put in.

'Oh! Do we know his wife?'

'No. She didn't come over with him. He's on his own here.'

'Well, she has only herself to blame then. Sending her man away like that was just asking for trouble. You can't blame a man for straying if his wife doesn't care enough to be with him.'

'Well, what about the husband of that woman — Evelyn? Does he know she's carrying on?'

'He was the one who found her — in bed I mean — with the other guard. They thought he was safely out of the way on duty, but he'd had a suspicion something was going on and came sneaking home to check.'

This revelation was followed by a lot of giggling and whispering.

'Whatever did he do?' Margaret asked.

'Percy said he gave the other fellow a beating and threw him

CHAPTER 12

out, naked as the day he was born. Now he's sent his wife back Across and she has to go and live with his mother until the war is over.'

Everyone laughed aloud then, picturing the scene. Even Voirrey, lurking in the corner and overlooked, furtively listened to the conversation and giggled quietly.

The piece of scandal, she felt had made a welcome escape from reality. Lately, it seemed, the laughter had been too shrill, the talk too stilted and loud. The adventure and excitement were over — the war had gone on too long for everyone. Many of the Island's youth were dead or permanently maimed and the fun had gone out of it.

Henry, with Voirrey propped on his chair arm, turned the tiny flowers between his fingers, studying them admiringly.

'How beautiful,' Voirrey whispered reverently. 'What're they made from?'

'Bone! They were given to Mrs Beckinsale by one of the prisoners. He begs the bones from the kitchen after the meat has been boiled off them. Then he bleaches them wi' soda, then carves them into ornaments, vases an' jewellery. Mrs Beckinsale tells me many of the prisoners do it. They seem to be a very talented lot. They also make beautiful, intricately designed medallions from the tinfoil lining of tea-chests.'

At that moment there was a sudden urgent banging on the door and without delay, Voirrey ran to open it.

Caesar stood framed in the doorway.

Henry looked up, startled.

'Caesar?' he looked questioningly at his friend.

The policeman nodded. 'I need to talk!'

'Aye? I'm listening.'

Caesar frowned towards Voirrey. 'Best the child doesn't hear.'

Henry caught his granddaughter's arm, pushing her gently. 'Go on upstairs, love.'

'But Daa.'........

'Go! Now!' He gave her another nudge. 'Don't argue.'

Voirrey rose and reluctantly left the room. Pulling the door gently, she left it slightly ajar, waiting noiselessly just beyond it.

'What's to do, Caesar?'

'I had word this afternoon about the *Ben-my-Chree!*'

Voirrey moved closer, putting her ear to the chink.

'Go on.' Henry encouraged.

"Twas sunk by the Turks, I heard!'

Sunk! Uncle Edward's ship — sunk? It couldn't be! Gasping, Voirrey clasped a hand to her mouth, choking. Unshed tears burned the back of her eyes.

'And Edward? Is there any news?' Henry's voice was harsh.

'The news is very sparse. No casualties I know of, but the ship was completely burned.'

Voirrey fled upstairs, taking the steps two at a time. Throwing herself on the bed, she clutched her knitted doll against her eyes, sobbing uncontrollably.

Minutes later she was roused by Henry's hand, gentle on her back. 'You heard?'

Voirrey nodded and bit her lip, incapable of speech. Whirling to clamp her arms tight around his comfortable bulk, she wept against his chest. Trembling violently herself, she felt him shaking also.

'Uncle Edward isn't dead, Daa! He can't be! He promised he'd come back. He promised! Daddy said so too. You all promised it would only last a few months. And now it's been two and a half years. You all promised! You all lied!' Shouting this last, she tore herself from his arms and threw herself face down on the bed.

· CHAPTER 12 ·

'Hush child!' Henry gathered her into his arms again, tightening the hug.

'He isn't dead, Daa! He isn't! Is he?'

Henry shrugged one shoulder, shaking his head forlornly. 'We can only pray, love. Just keep praying.'

Pray they did! Before every meal and every bedtime, they prayed. For all the Manxmen whose lives were in danger, but especially for John and Edward. For once Voirrey, feeling it might improve her chances of catching God's ear, was glad of all the religion which had been forced upon her.

Even Henry, usually keen to find any excuse to avoid church, was happy to attend twice every Sunday. And pray!

Gradually, without a word for many weeks of either John or Edward, Voirrey saw her family age perceptibly. There was no sparkle or laughter, and life only went on because it had to. Because it just didn't come to a standstill when people were unhappy, or worried, or frightened.

Eleanor appeared to wear a permanent frown, her mouth puckered at the corners as though she constantly sucked a lemon.

Henry became very stooped, frail and, somehow vulnerable.

Margaret's eyes became dull and lifeless, and imperceptibly the crow's feet of laughter changed to worry lines. Voirrey saw white appear in her mother's hair and wished she could make everything all right for everyone. But she could not. Couldn't even cope with her own heartache and fear.

Lily tried hard to cheer her up, often inviting her to visit after school. But Voirrey's only thought was to rush straight home, in the hope that there might have been news during the day.

'Please come to tea.' Emily had met the girls at the school gate. 'I have spoken to your mother, Voirrey, and she says you may.'

'Thank you, but I'd rather go home. They might have heard from Daddy or Uncle Edward.'

Emily's face shadowed. 'I am sorry, Voirrey, there is still no news. I have just now come from talking to your mother.'

Eyes misting, Voirrey clenched her top lip between her teeth. How long could this horror and fear last? It had gone on for so long already. So very long! A tear escaped and trickled down her face to drip, unheeded, from her chin.

Suddenly a familiar voice shouted, 'Voirrey! Voirrey Kelly come here!' Spinning, she saw him just coming into sight around the bend.

For a moment she hesitated, scared to believe the evidence of her own eyes. Was he real? Had hope dreamed him up for her?

'Uncle Edward!' she screamed, her heart leaping wildly against her ribs. Dropping her schoolbag, she sped to meet him, her feet flying across the ground.

Edward ran too and as their bodies impacted he threw his arms around her, swinging her off her feet and high in the air.

Wrapping her thin arms around his neck, Voirrey clung to him and pressed her face in against the curve of his neck and burst into tears.

'We thought you was dead! Mr Quine said your ship sank!' she sobbed.

Edward frowned. 'You heard about that, did you? Well, it would take a lot more than a few Turks to kill me!'

Setting her back on her feet, he held her at arms' length. 'Let me look at you. My, how you've grown! You're quite a young lady now!' He hugged her tightly again.

Voirrey grabbed his hand in both of hers. Skipping sideways, she dragged him along the footpath.

Emily and Lily stood spellbound, watching the scene through watery eyes.

· CHAPTER 12 ·

'Mrs Beckinsale! Lily! It's Uncle Edward! He's alive! He's come back!' Voirrey screeched, hurrying him to them.

'I'm so pleased,' Emily smiled, 'So very pleased. We have all been terribly worried about you. Your family have been so distressed.'

'Uncle Edward, we must hurry home and let them know you're alive.' Voirrey tugged at his hand. She danced down the road, hustling, pulling, stopping every now and again to throw her arms around him, hug him tight and press a happy kiss to his cheek.

At the garden gate, she relinquished her grip on his hand, racing ahead of him into the house.

'Mammy! Granny! Daa! Look who's here! See who I found!'

Margaret thrust her head around the kitchen door, her mouth opening to scold her daughter. Her eyes popping and her jaw sagging even further when she saw who Voirrey was clinging to.

'Edward!' she whispered. 'Is it really you? Oh, thank God!' Raising her voice, she shouted, 'Mammy, come here. Come quickly — Edward's home safe!'

There followed a clattering on the stair, followed by Eleanor exploding into the room, to throw herself into her son's arms.

'We heard a bit, but news is hard to come by', Henry explained later. 'We hear stories, but don't know how much of it is true. Tell us all about it.'

'Well, we was at anchor off Castellorizo, an island occupied by the French. Of course, we thought we was safe there, but the Frenchies had forgot to tell us there was a Turkish battery just taken up position on the mainland across from us.'

'You should ha' bin told!' Henry scowled.

'Aye. 'Course we should, but we wasn't. Anyway, the Turks opened fire on us, destroyin' the hangar an' settin' the ship ablaze. The steerin' gear was wrecked, so we couldn' get away.'

'How awful!' Voirrey whispered. She noticed her grandmother's fists clenched tightly on her lap, her face pale, eyes wide and brimming with unshed tears.

'We had three lifeboats undamaged an' we all managed to escape in them — all two hundred and fifty or so of us. It was awful! Shells were explodin' in the sea all around us. Our time hadn't come though. By some miracle, only four of us were hurt an' none killed.' Edward's words trailed off, his mind and soul back in the battle.

'Shells? Explodin' in the sea?' Voirrey questioned.

Edward looked blank for a moment, then laughed. 'Not seashells, dopey! A type of missile!'

'Oh!' Voirrey nodded absently — not much the wiser. What was a missile?

'For five hours,' Edward continued, 'The Turks shelled the *'Ben'* until finally, she sank in shallow water. Later two officers, two other men an' me went out to remove the breech-blocks from the guns so they wouldn' be no use to the enemy. The ship's cat an' two dogs were still alive on board, so we took 'em off. The *'Ben'* was just a burnt-out hulk. No more.'

'So what's to do wi' you now? Is your war over? Are you home to stay?' The lemons had gone from Eleanor's lips and she looked alive again.

Edward grimly shook his head. 'Sorry Mammy, no. I have to report back in eight days to a cruiser called *'Champagne'*. I'll miss the planes, though.' His eyes were distant again.

During the week Voirrey clung to Edward, spending every spare moment in his company. Walking hand in hand through the woods and over fields with him. She even walked with him through Barnell Glen without once voicing her fears about the fairies.

On occasions she grudgingly allowed Lily to come with them,

CHAPTER 12

but being in a possessive frame of mind she did not encourage her.

Edward was able to tell them nothing about John. Although the *'Ben'* had been engaged along the Greek, Bulgarian and Turkish coastline, the men aboard learned little of those ashore. They had heard, of course, of the depletion of both allied and enemy forces by disease.

'We did hear that the enemy is also stricken with Cholera. The British have escaped that, I believe, because of inoculations and better sanitary conditions.'

Edward related, with a husky tremor in his voice, of tales he had been told by soldiers he had talked to after his shipwreck. Even in winter, he had felt it warm on those foreign shores. But the artillerymen had told him of summer when the heat had been unbearable, the trenches like ovens. With the grass withered, the hot winds had blown it away, covering everything with dust. Even their food and drinks had a coating of dust.

Everywhere, the pungent smell of war and death pervaded.

'Where'er you looked in that Hell hole,' Edward absently twisted a blade of grass, 'were ugly, bloated, hateful green flies. Corpse flies, the soldiers called them. In the *'No Man's Land'*, in the war zones, they came in millions, feastin' on the corpses of the unclaimable dead!' Edward's voice broke in a sob. 'The hideous creatures swarmed in the latrines, in every dug-out and trench. On the food, too, spreadin' dreadful dysentery.' He shuddered

'You must have been glad to get yourself back to sea,' Voirrey said thoughtfully.

Edward roused himself, nodding.

Voirrey sensed a difference in him. Gone was the eager youth she had waved to as he sailed away from Victoria Pier. This was a man a hundred years older and wiser. War was not exciting.

It was awful! Yet she could tell Edward was eager to get back to it — to help get it over with.

'It wasn't too good at sea either,' he continued his story. 'We had some sickening jobs to do. Off the beaches of Gallipoli, in Turkey, ships had been sunk carryin' horses an' mules. The corpses of these poor unfortunate animals floated in the warm, limpid waters of the ocean, bloated an' addin' to the smell an' pollution. We towed away many of the bodies, piercing them with bayonets lashed to broom handles, in an effort to make them sink. If that didn't work we chopped them up wi' the propellors. Many o' them still wouldn't sink an' the mangled corpses drifted back onto the beaches. It was all too dreadful for belief.'

A million worms squirmed in Voirrey's stomach. 'Poor Uncle Edward.' She slipped her hand into his and gave it a squeeze.

Edward smiled and gently ruffled her hair.

'There was one good occurrence I heard o' on my way home. It was the *Mona's Queen*, you know, our little Isle of Man paddle steamer. Well, a few weeks after the *'Ben'* was sunk, I heard that *Mona's Queen*, wi' over a thousand troops aboard, was headin' to Le Havre from Southampton. The connin' tower of a German U-boat suddenly appeared dead ahead, only about five hundred yards away, an' the *Queen* had no weapons. With great courage, her Master, Captain Cain — a Manxman, I'm proud to say — held course. The submarine loosed a torpedo when the Queen was only about ten yards away, but it passed safely below the ship. In seconds, the paddle box on *Mona's Queen* struck the U-boat, the steel paddles destroyin' the connin' tower. The submarine was sunk.'

'Our little ferry did that?' Voirrey asked in awe.

Edward nodded proudly. 'Indeed it did!'

· CHAPTER 12 ·

All too soon, it was time for Edward to leave. Back to the horrors of war in another ship.

He left on foot from Patrick, this time, pack on back, not wishing anyone to see him off.

Voirrey, watched from the gate with tears streaming and dripping unheeded onto her dress, until he turned the corner. This time she felt his loss even more than before.

CHAPTER 13

There appeared to be a great deal of enemy activity in the seas around the Isle of Man. German U-boats were continually seen, fishermen reported being fired upon, some boats were sunk.

Caesar stopped by often to regale Henry with the latest snippets of war information. On the 10th day of April, he caught up with Voirrey as she walked home from the post box.

'Is your grandfather home?'

'Aye.'

'I have news.'

Voirrey waited expectantly, but he said no more until he spied Henry, spade in hand, scratching his head.

'Diggin' for the vegetables are you, Henry?'

The old man shook his head thoughtfully. 'Them's already in aroun' the back. I was of a mind to plant a couple o' apple trees, but I can't think where's best to put 'em. What brings you, Caesar?'

'I heard there was an American ship sunk last night, just Nor' West o' the Bar Lightship. Passenger liner 'twas. Called New York. She struck a mine, tearin' a great hole in the hull, below the waterline.'

'That's bad!' Henry grimaced.

'Aye. Well luckily the 'Tynwald' was passin' about a mile away, headin' from Douglas to Liverpool. Captain Cregeen took the Tynwald to the rescue, an' was the first to arrive.'

''Twas a nasty night for a shipwreck,' Henry interrupted.

'Aye, there was a blizzard blowin' an' a perilous sea runnin'. Jus' the same they managed to take on board folks from five o' the 'New York's' boats. One o' them bumped hard against the Tynwald's side, but by a miracle stayed upright.'

'Fortunately, the captain o' the New York had insisted on daily drills, so apart from the first confusion after the explosion, all was calm an' well ordered.'

Voirrey, fearing for Edward, now patrolling in these violent waters, moved indoors.

'Granny?'

Eleanor looked up, her hands hovering over a bowl of bonnag mix. 'Do you think it's like that for Daddy?'

'Like what?'

'What Uncle Edward said it was like on the shore. All those flies an' disease an' things?'

Eleanor shrugged, shaking her head slightly. 'Who knows? We must just keep prayin'.' Her chest rose on a mighty sigh.

'I wish the war was over. I wish I could just go to sleep an' not wake up until next month, or next year, or ten years, or whenever the war is ended!' Voirrey burst into tears.

Eleanor bustled round the table, rubbing flour from her hands. Taking the child in her arms, she pressed her face against her ample bosom.

'Is it ever goin' to end, Granny? I want Daddy an' Uncle Edward back! I want things the way they used to be!'

'Hush child. We all want that, but there's no use desirin' what you can't have. I heard a sayin' once what stuck in my mind. It goes:

Time was, 'tis past, Thou canst not it recall.
Time is, thou hast, employ thy portion small.
Time future is not, an' may never be.
Time present is the only time for thee.
Voirrey listened thoughtfully.

'Do you understand it, child?' Eleanor asked softly. 'Do you know what it means.'

'I think so. It means the past has gone an' you can't bring it back, the future may never come, so you have to do the best you can with the present.'

Eleanor nodded. 'It's now that matters! So go out right *now* and enjoy yourself. Be happy, child.'

Voirrey nodded, went outside and took her bike from against the back wall. Perhaps Lily would come with her to Traie Cabbag and they could collect some flithers for tea.

As she pedalled up the track to Knockaloe farm and the guards' quarters, Voirrey saw *the* prisoner near the fence. Looking around furtively, she could see no sign of a guard, so stopped and crossed to the fence.

The man smiled and winked. 'How are you on this fine day, young lady?'

Voirrey giggled shyly. 'Very well, thank you. How are you?'

'Well, but just a little worried.'

'Why so? What has happened?'

'I have had no word from my wife and daughter for quite some weeks now. They have not visited, nor even written.'

'Oh, I'm sorry. I know how worrying that must be for you. It is months since we had news o' my father too. We are all quite fearful for his safety.'

'Where is he?'

'He's in …!' Voirrey broke off, warning bells ringing in her head. She really shouldn't tell the enemy too much. 'I can't

CHAPTER 13

remember the name, but there is a lot o' fightin',' she finished rather lamely.

The man smiled understandingly. 'It is hard for us to imagine, is it not, little one — the real horrors of war. When we are shut away here, safely cocooned.'

'Uncle Edward says it's awful. Dead bodies rottin' an' smellin' an' flies eatin' them!'

The prisoner grimaced and blanched. 'And what's it all about? What is it all for? Who will gain anything from it? All the suffering and pain and death! Why? It is a wicked, senseless world, my little friend!'

Voirrey gazed up at this man who was so much like her father. 'What is your name?'

'Kurt. Kurt Mueller. And yours?'

'Voirrey Kelly. That's Manx for Mary, I think.'

Kurt smiled gently. 'Well, Voirrey Kelly, I think you had best leave before a guard sees you. But before you do — I have something for you.'

He carefully eased a small roll of paper through the wire to her. 'Look at it later,' he cautioned when he saw her about to unroll it.

Voirrey nodded, pushed the paper inside her jersey and cycled off, waving to him as she went.

Lily was home but claimed to be feeling sick. Voirrey suspected the illness had its onset at the mention of a bike ride. It seemed to her that, of late, Lily had become less keen on cycling. Perhaps because Voirrey's influence always led her to arrive home tired, sore and covered in mud and to a scolding. Besides which she seemed none too keen on the salty flithers!

After several hours of board games, most of which Voirrey won, she left for home in a happier frame of mind.

Caesar was standing at the end of the track as she turned

onto the road. 'I want a word wi' you, Voirrey Kelly,' He said grimly.

Voirrey dismounted. 'What's wrong, Mr Quine?'

'I watched! I saw you.'

'Oh!' Voirrey studied her boots, shuffling uncomfortably.

'You stay away from them fellows, girl. They're dangerous!'

'He reminds me of Daddy.' Voirrey's eyes misted. 'He has a daughter near my age an' he's worried about her.'

'Well, he's *not* your Daddy! He's a prisoner. He's the enemy an' he's dangerous. They're all dangerous. Stay well clear. He's the sort of fellow your Daddy an' uncle are away fightin'.'

'Yes, Mr Quine,' Voirrey whispered. She found it hard to believe Kurt could be evil.

'Get away home quickly now, Voirrey, Amos the postie tells me he delivered a letter he thinks may be from your father.'

Voirrey raced away, sliding her bicycle recklessly round the corner from the main road, pedalling crazily down the lane. Dropping the bike roughly just inside the gate, she ran into the house.

'Mammy! Granny! Daa! Mr Quine says there's a letter!'

Margaret, sitting at the kitchen table with a letter spread before her, nodded mutely.

Voirrey sat, apprehensively fingering the edge of the paper. 'Is this it?'

'Yes.' Margaret nodded.

'What's wrong?' Voirrey looked from one downcast face to another.

'Your daddy is very ill.' Margaret's voice was thin, choking as she stumbled over the words.

Voirrey fearfully picked up the letter. 'Can I read it?'

Margaret nodded.

Automatically Voirrey slipped an old shoebox, with the

centre cut out, over the glass of the oil lamp. With the light now cast downward onto the paper, she started to read.

'My dear family,

It is with regret I have to tell you I am now in hospital in Malta.

I'm sorry I have not written sooner, but I really have been going through the most awful of times. Through summer and autumn, the battle raged on endlessly in the searing heat. Men fell all around, with malaria and dysentery mainly, though many were stricken with heat exhaustion.

We were plagued constantly with loathsome clouds of flies. They were attracted in millions by all the human waste and the rotting corpses in 'No Man's Land'. Corpses we couldn't bring in to give a decent burial. They got everywhere, those flies — in our eyes, ears, mouths and they crawled up our noses.

Wherever I looked, it seemed, I saw death. Grotesquely twisted bodies lay all around, sprawled everywhere in various stages of decomposition.

The scorching sun burning on them made the air fetid and unbearable to breathe. But breathe, we had to.

In all this, it was difficult to stay sane. Many failed. I was relieved young Stanley was out of it, sent to the safety of Malta. It was not a sight any young mind should have to endure.'

Voirrey put the paper down for a moment, eyes aching with the horror of what she had read.

'Oh, poor Daddy,' she whispered as she choked back a sob.

Drawing a trembling hand across her face, she picked the letter up and read on:-

'The battle and the sniping dragged through eternity until we were all completely exhausted. Even at night, there could be no rest. Our troops, in a super-human effort, fired ceaselessly at the Bulgars, who were rapidly approaching.

The sky was lit up like a great flame by the gunfire and against it I saw, silhouetted, an enemy soldier. As he leapt at me I raised my rifle and he fell on to my bayonet. We toppled to the ground, he on top, screaming and writhing in the agonies of death. Eventually, he was still and I struggled out from under.

Till my dying day, that scene will live on in my nightmares.

We snatched sleep in odd moments, only if we were lucky. Many men simply, through sheer exhaustion, collapsed where they walked.

Often when we were on the march we had little idea where we were bound for. We scrambled in full battle dress, carrying heavy ammunition, through hot, dusty gullies or ravines, knowing not why!

The fighting went on without ceasing. All through the night, the rifles barked and the big guns and howitzers boomed. All the time there was the ever-present flash of guns, the blaze of searchlights and the blood-red light of exploding bombs. I saw men with their heads and arms and legs blown off.

All the time, as well as the injured, men were being evacuated in vast numbers with all sorts of fevers. Few of us escaped all the ills, but those who did were sick to death of the flies, the monotonous, rancid food and the endless shelling.

The seasons drew on into winter and at first, we were glad of the relief from the oppressive heat. Then one night a violent thunderstorm broke. In the violence of the tempest, rain flowed from the sky like a torrent. A mighty sheet of flame would flash across the heavens, roaring like some awful monster.

A strange slapping noise came from further along the dug-out and a great runnel of water snaked round the bend, waist-high, washing me backwards.

I clambered quickly onto a parapet and saw dead mules, dead

CHAPTER 13

Bulgars and all sorts of other debris sweeping past me down the trench.

Men were struggling, shivering and blue with cold, in putrid water up to their chests.

Many of us stood atop the parapets and across 'No Man's Land', which had become a lake, we could see the Bulgars doing the same.

All thoughts of fighting vanished in the general struggle to stay alive.

For the moment the weather had become our deadliest enemy.

Before we could recover from this the wind veered to the north and we were caught in a blizzard that raged for days. We had little protective clothing and what we had was drenched. The snow and frost hit us with the ferocity of an explosion.

Sentries froze to death at their posts. Blankets froze solid and many rifles jammed, making them useless. Many men lost limbs with frostbite, some so badly affected by the cold they lost their minds.

And to think I was actually excited about coming to this!

Well, after that my body finally could take no more. I fell sick with dysentery and very severe pneumonia. I knew little of the next few weeks, but eventually recovered and was sent back to the front.

But I was weakened. When the weather warmed and the mosquitos returned, I was quickly taken with malaria.

After a while, I was evacuated here, to Malta. I am getting the better of the fever, I think, but it is taking time. On some days I feel quite well, then suddenly it strikes me down again.

I hope this letter finds you all happy and in good health.

My love to you all, John.

With shaking hands Voirrey painstakingly folded the letter.

Repeatedly she ran her thumbnail along the crease before placing it deliberately on the table.

With blank, unseeing eyes, she looked from one shocked face to another.

'How can it be?' She rasped through dry lips. 'How can anyone bear all that? They won't make Daddy go back to the war, will they? Surely they'll see he's had enough an' send him home now?' A tear ran down her cheek and she licked it away from the corner of her mouth.

Henry shook his head grimly. 'No, child, it doesn't work like that in the army. If they bring him to health they'll send him back. Again, and again and yet again if need be!'

Voirrey stood dejectedly by her attic window that night. The lights were no less bright, but somehow they were less magical. The music, quieter now, seemed to reflect the sadness of her mood.

Remembering, at last, the roll of paper Kurt had given her, she smoothed it. Gasping, she gazed in awe at a delicate pen drawing of the Knockaloe camp. It must have been made from a vantage point on the Creggans and there was no detail missing from it. In the background were the sea, Peel Castle and the buildings of Peel itself. The foreground was of the camp, with men playing tennis; even their racquets visible; while others exercised. To the right of the drawing was Patrick village, with the church and even her own cottage shown. The part of it that rose from the picture to make Voirrey shudder was the clearly marked hedge of thorns that ran around the perimeter of the camp and divided each compound!

This was a real treasure. A work of art. One of the most special presents she had ever received and she resolved she would keep it forever.

CHAPTER 14

'Well, children, before you leave I'd just like to wish you all a very happy holiday.'

Sage Quayle was systematically clearing her desk. Why she always did this, Voirrey could not quite understand. In less than two months she would be returning all her papers and writing implements, exactly as they were now. Did she even look at any of them during the holidays?

'To the few of you who have won scholarships and will be attending Secondary school in Douglas next term — I wish you good luck. I hope you will all enjoy it and do well there. I would just like you to know how proud of you I am.'

'Thank you, Miss Quayle,' the children chorused.

Voirrey and Lily lingered at the school gate for a while, talking excitedly about their plans for the holidays.

'We can take sandwiches and cycle to the beaches for picnics. And climb the hills and glens' Voirrey suggested.

'If the day is warm enough we can swim in the sea.' Lily continued.

Voirrey's face fell. 'I have no swimming costume.'

Lily laughed. 'I have two. You can borrow one of mine,' she said cheerfully.

'Would it fit?' Voirrey looked doubtfully at her friend — much shorter, though plumper than she.

Lily shrugged nonchalantly. 'Come home with me now and try it on.'

Voirrey hesitated. 'Well, all right. But not for long. Mammy will worry if I'm late. An' I want to know if there's any news from Daddy yet.'

The swimming costume, much to Voirrey's surprise, fitted well. Going home afterwards, she skipped dreamily down the track by the high barbed wire fence.

'Good afternoon, Voirrey Kelly, you're something of a stranger lately.' She started as a voice woke her from her reverie.

Looking around, she saw Kurt standing by the wire, smiling. After glancing around furtively, she approached him.

'I've had exams at school and I had to study a lot, but it was hard to think properly, knowing Daddy was so ill.'

'You have had word of him then?'

'Yes. We had a letter.' Voirrey felt her lips quiver and drew in a deep, tremulous breath before continuing. 'He's in hospital in some foreign place. Have you had any news about your family?'

'My daughter, too, has been unwell. Some trouble with her lungs, so she has been unable to travel. My wife writes that she is recovering and they hope to pay me a visit soon.'

'That will be nice for you.' Voirrey's eyes brimmed with tears. 'Daa says that when Daddy is well again he will be sent back to fight. Why did those nasty Germans have to start this stupid, evil war?' She ended vehemently.

Kurt reddened, shifting uncomfortably. 'I'm sorry, Voirrey. I would willingly give my life to see an end to it.'

Stricken, Voirrey looked up at him. Then, turning on her heel, she picked up her skirts and fled, sobbing. She knew she had hurt him, but after all, he was one of them!

· CHAPTER 14 ·

'May we go to Niarbyl Daa?'

Henry straightened, grunting slightly, and emptied a spade full of waste into the pail that stood outside the door of the dry closet.

Lily gasped, taking a step backwards, her lip curling in distaste.

'Here, will you take this pail an' empty it, lass.' Henry asked, holding the pail out to Voirrey. 'I'll dig it in for the priddas next year. Take care you don't get it on your skirt!' He added as an afterthought.

Voirrey took the pail of human waste and emptied it where she knew next year's potato patch was to be.

Digging his fingers into his lower back, Henry flexed it painfully. 'Well, I s'pose you could go, lass. Just so long as you both ask your mothers and they say you can.' He finally answered her question.

Margaret, when asked, was thoughtful for a moment. 'Yes — if you're careful.' she agreed finally. 'But don't go climbin' around the rocks, they're perilously slippery.'

'No, Mammy.'

'An' don't go in the sea! It's too rough there an' you can easy get washed against a sharp edge.'

'No, Mammy, we won't.' So promising, Voirrey edged through the door, pushing Lily ahead of her.

Voirrey went to her grandfather before she left, 'I'm takin' a bag an' I'll see if I can get some crabs, Daa.'

Henry turned, holding another shovel of muck above the pail. 'Stand back a bit, lass. Watch you don't get splashed.'

Voirrey leapt away quickly.

'Some crabs would be nice. But you two be a bit careful there.'

'We will!' They promised together.

'What *is* he doing?' Lily asked, her nose screwed up in distaste.

'Who?'

'Your grandfather.'

'Cleanin' the dry closet.'

'Why?'

'Because it gets full sometimes, an' if he didn't empty it there'd be nowhere for us to — well — you know! An' he uses the muck out of it to make the vegetables an' the fruit grow better. That's why our gooseberries are so big.'

'It smells awful!'

'That's why you always have to remember to put the lid on after you've been. To keep the smell an' the flies out. It doesn't stink too much, though, until you have to dig it out.'

'I didn't know anyone had to empty the closet.'

'Where does yours go then?'

'Daddy says all the waste from the camp is pumped over the cliff into the sea!'

Voirrey was aghast. 'All that? For all those thousands o' men?'

Lily nodded.

'I won't ever go in the sea near here again!' Voirrey shuddered.

'We'd better go and ask Mummy if I may go to Niarbyl,' Lily suggested.

'Must you?' Voirrey frowned. 'She might say no!'

'I shouldn't go without asking her. She would be angry.'

'She won't know. Come on. Let's go.' Voirrey urged impatiently.

'Oh — all right.' Lily sighed and collected her bicycle from where it leant on the gate.

The ride to Niarbyl was long and rough, but the girls enjoyed the exhilaration of the warm sun on their faces and the wind in their hair. The freedom of it! To be free to roam, or run or just rest and enjoy the scenery.

They sat on the hilltop above the tail of rocks at Niarbyl,

CHAPTER 14

watching the white horses on the wave tops leaping over the jagged rocks and prancing up onto the pebbled beach.

Seagulls circled slowly, wailing like mournful banshees at a deathbed, watching eagerly for an unwary fish. Then they would swoop like bolts of grey lightning, dredging the surface with their beaks.'

Below them, an old cannon, fixed to the sea wall, still stood its ground, pointing out to sea, a silent reminder of the Island's criminal past, waiting for a smugglers' ship it might sink.

'This used to be a favourite place for smugglers,' Voirrey said.'

'What did they smuggle?'

'Oh — all sorts. Gold. Money. Tea. Brandy. Silks. Everything they should ha' paid taxes on,' Voirrey replied airily — not really knowing. 'There's a cave just down there!' She pointed beyond the cannon.

'Let's look!'

The girls left their bikes and scrambled down the steep, slippery track to the beach.

Lily gazed round the cave. Huge, high and fairly wide at the front, it narrowed to a slit further back. Straining her eyes, she struggled to see into its deeper, darker reaches.

How far back does it go?'

'A long, long way. Shall we go in?

Lily hesitated. 'Perhaps not without a candle. It's huge, isn't it? I've never seen a cave before .'

'There are hundreds o' them on the Island — all around the coast. I think that's why the smugglers did so well here. Some day we must bring some candles an' explore a cave properly.' Voirrey's voice echoed eerily in the damp darkness.

Lily ventured a few timid steps further. 'It smells dreadful.'

'It'll be dead fish an' sea-weed rottin'.'

'Ugh!' Lily fled into the daylight. 'I don't think I want to look any further.'

'I wish there still were smugglers.' Voirrey stopped to caress the cold barrel of the cannon. 'I'd like it better if Daddy an' Uncle Edward were doin' that instead o' the war.'

'Daddy could help them! He doesn't much like being a guard.'

'Why is he then?'

'He was too old to go and fight. I'm glad he was!' she finished with feeling.

Voirrey nodded sympathetically. 'Let's get some crabs.'

They spent a long time overturning rocks, but any crustaceans of a decent size eluded them. In the end, the girls had to admit defeat and leave Niarbyl empty-handed.

A lone skylark hung motionless in the summer sky, watchful, trilling his cheerful song. Beyond him, fleecy white clouds danced across a translucent blue sky.

'Wouldn't it be nice to be so carefree?' Voirrey thought aloud. 'Just to soar to heaven an' not have to worry about this awful war.'

'It shouldn't last much longer. Daddy says so many have died there can be few men left alive to fight!' Seeing Voirrey's stricken look, she clamped a hand over her mouth, a tear falling.

'Lets' go home,' Voirey suggested wretchedly. How could Lily say something like that? *How could she?*

A dark cloud passed before the sun: the lark stopped singing.

The girls cycled back to Patrick in an uncomfortable silence.

Voirrey pedalled wildly in an attempt to burn the anguish from her mind in a fury of activity.

Lily, trailing behind, sweated freely inside all her layers of clothing, losing the battle to keep up. Her front wheel hitting a rock, she was pitched headlong over the handlebars, landing halfway into a waterfilled ditch.

· CHAPTER 14 ·

Ignoring her friend's tormented yell, Voirrey raced on without slackening her pace. She prayed Lily was right — about the war ending soon, that was. But it was over three years since she'd first been promised the end of it would not be long away. Before Uncle Edward left they had promised her only months of waiting. Promises. Always promises! Promises never kept; always broken! Sometimes it seemed the war was forever. How she hated the Germans! And the Bulgars too — whoever they were — for what they had done to Daddy. If only she were a witch she would curse them all dead! Then Daddy and Uncle Edward could come home. She would care for Daddy and love him till he was well again .

A hot tear burned a channel to her mouth and she put on an extra spurt as she topped the rise.

'Hey! Voirrey Kelly!'

Awareness returning, Voirrey found herself alongside the camp's boundary. Kurt smiled wanly from behind the barbed wire.

Braking abruptly, Voirrey bucked the bike onto its front wheel, skidding wildly to a halt.

'Kurt! I didn't see you there,' Voirrey glanced around. Dropping her bike she moved closer to the wire. He looked ill. Almost grey — and thinner. His eyes had lost their smile.

Nervously he ran his fingers through his hair. 'I've seen you from a distance Voirrey, but I thought perchance you didn't wish to speak to me.'

Voirrey hung her head, her curls dropping to hide the shame on her face. 'I didn't mean the things I said. I was upset.'

'We are all upset. I understand. Is there any more news of your father?'

'A letter came last week, but it told us little.' Voirrey thought about it, her lip trembling. Just two short pages; very polite and slightly curt. Like a letter from a stranger. Her mother had been dreadfully upset. 'Have your wife and daughter been to visit yet?'

Kurt's face clouded and his eyes glazed and became pained. Biting his lip, he shook his head disconsolately. 'My daughter's illness has worsened.'

'I'm sorry.' She longed to reach out to him, but the wire was there!

'This war is hurting us all. I had no wish of it. It gives me great pain. Germany is no longer my country, you know. England is my country now. That is where my home is. My wife is English, as is my daughter.'

'I know,' Voirrey smiled and nodded.

Kurt's mood brightened suddenly and digging a hand deep into his pocket he said, 'I have a little present for you.'

'For me? Another gift? I don't think I thanked you for the lovely drawing you gave me, did I?'

Swiftly Kurt reached through the fence to press something into her hand. Withdrawing, he caught his arm, wincing as he tore it on a barb.

Voirrey gazed through a salty mist at the tiny creation in her hand — an intricate replica of a rose, carved in bone and perfect in every detail.

Lily limped around the corner pushing her bike, the front wheel buckled. Face grubby and tearstained, pinafore torn, she approached but lowered her eyes to ignore Voirrey.

Seeing her, Voirrey stepped guiltily away from the fence and picked up her bike.

Kurt drifted away raising his hand slightly in farewell.

'I'm sorry I went off and left you,' Voirrey said, realising belatedly how mean she had been.

Lily refused to speak, blaming Voirrey, perhaps not altogether unreasonably, for her accident.

· CHAPTER 14 ·

Henry, to Voirrey's relief, had finished cleaning the closet and the muck was well dug in by the time she got home. No amount of scrubbing however could quite take the smell away and Voirrey found a wide range of excuses to avoid her grandfather that evening.

June and July, mainly dry and warm, swept past in a flurry of activity for the two girls, now friends again. Determined to make the most of their last summer of childhood, they spent the pleasant, balmy days together, cycling the country tracks and rambling through the hills in warm companionship.

As the end of their holidays drew close, they looked forward to Secondary school in Douglas with a mixture of excitement and trepidation.

'It's a long while since we went to Douglas. I think a day out would make us all more cheerful,' Margaret suggested.

'Oh yes, please,' Voirrey jumped to her feet. 'May we go tomorrow?'

Eleanor shook her head. 'The walk is too far for me. But it would do the girl good to go.'

'Seein' you're startin' at secondary school on Monday it would be nice if we could have a special day together first. If the mornin' is dry we'll go then, an' if there's a good film on, we'll go to the picture house too.' Margaret said.

Voirrey went to bed excited, the war pushed to a far recess of her mind. Blowing out the candle the moment they entered the attic bedroom, Margaret pulled back the blankets, then tucked her daughter into bed.

'We'll make tomorrow a special day. Wear our best clothes, forget, for a day, about the war and how poor we are. We'll have a lovely, happy time.' For a few moments, she stood motionless by the attic window. 'They have the floodlights on in the camp and 'tis still daylight! Listen to their music. How well they play.' She observed dreamily.

After she had gone, Voirrey left her bed to set the window ajar. Tonight was a special night. A night to listen to the angels' orchestra — perhaps to dance to it a little. Quietly, lightly, she pirouetted in the little room, ducking her head occasionally when she spun too close to the sloping roof.

The old boards creaked and groaned under her weight until, finally, she heard her mother shouting to her to get back into bed. Abashed, she crept under the covers.

On the dresser, basking in the changing light crouched the sugar mouse she had received that last Christmas her father had spent with them. Voirrey had never quite had the heart to eat the little mouse. So, often she had longingly picked him up, turned him over a few times, then replaced him unharmed. Now, as she snuggled under the blankets, peeping at him, he watched over her, appearing to twitch his whiskers.

'I'll never eat you,' she vowed, 'Please help me pray for Daddy to get well and the war to end so we can all be together next Christmas.'

The melancholy music faded and Voirrey drifted into a troubled sleep.

Morning dawned bright and beautiful, with just an occasional puff of white cloud scudding across a clear blue sky.

In a fever of excitement, Voirrey gulped down her porridge, without argument, then rushed to take the cows up to the lhergy.

Impatiently she waited while Margaret made her final preparations. 'Why do we have to get so dressed up?' She pouted.

'On such a special occasion we must look our best,' Margaret explained for the umpteenth time. Pinning her new red felt hat

CHAPTER 14

carefully on her head, she plucked at the long feather until it was in a proper, jaunty position. 'We must not let the people in Douglas see how poor we are.'

Voirrey didn't really care what the people of Douglas thought. She just wanted to *get* there! And the sooner the better.

At last, the hat was securely in place, the wide brim twisted just so, and they were able to leave.

The walk to St John's, was a bit arduous, though Voirrey tended to skip ahead, then wait, kicking her toes impatiently until her mother caught up. With her best shoes beginning to pinch a little, Margaret was limping a bit by the time they reached the railway station. Caught by a strong gust, the new red hat was slightly askew. Squinting at her reflection in the grimy window, Margaret straightened it. Pinning it at exactly the correct angle, she gave the brim an extra tweak.

The train was late, crowded and filled with foul-smelling tobacco smoke. Voirrey stood on tip-toe, clinging to a strap for the threequarter-hour journey.

Douglas was strangely quiet and subdued.

'Like a ghost town,' Voirrey thought.

No one smiled. There were no cheerful greetings from brightly dressed, holidaying visitors. Landladies stood at windows and doorways hopefully studying all who approached. Silently they prayed for someone to request lodgings. How were they to feed their families with no money coming in?

Hurrying past, Margaret voiced her sympathy for those poor ladies, many of whom had been bankrupted by the war. 'It has been hard for us,' she said, 'But so much worse for these poor folk.'

They sat on the beach, under a rapidly clouding sky, to eat their sandwiches. Then brushing the sand from their skirts, strolled, hand in hand, towards the picture house.

Margaret, limping worse by now, scraped through her purse,

managing to find enough spare farthings to buy her daughter an ice cream. This Voirrey ate slowly, licking gently to make it last as long as possible. It melted quickly in the warmth of the afternoon so, in danger of wasting some, she had to finish it quickly.

The flickering images, so much larger than life on the huge silver screen, held her spellbound and wide-eyed. Imagination well fired and out of control, she became the beautiful heroine, being wooed by her handsome young suitor. The escape was total! Voirrey was completely removed from the draughty, dowdy picture house and drifting out in a wonderful, magical world filled with love and happiness. There was no war in this world. No hatred! No suffering! No killing!

Suddenly it was over. The film finished. The lights came on. Voirrey was catapulted painfully back into the real world.

Rubbing her eyes, she looked around and stood to attention as the national anthem was played.

It was raining lightly when they went outside. For a while they stood on the picture house steps, taking shelter. Margaret looked despairingly at the menacing clouds scudding across the moon. Finally, the rain slowed to a light drizzle and she caught Voirrey's arm.

'We must go or we'll surely miss the train.'

After scurrying down the hill, they reached the station in time, with Margaret limping quite badly by now. Once settled on the train, she removed her shoes, sighing thankfully. "Tis a painful business havin' to look smart for Douglas,' she muttered, adding, as a heavy smattering of raindrops hit the carriage window, 'I do hope this stops before we reach St John's.'

Within minutes miniature rivers flowed cornerwise across the window and their hearts sank at the thought of the walk home that lay before them.

· CHAPTER 14 ·

Margaret had an agonising few moments forcing her swollen feet back into her shoes just before St John's. To make matters worse, a gust of wind, as they stepped off the train, snatched the new red hat. Margaret desperately grabbed the brim with both hands, dragging it as tightly on her head as it would go.

For quite some distance the River Neb ran alongside the road, with no hedge or wall dividing the two. Margaret nervously held onto her daughter.

'Keep well over to the left,' she warned constantly. 'If you slip into the river when it's running so fast there'll be no saving you!'

Torrents ran in the cart tracks as they battled, heads down, into the oncoming deluge. Voirrey tripped on stones, sliding to the nadir of the ruts, while Margaret stumbled, limping ever more painfully with every minute that passed, in her wake.

'Hold up a minute, Voirrey.'

'What's wrong, Mammy?' The girl swung round, relieved to turn her back on the storm for a moment.

'I must take my shoes off. I can walk no further with them.' Still clutching her hat, she struggled to unbutton the offending footwear. 'Will you carry them, love? I must keep a good grip on my hat.'

Voirrey took them, allowing her mother to move ahead. Stepping in close behind, she hoped for a little protection from the cold rain.

Approaching the corner before the Vicarage lane, Margaret stopped and, reaching behind her, took hold of her daughter's hand. 'Walk beside me, love, lest the hearse should come.'

Voirrey looked around fearfully. There had been much talk in the village recently of an ethereal hearse, which was usually seen first at the corner they were approaching. Then without passing, it would be waiting at the bottom of Vicarage Lane. Finally, it was seen, standing motionless, at the end of Barnell.

Some said it was the ghosts of the Manx lads killed in the war! Thankfully it wasn't at the corner that night!

Voirrey clung close against her mother, nervously peering ahead. 'There's someone there!'

She stopped, staring in terror, toward the bottom of Vicarage Lane.

'Where?' Margaret's arms tightened around her.

'I saw someone move! I did, Mammy! It looked like a man!'

They stood motionless for several minutes, then timidly edged forward, stumbling in the slippery ruts.

There was no spirit hearse at the Vicarage, but there was a presence. Voirrey felt it sharply. Some sort of being, almost close enough, she sensed, to touch. Someone — or thing — watching. Just watching!

The huge trees bent with the wind. Bowing, then straightening. They screeched and squeaked with the pain of the lashing storm.

'It's the bugganes!' Margaret spoke through chattering teeth. 'They're angry with this weather.'

It was common knowledge the bugganes lived in this corner of woodland. Mostly the people stayed away from it.

A twig snapped amongst the trees and with a terrified scream, Voirrey took flight. Without a backward glance, she fled and could hear Margaret stumbling and splashing behind.

Slackening her pace only as she approached Barnell, to check there was no hearse full of ghosts there, she arrived at the cottage only a moment before her mother.

Henry and Eleanor jerked around as the two sodden bodies hurtled into the kitchen, crying hysterically.

'Oh, my dear God! What has happened?' Eleanor had her hand to her mouth, staring in horror.

CHAPTER 14

'Who did this terrible thing?' Henry had stopped, half out of his chair. 'Was it the bugganes?'

'They tried to get us!' Voirrey glanced up at her mother and screamed. 'They got you, Mammy! The blood! On your face! the blood!'

Margaret took her hands from her hat, saw them dripping blood red and swayed, reaching blindly for a chair.

Henry helped her to sit, handing the hat to Eleanor, while he checked for the injury. Margaret sat, sobbing, her face red and with bloody streaks all down her clothing.

Henry frowned. 'Strange. I can see nothing. No sign of any injury.'

Eleanor stared, puzzled, at the object in her hand. "Tis the hat!' She spoke quietly.

Voirrey turned anxious eyes away from her mother — to see red dye dripping from the new red hat to the stone floor. The once-proud feather now hung, limp and dead.

'Oh, put it in the fire, Mammy!' Margaret said sadly. "Twill never be fit to wear again.'

Voirrey shivered sleeplessly in her bed that night. There was no light even from the camp, for some reason, and her room was black as death.

CHAPTER 15

Caesar knocked early the following morning. 'Jus' thought I oughter warn you there's another prisoner got out.' There was a certain smug satisfaction in the way he spoke. Voirrey always suspected he was pleased to have this sort of news to impart. It proved him right, didn't it?

'I said them guards was too old. Allus lettin' 'em out, they are.'

'They gets 'em back, though. None o' 'em ever gets off the Island does they?'

'No,' Caesar admitted grudgingly. 'But it's not good havin' 'em runnin' aroun' loose. This 'un got away las' night when the storm put the lights out. Better you keep an eye on the girl till they catch him.'

'I don't know why they bother trying to get away. It seems to me they're well looked after where they are.' Henry grimaced and shook his head.

Caeser nodded in agreement.

'That must be who I saw near the Vicarage last night,' Voirrey said, and Caesar looked searchingly at her.

'You saw someone las' night? What did he look like — this feller?'

Voirrey shrugged, suddenly uncomfortable and wishing she'd said nothing. 'Well — I didn't really see right. 'Twas dark

· CHAPTER 15 ·

you see, 'cos the lights was out in the camp. I jus' saw someone move among the trees.'

'You was lucky you wasn't murdered!' Caesar said grimly.

'I'd best walk wi' you an' the girlie to Peel in the mornin' if there's a villain on the loose,' Henry told Margaret during tea.

'Emily will be with us, Daa. Lily's startin' school in Douglas too.'

'Aye. I know, but I feel you would best have a man wi' you. I'll be happier if I see you all safe on the train.'

'I'm sure we'll all be less nervous to have you there,' Margaret agreed.

Voirrey was up early and rushing around. They would have to leave home, she knew, well before seven o'clock if they were to be at Peel in time for the train. It was a huge, exciting adventure to go all the way to Douglas every day.

In spite of Eleanor continually pressing her to have a big breakfast, the knot in her stomach would not allow her to eat much. When it was almost time to leave she carefully put on her head the straw hat with the letters E.D.S.S. Wearing that hat, and, with it, the uniform of the Eastern Districts Secondary School, swelled her heart with pride. To her mind, it was the tangible sign that she was grown up. No longer a child at the little local school. A woman now!

'Here, put this in your school-bag. I've put cress and scallions in your butties. Now have you got everything? Pencil? Rubber?' Margaret handed her a paper bag.

Cramming it into her school-bag, Voirrey nodded. 'Yes, I have all I need.'

'Are you sure? Have you checked?'

'Yes!' Voirrey scowled. Why must her mother still insist on treating her like a mindless child?

'Well, put your coat on an' we'll go.'

Voirrey held Henry's hand as they walked along the road. Now and again she excitedly skipped a few steps, almost pulling the old man off balance.

Caesar stood watchfully on the corner.

'They caught 'im yet?' Henry asked.

Caesar shook his head. 'No. We've searched everywhere. Turned the church inside out an' all. He'll be long gone from here. I reckon he'll be halfway to Douglas by now.'

'Jus' the same, it will keep my mind at rest to make sure the women-folk get on the train safe.'

'Aye. 'Tis best.' Caesar agreed.

Emily and Lily were waiting for them by the camp gate. The two girls giggled and pranced ahead, while the grown-ups followed, chatting comfortably.

'Who's the prisoner who got out? '

'I don't really know. Daddy said his name was Mullen or something like that. A German..'

'Mullen doesn't sound German.'

Lily shrugged. 'Well, it was something like that.'

Suddenly Voirrey blanched, stopping dead in her tracks. 'It wasn't Mueller, was it?'

'Could have been. Why?'

'That's Kurt's name.'

'Kurt?'

'Yes. You know!' The one who looks like my Daddy!'

'Oh, the one you keep waving to?'

'Yes. Have you seen him since?'

'Since when?'

Voirrey sighed impatiently. 'Since he escaped — stupid. Or whoever it was.'

· CHAPTER 15 ·

'I don't know, but I haven't been looking. I don't think I would recognise him anyway. They all look the same to me.'

Voirrey sighed again and hurried on, with Lily trotting behind.

'Well if it is him I hope he can get away off the Island!' Voirrey said feelingly. 'His little girl's bad sick an' he's awful worried about her.'

'Don't you girls get too far ahead,' Henry called. 'Stay where we can see you. You know the train won't go any sooner, an' school won't start any earlier jus' because you're at the station ten minutes early.'

The girls slowed their pace.

On Peel station the waiting passengers gathered into little groups, all discussing the latest escape. All were of the firm opinion that he had no chance of leaving the Island.

Voirrey and Lily sat together on the train, heads almost touching and eyes sparkling as they chattered excitedly and wondered aloud what secondary school would be like.

The walk from Douglas railway station to the school, uphill all the way it felt, seemed longer than from Patrick to Peel. It was not far enough to dampen the girls' spirits though, nothing short of black magic could have done that.

As they approached, Voirrey saw that a high fence surrounded the tall, dark school. The girls and their mothers stopped just inside the huge iron gates, gazing up in awe at its looming dark height.

'It's so big!' Voirrey said huskily, a trace of apprehension creeping in.

'Not so very big,' the more worldly Lily assured her. 'The schools in Manchester are much larger than this.'

Children milled everywhere, most of them older than Voirrey and Lily. They chased each other around, giggling and squealing excitedly, happy to be back at school after the long summer holiday. Some of the older children stood in more sedate groups, talking quietly, with just the odd burst of laughter.

Younger children, arriving at the secondary school for the first time, came hesitantly through the gates, accompanied by their mothers. Instinctively these all seemed to gather in the same corner, just a few steps inside the gateway.

Suddenly a teacher came through the huge double doorway, stood atop the steps ringing a loud bell, calling the children into line.

Another teacher came to herd the new arrivals into a row at the side.

'Now, are you sure you know your way back to the station?' asked Margaret.

'Yes.'

'Well, mind you go straight there after school. Don't play around or you'll miss your train,' Emily warned.

'We won't.'

'And remember not to get off at St John's. Go right through to Peel an' Daa will meet you there.' Margaret called this last instruction as the line started to move, crocodile fashion, into the building.

Voirrey passed through the quick, exciting, but oftentimes scary day in a sort of daze. Such huge rooms and wide corridors. So many children. The blackboards looked bigger. And the windows. Even the teachers seemed larger than life.

After school, the girls, still in high spirits, raced each other to the railway station.

· CHAPTER 15 ·

On the train, they chattered and laughed about their day and the people they had seen, the new things they had learned.

'That boy kept looking at you!' Lily said, giggling.

'What boy?'

'The big one with the red face.'

'And buck teeth?'

'Yes. He kept smiling at you!'

'Ugh! He looked horrible, *and* he had a hole in the back of his trousers,' Voirrey added, as though this were the greatest crime of all time. 'I don't like boys anyway. They always have runny noses!' She screwed her face up.

Henry was waiting anxiously at Peel station when the train drew in.

'Seeing them, his face brightened. 'Did your day go well?'

The girls fell in on either side of him. They prattled girlishly and sometimes cattily.

Henry enjoyed it all, laughing deeply over the boy with buck teeth and a hole in his pants.

'What an unfortunate lad. They must be a poor family to send him to school wi' his clothes in rags. But don't think too harshly of him 'cos it must have been hard for a boy with that sort of background to win a scholarship to secondary school. He must have studied hard.'

Voirrey thought about this and felt a little bit ashamed.

In the following two weeks, while the search for the escapee continued, Henry walked to Peel every morning to see the girls safely away on the train. Ever reliable, he was there, waiting patiently to take them home in the early autumn dusk, no matter what the weather.

Voirrey found it tedious being taken under guard, almost, wherever she wanted to go. Although it gave her a sense of security to have Henry always at her side, she found herself, on occasions, wondering vaguely just how much help he would be if attacked by a younger man, as the escaped prisoner was almost certain to be.

Whenever she passed the camp Voirrey covertly watched the prisoners, studying their faces. Kurt was never there. *'It must be him'*, she thought, a thrill of joy shimmering through her heart. *'I do hope he has made it home to Catherine. I'd want my Daddy if I was real sick.'*

It didn't occur to her that even if he did make it home the police would almost certainly be waiting for him when he got there.

From then on, as soon as Margaret had left her bedroom each night, Voirrey slid out of bed and onto her knees to add a rider to her prayers 'And please, God, look after Kurt. Keep him safe an' well and help him get home quickly. Thank you, God.'

After that, she stood by the window, listening to the gentle music of the orchestra, thinking of the men she loved and was missing so badly.

All the while, as the search continued the village folks were wary about leaving their homes, always looking around carefully before venturing outside.

Whenever Eleanor, Margaret or Voirrey wished to make use of the closet, Henry went out first to check it. Then he felt it his duty to stand guard at the back door until they were safely back indoors.

Eventually, the hullaballoo died down. The hunt seemed to be called off and Caesar strutted smugly back and forth along the perimeter wire.

'They lost this 'un!' He said cockily, leaning on the gate. 'Allus said it would happen. My bet is he bribed a fisherman from Peel to take him Across.

CHAPTER 15

'No one'd do that!' Henry frowned. 'No one'd take a German off the island.'

"S my bet he's not on the Island.'

Percy Beckinsale's opinion was the same and the vigilant watch on the girls relaxed.

Voirrey's free spirit, aching after its confinement, agitated to be let loose. She had felt like a lark imprisoned in a tiny cage. It had given her a strong inkling of how the men in the camp must feel.

On the first Saturday after that Voirrey rushed down for breakfast. 'Please, may I go out on my bike today?'

'Not alone.' Margaret shook her head.

'Lily will come wi' me'

'If Lily is allowed, then you may go.'

Eleanor scowled. "Tisn't right. Two young girls out on their own with this prisoner loose. 'Tisn't safe.'

'Escapee's gone. Caesar said so. Either made it *across* or fell off a cliff. Can't keep the young 'uns locked up for ever.'

Eleanor sighed, defeated and shook her head disapprovingly, lips clamped tightly together.

Voirrey bolted her porridge, screwing her nose a bit at its yellow buttermilk, then rushed to take the cows to the lhergy. As ever, when *she* was in a hurry *they* were not. Even with her slapping their rumps with a stout stick, and Dog nipping their heels, it proved to be a long job. Why, she wondered, was it safe for her to take the cows to the lhergy on her own — but not to go on a bicycle ride? It didn't make sense! She didn't have much faith that the cowardly Dog would protect her. More likely he'd put his tail between his legs and flee!

Turning to hurry home, she noticed Dog half-way through the gap in the hedge. He was on tip-toe, hackles raised, teeth bared, staring intently at the tholtans.

When Voirrey called him he sidled to her, constantly looking back over his shoulder.

'You know, don't you Dog? You can feel them there too.' He had never dared venture into the glen since the day the fairies had chased him out.

After a substantial amount of pleading and cajoling, Emily was persuaded to permit Lily to cycle. 'Don't you two go wandering in the meadows,' she warned. 'Just in case that villain *is* still at large.'

'Oh, Mummy! Even if he is still alive and on the island, he will be a long way from here by now!'

'Just the same — be careful.'

'Let's get a pail an' we'll go to Traie Cabbag for flithers,' Voirrey suggested.

Lily wrinkled her nose.

'You don't have to eat 'em. Just help me get 'em.'

Dog attached himself to the girls and refused to be sent home. Ever since the episode on the cliff, it seemed, he considered it his responsibility to tag along and take care of Voirrey. Most days when she arrived home from school he was at the gate, eagerly waiting, his tail flapping so wildly it almost lifted his back feet from the ground.

With the pail hooked awkwardly over Voirrey's handlebars, the trio rushed off excitedly.

Caesar was at the corner by the shop. He held up a meaty hand as they approached.

'Where're you young 'uns off to?'

'Just to get some flithers, Mr Quine.'

'Take care an' don't talk to no strangers.'

'We won't,' the girls promised, in one voice.

Dog had run on ahead, but stopped and stood looking impatiently back toward them.

· CHAPTER 15 ·

'I thought the prisoner had got off the Island?'

'He most likely has, but we don't know for sure. Stay well clear of any person you don't know.'

Dog bounded back, then danced around the group, barking excitedly as he tried to hurry them up.

'We will,' Voirrey promised. 'Anyway, we have Dog to take care of us.'

Caesar frowned doubtfully at the collie. 'Well a'right. Off you go then.'

They sped away, anxious to make good their escape before he changed his mind. The bikes bounced wildly on the rough road, the metal pail clanging against the bike and banging painfully on Voirrey's knee. Dog bounded beside them, sometimes racing ahead, barking excitedly all the while.

The tide was fairly well out and the flithers easy to find. It took little time for the girls to fill the pail three-quarters full, then they sat on the rocks, gazing wistfully out to sea.

'The Mountains of Mourne are very clear to-day,' Voirrey said dreamily.

Lily followed her friend's gaze toward Ireland. 'They look close. Perhaps the escaped prisoner swam across.'

"Tis no nearer than England. He would have died of the cold.'

'Maybe that's what did happen.'

Voirrey shrugged. 'I dunno.' But she prayed Lily was wrong.

'Have you heard from your Daddy?' Lily changed the subject.

Voirrey's eyes misted and she shook her head miserably. 'His last letter was a long while ago. There's been only one since he wrote to us from Malta. He sounded very odd, as though he was writing to strangers. Made Mammy cry, it did.' She picked up a pebble and lobbed it into the sea. Dog leapt to his feet and raced after it.

'You told me already. Nothing since then?'

Wordlessly, Voirrey shook her head.

Dog gave up his search amongst the thousands of pebbles at the water's edge and returned to lie at his mistress's feet.

'Wouldn't it be nice if this awful war could be over an' we could all be together again?' Voirrey absently addressed the distant blue outline of the Mountains of Mourne.

Lily gazed sadly at her friend's profile. 'Then I would be gone too. Back to Manchester.'

'Must you go?'

' Lily nodded dejectedly.

'Why? Can't you stay here?'

'No. Daddy says once the camp has gone he will have no job. And our home here goes with the job.'

Voirrey frowned. 'But surely he can find work on the island. And a place to live.'

'He says not. I think Mummy would be happier in Manchester.'

'I thought she liked it here?' Voirrey could not imagine how anyone could not like the Isle of Man better than any other place on earth.

'Oh, she does, but she's homesick sometimes. My grandparents and uncles and aunts are all there. Mummy misses her friends too. All my friends are there also.'

Voirrey felt a stab to her heart. 'Aren't I, your friend?'

'Oh, yes! You're the best friend I've ever had. But I had lots of friends in Manchester.' Lily flushed.

Voirrey studied her through the curls which had flopped over her face. 'You want to go back, don't you?'

Lily shrugged. 'Well — in some ways — yes. All my cousins are there. And Grandma and Grandad. We were all quite close, you know. Visited all the time. Every Sunday we went to Grandma's for tea. Then in the evening, she would play the piano and we'd all gather round and sing. There was always a huge log fire in the hearth — even in the summer. They were cosy times, Voirrey, and I miss them. There is none of that warmth and love and togetherness in the camp.'

'I understand.' Drawing her lips between her teeth, Voirrey nodded sadly, sighing. 'I'll miss you. But I still wish the war would finish.'

The girls sat in dreamy silence for a while, watching the hungry ocean roll in on the rocks, sucking and seeking into every little crevice. The sound of the water lunging and receding, frothing over the rocks, was almost hypnotic.

Dog, sensing the melancholy mood, mournfully watched the girls and whined. His gentle brown eyes fixed lovingly on Voirrey, he pressed close against her legs. Absently she reached down to scratch behind his ear.

'Do you ever wonder what's beneath the water? I don't mean fish and things. I could be looking straight at a submarine and not even know it. There could be one just down there waiting for a British ship it might sink!' Lily was looking to a point just beyond the water 's edge.

'It'd be too shallow, wouldn't it? Besides — it'd get wrecked on the rocks!'

'Yes,' Lily frowned irritably, 'But you know what I mean.'

'Aye.' Voirrey poked at a few flithers which were trying to climb the bucket wall. 'Should we try an' find some crabs, too? There should be plenty around wi' the tide just gone out.'

'Ugh!' Lily shuddered. 'I'm not! Ugly things!'

'A'right then. 'Tis so quiet an' peaceful here you'd never know there was a war on.'

Black clouds started to gather over the Irish Mountains, which disappeared gradually in a dark haze.

'I think we might best go before it rains.'

They picked up the pail, carrying it between them toward the path.

Dog, trotting just ahead, stopped suddenly and took two quick steps backwards, almost tripping Voirrey. Growling, he crept forward, just a few inches at a time, dragging his belly on the ground. His lip curled right back, showing all his fangs and his hackles fully risen. With his stare fixed intently to a nearby bluff, he crept yet further forward. Then with a sudden flurry of action, he leapt to his feet and in his peculiar hobbling fashion, raced, snarling and snapping around the rocks and out of sight.

'What's wrong with him?'

Voirrey shrugged. 'I dunno. Dog! Dog! Come back here, Dog!'

There was no response, though they could hear him barking in the near distance.

'I'll go an' get him. You stay here wi' the pail.' Tutting her annoyance, she dumped the bucket on the ground and ran off in pursuit of the dog.

She found him looking eagerly into a cave-mouth when she caught up with him, his tail twitching nervously. Taking a few tentative steps forward, head alertly tilted sideways, he stared intently into the blackness. Suddenly, swiftly, barking wildly he leapt backwards, dancing then cowering.

'What is it, Dog? What have you seen?'

Dog allowed her a brief glance when she laid her hand on his head. 'Is it a rabbit? Or a crab?'

Voirrey ventured toward the cave-mouth, Dog creeping, almost on his belly, behind her.

The floor sloped gently upward and, toward the back, narrowed to a slit not much higher than Voirrey. Reaching it, she squeezed through, carefully testing the ground before each step

CHAPTER 15

lest it should unexpectedly fall away. As she straightened she suddenly sensed a presence. Screwing her eyes up, she peered into the impenetrable darkness, her heart like a drum in her ears. A scuffling sounded nearby and something wet touched her hand. With a squeal, she cringed away, but at the moment she realized it had been Dog, she also became aware that the object she had backed up against was soft and yielding.

In an instant, before she could recover her senses, a hand was clasped over her mouth. A strong arm snaked around her waist and arms held her against a firm body.

Voirrey wriggled wildly, vainly trying to break free. Her left heel lashed backwards, beating at his shin — for she was sure it was a man. He grunted in pain but did not loosen his grip.

Dog was dancing, whimpering, desperately craving to help his mistress, but in the darkness knew not where to bite.

Voirrey managed to work a fleshy part of her assailant's hand between her teeth, biting with all her strength. The man gasped and managed to pull free. Before she had time to scream, her mouth was firmly clamped again.

CHAPTER 16

'I'll take my hand away if you promise not to scream. I give you my word I won't harm you.'

Recognising Kurt's voice, Voirrey nodded, her terror abating.

The hand was removed from her mouth and the arm around her body slackened. As she moved away a little, Dog sorted out the separate bodies in the darkness and leapt to the rescue. The man gave a muffled, agonized yell as the collie's teeth sank into his thigh.

'No, Dog! It's all right!' Voirrey grabbed the animal's collar, pulling him away, but keeping him between her and the man.

'It's you, Kurt!' she accused. 'You're the escaped prisoner they're all looking for! I thought it might be.' Voirrey's eyes had adjusted to the darkness and she could just make out the movement of his head nodding. 'But why? Why have you run away? You won't get off the Island! No one ever has! They all get caught!'

'I must! I have to get back to England. My daughter's sickness is worse and neither she nor my wife can visit me. It is necessary. I *must* get off the island!'

'Voirrey!' Lily's voice drifted in.

'I have to go,' Voirrey said urgently.

'Please don't tell her I'm here. Don't tell anyone. I beg you to

CHAPTER 16

give me my chance to reach my family. I promise you I'll hurt no one.'

'I won't tell. Stay here an' I'll try to come back later. Together we may think of a way to get you home.'

'Voirrey, where have you been? I was worried.' Lily was only yards away from the cave-mouth when Voirrey, blinking at the brightness of the day, stumbled out into the daylight,

'I thought there might be some crabs in there.'

Lily gazed doubtfully towards the cave. 'Were there?'

Voirrey shook her head, wandering nonchalantly away along the beach.

'We have plenty of flithers.' When she glanced back she could just make out Kurt's shadowy form lingering well inside the cave. Her heart lurched. From what she could see, he looked so grey, thin and ill.

Voirrey puzzled what to do.

First, she must get rid of Lily. Much as she would like to trust her, to be able to tell her about Kurt and to ask for her help, she dared not. After all, her father was a guard and she might feel it her duty to tell him. Kurt had begged her not to tell anyone and she had given her word! Best to leave Lily in ignorance.

But how to get away from her?

'I'm goin' to help Daa clean the closet when we get home. Do you want to come an' help?' Voirrey lied.

Lily blanched, her stomach giving a little kick. 'Er — no. I promised Mummy I would help her with some sewing.'

'Oh! Very well then.' Voirrey's grin was evil and triumphant as she turned her head away to hide it. At the corner, she gave a quick wave, called, 'I'll see you tomorra,' then pedalled quickly down to the cottage.

'Look at all the flithers we got!' She banged the bucket down on the floor at her grandmother's feet.

'Careful. You'll crack the slates. Lily not with you?'

'Gone home. She has to help her Mammy wi' some sewin'.'

Eleanor eyed her suspiciously. 'She did go wi' you, didn't she? You didn't go alone?'

'Oh, yes. She came all right. Ask her Mammy.'

'Hm. I'll take your word for it.' Eleanor still did not look entirely convinced.

'I said I might go up an' help after I'd brought these home.' She nodded toward the bucket, her fingers firmly crossed. 'Can I go?'

'I didn't know you were so keen on sewin'?'

'I thought maybe Mrs Beckinsale might teach me some new stitches.'

Eleanor thought for a moment, while Voirrey crossed her fingers behind her back.

'Go then. But don't you be late for tea.'

'I won't!' Voirrey strolled until she had the kitchen door closed behind her then, afraid lest her grandmother should change her mind, she grabbed her bike from against the wall, pedalling frantically out through the gateway and up the road.

At the corner she stopped, looking carefully in case Caesar should be watching, or Lily anywhere in sight.

A beautiful aroma drifted across from the chip shop. Through the steamed windows, Voirrey could see the vague forms of soldiers queueing inside. An occasional burst of laughter floated across the road.

Caesar stood down near the camp entrance. His back turned towards Voirrey, he was deeply engaged in conversation with Joseph Callow.

Quickly she stood on the pedal, setting the bike in rapid motion and was soon out of sight round the bend. With a relieved sigh, she slowed her pace when she turned up the little-used track to Traie Cabbag.

· CHAPTER 16 ·

The old bike rattled and jolted over the slippery stones of the rough lane. Voirrey feared the bumping might break some part of the bike, but speed was essential, so she rode on a prayer.

Reaching the top of the rubble-strewn rise, she dropped the bike and ran, slithering on loose stone, hair flying behind her, to the rocky beach. Round the headland, she hurried, slowing only as she approached the cave-mouth.

Stopping outside, she scanned along the shore and cliff-tops, making sure no one was watching.

Dog, who had run frantically along behind her all the way, dashed eagerly into the cave, barking wildly.

'Quiet Dog!' She commanded and he slunk out looking dismayed. Satisfied the coast was clear, she edged into the cave and, squeezing through the cleft to the rear, she called Kurt's name.

There was no reply. She called again. Still nothing!

'Oh Dog, he's gone,' Voirrey said in dismay. 'He didn't trust me. He must have thought I would tell.'

Voirrey sat disconsolately on a rock close to the water's edge, absently chipping pebbles into the sea. 'Maybe he's just gone for a walk. We'll wait a while.'

Silently, sadly, her eyes scanned the cliff-tops and the tangle of dying gorse bushes for any sign of life. Apart from the mournful, wheeling gulls, all was still.

Finally, with an unhappy sigh, she stood up. 'C'mon Dog. We'd better get home or we'll be late for tea.'

They trailed up the crumbling pathway to where she had abandoned her bike. Bending to pick it up, a movement caught her eye and she saw Kurt rising from behind a dense clump of gorse.

He stood looking at her, Voirrey thought, like a hunted animal. He seemed tense, ready to leap, his eyes sunk deep in his head. His face — what she could see of it beyond a scruffy growth of beard — was grey and drawn. Suffering was etched into every line of his countenance.

Slowly she straightened, watching him warily through frightened, frozen blue eyes.

For long moments they studied each other uncertainly. He had such a wild look, Voirrey found herself suddenly very afraid of him. A chill wind blew down the coast and her teeth chattered like dice in a glass.

'You came.' He finally found his voice.

Voirrey nodded mutely, feeling the fingers of wind wisping her hair around her face, catching the curls in the corner of her mouth. Her skirts flapped noisily around her legs, tugging at her, while overhead a solitary gull mewled its song of misery.

A pall of silence fell between them, lingering like the heavy, humid air right before a summer thunderstorm.

'You came alone!' Kurt sounded surprised. 'I had to hide until I was sure you had brought no guards.'

Voirrey shook her head sadly. 'I promised I would tell no one. Don't you trust me?'

Suddenly he sank to his knees. Bowing his head he put his face in his hands, sobbing loudly. His shoulders heaved with every sob which racked through his body.

Running to him, she knelt and put her arms around him.

His clothes, she noticed, were damp and cold, hanging from him as though they were cast-offs from someone much larger. He was shivering, and when she laid her cheek against his it was cold and clammy.

Suddenly he put his arms tight around her, crushing her uncomfortably. His tears were wet and cold on her face.

Wriggling, she managed to loosen his grip a little.

'Thank God you came, Voirrey Kelly, to bring some warmth

CHAPTER 16

back into my life. I've prayed to God for help — for salvation. And He has sent you to me. Thank you for coming.'

'I must go home now or Daa will go to look for me an' find I'm not where I said I would be. You can't stay here, though, in the damp an' cold. Have you been able to find much food?'

'Very little. But where else can I go? Nowhere is safe.'

'Do you know the church in Patrick?'

Kurt nodded.

'Well, when it's dark, go there. Stay in the shadows o' the hedges an' you won't be seen. At the back o' the church is a doorway that is never locked. Just inside is another door with stairs that go down under the church. All sorts are stored in there. You can stay safely hidden, an' it's dry an' out o' the wind.'

'The church in Patrick?' Kurt shook his head decisively. 'That's right across the road from the camp. They'll easily find me there.'

'They won't!' Voirrey tried to sound more definite than she felt, but she could think of nowhere safer, and at least it would be dry and much warmer than the cave. 'They have already searched there. Anyway, they think you're either dead or gone off the Island now. They're not lookin' for you any more.'

Kurt looked thoughtful for a moment. 'All right. I'll trust you. I'll go to the church as soon as it is dark enough to be safe.'

'I'll try to sneak out tonight wi' some food for you. Now I must go.'

Kurt nodded. 'Go safely, little one.'

Voirrey cycled off and when she glanced over her shoulder, Kurt had disappeared.

'Watch out for Mr Quine!' She called back to thin air as she hurtled down the slope.

Henry was just outside the gate when she arrived home. 'You're late!' he said crossly. 'I was jus' comin' to look for you.'

'Sorry, Daa. I forgot the time.' Walking ahead of him up the garden path, she drew in a deep breath. Rolling her eyes toward heaven, she puffed out her cheeks and let the air escape slowly from her lungs.

During tea, Voirrey longingly watched the herring and potatoes vanish from the plates, the juice mopped up by the one slice of bread each, which was all their meagre finances could afford. Hopefully, she willed someone to leave a scrap on their plate but knew it would not happen.

When the grown-ups were engrossed in conversation, she slipped half of her bread into her pocket.

Sitting in the parlour later, Voirrey fidgeted, longing to find a way to escape and go to Kurt. The morsel of bread was nestled safely in her drawer upstairs, tucked safely away under her bloomers.

'I'm goin' up to do my homework.'

Henry raised one eyebrow, quizzically. 'Up?' he questioned.

'In my bedroom.'

'Bring it down here like you allus do. 'Tis too cold in your bedroom.'

'The work's quite hard an' I can't think proper wi' folks about' me talkin'. I won't be cold if I wrap a blanket aroun' myself.'

Margaret nodded her approval.

With a sigh of relief, Voirrey hurried upstairs. Taking the bread from the drawer, she sneaked quietly back down. Placing her feet flat on each step, she counted every one, holding tightly to the stair rail to help her silently reach past the squeaky sixth.

Pausing briefly by the parlour door, she listened to the voices droning, but could hear no sound of movement. Everyone seemed settled.

She slipped quietly into the kitchen and took the bonnag tin

· CHAPTER 16 ·

from the larder shelf. Cutting a generous slice, she dropped it into her pocket.

It didn't seem much. Better than nothing though. Passing the herring crock, she stopped, looking at it thoughtfully. Yes, she patted an empty pocket, perhaps a herrin' too.

Lifting the lid of the crock, she dug her arm down. It was coming close to empty and she had to grope deep down through inches of foul-smelling, fishy, salty water to reach the fish. Struggling to keep a grip on the slimy creature, she replaced the lid on the jar. Only in the nick of time did she stop herself dropping the herring in beside the bread and cake. Quietly she lifted the latch on the back door and sneaked outside. Stopping by the front corner, she listened outside the house for a few moments, then ran lightly to the gate. Halting in the gateway, she watched along the road to ensure no one was coming.

All was clear! Keeping close in against the hedges, heart drumming against her ribs, she crept the few yards up towards the church then ran across the road.

The huge, black-painted iron gate groaned loudly as she moved it. Freezing, she darted fearful looks around. The noise surely must have wakened even the souls of those buried in the graveyard.

For a long moment, she stood with her back against the gate. Gravestones stood like huge, silent sentinels at attention to guard the churchyard.

A twig somewhere cracked like whiplash and she started like a nervous filly, pressing herself into the corner against the stone gatepost. An icy wind cut through her clothing and, shivering, she wished she had brought her coat. There was no other sound, so after a moment she forced her feet to carry her forward between the looming gravestones and along beside the church to its rear door.

Peering warily behind her in the blackness, she carefully turned the knob, gently sliding the door open. Once inside, she felt for the handle to the cellar door. It was stiff to move, but she edged it wide enough, then feeling carefully for each creaking step, moved quietly downward.

There was no sound save the occasional scuffling of a mouse or rat. Voirrey gave an involuntary shudder. 'Kurt!' she whispered and her voice rasped back at her from the stone walls.

'Voirrey.' His voice, only inches from her ear, made her jump and her throat constricted with fright.

'Oh! You're here safely!' she said breathlessly. 'I've brought you some food. Just a little. I couldn't get much.' She could smell the fishy saline on her arm. 'I got a herrin', but it's not cooked at all.'

'That's fine, Voirrey. I've grown used to food not cooked this last two weeks. I've had nothing to eat except an occasional turnip and mussels from the rocks. I've had no means of cooking any of it.'

Voirrey's stomach somersaulted at the mere thought of raw flithers.

Kurt's hand, when she found it to give him his food, was icy cold. Again she felt the winter dampness of his clothes and noticed him shivering.

'There must be something in here to keep you warmer.'

'The room is full of objects, but it's too dark to find anything.'

Voirrey tried to visualise the room. She had been down here many a Christmas time, helping the vicar and the ladies to find the props they needed for the nativity play. There was, she knew, a large pair of faded brown velvet curtains somewhere.

'At the far end of this room,' she said, frowning thoughtfully, 'Should be a large box with curtains in. If you can find them you could wrap them around yourself. I don't think the box has a lid. I must go now before I'm missed. I'll try to bring you some dry clothes as soon as possible.' So saying, she slipped quietly backwards from the room, retracing her steps until she was back out amongst the graves.

Pausing briefly to listen to the sounds of the night, she hurried to the gate, starting as it squealed again. Glancing up toward the corner, she could see no sign of Caesar Quine, so ran across the road and back to the cottage.

Outside the window, she paused to peep through the chink in the curtain. To her relief, the three grown-ups were still sitting quietly engrossed in their conversation.

Letting herself in through the kitchen, she picked up the bar of red carbolic soap; Granny's cure for everything; and tried to scrub the herring stink from her arm. It helped, but not a lot and she wasn't even sure which smell she liked least. Once clean she crept furtively back to her bedroom, again avoiding the sixth step from the top.

Picking up the knitted doll, she cuddled it to her and snuggled under the blankets, pulling them up around her ears.

'We've got to get Kurt some dry clothes,' she told the sugar mouse. 'An' a candle. An' some matches to light it wi'.'

The mouse twitched his whiskers and nodded his agreement. His pink eyes gleamed in the glow from the floodlights.

'I know!' Voirrey sat bolt upright. 'Uncle Edward 's clothes! He doesn't need them just now an' they should fit Kurt.'

The sixth step from the top creaked and Voirrey lunged for her school bag, tipping the books onto the bed. By the time Margaret came into the room, her daughter was chewing a pencil while she thoughtfully studied an exercise book.

'Are you near finished?'

Voirrey looked up dazedly. 'Pardon? Oh, yes. I'm just doin' the last sum.' She guiltily hoped her mother wouldn't notice the book was upside down. Making a quick scribble, she snapped shut the jotter, throwing it down on the bed.

'There! Finished!' She slipped off the bed.

'Good. Come down for a cup o' tea an' get warmed by the fire. It's so cold up here.'

Voirrey sat close against the parlour fire, her hands wrapped around the hot cup of thick black brew. Slowly, feeling returned to her fingers and she could feel the blood coursing more hotly through her veins.

'How much longer is this awful war goin' to last?' Voirrey asked later as she scrambled into bed.

Margaret, engaged in tucking her daughter in for the night, paused, shaking her head dismally. 'I don't know, love. I really don't. I thought it would ha' been ended long ago. It *should* ha' been ended long ago.'

'I want Daddy home. An' Uncle Edward.' Virrey tried to hide the tremor in her voice.

'We all do, love,' Margaret agreed. 'I'm sure those awful Germans can't hold out much longer.'

When her mother's footsteps had receded downstairs, Voirrey climbed out of bed, wrapped a blanket around herself and stood at the skylight window, gazing at the brightened sky. The camp's lights were still as bright, but the music seemed, somehow, sadder now. It no longer inspired the dreams of handsome princes and magical ice palaces.

Voirrey lay wide awake, huddled under her blankets, long after the music had stopped and she had heard all the grown-ups go to bed. When there had been no sound for quite some time, she sat on the edge of the bed, pulled on her stockings and laced her boots. Dragging a jersey and coat on top of her nightdress, she tip-toed to the bedroom door, edging it open.

· CHAPTER 16 ·

At the top of the stairs, she stood for a while listening to the house. Satisfied there was no one awake, she crept quietly down to the next landing.

Outside Edward's door, she stopped to listen yet again. Turning the knob firmly, she pushed the door slowly open. The hinge groaned quietly and she froze, one foot raised slightly in the arrested act of stepping forward.

No sound followed, so Voirrey moved swiftly into the room, feeling her way to where she knew Edward's wardrobe to be.

First trousers and a jacket. They were easy to find. Then the thick, heavy fisherman's oilskin coat. On the wardrobe floor, she found a pair of boots. Easing open a drawer, she located a warm oily wool gansey and socks. Wrapping everything in the coat, she carried it all to the landing.

The door moaned again as she closed it, but it went unheard. After struggling down the last flight of stairs with her cumbersome bundle, Voirrey slipped quietly through the kitchen and out into the night.

When she found the church gate lying open, she faltered there. Had she closed it when she left? Standing with one hand on the offending gate, she studied it thoughtfully. It had creaked when she opened it, but she could not recall a sound of it closing. Without moving it, she sidled through with her bundle.

Something moved ahead of her. Frozen with fear, Voirrey peered into the darkness, straining her ears to hear any sound.

The only light came from the camp. Shining low through the waving trees it made strange shadows amongst the gravestones.

Another movement came. To her left a bit. It was clear this time, but she couldn't make out what it was. If only there were moonlight to dispel the dark fantasies her mind insisted on inventing!

A sudden flurry of movement from the crest of a gravestone

caused Voirrey almost to drop her bundle of clothes. It flew close overhead, slipping furtively past, almost touching her hair. When it cried, its strange call revealed it to be nothing more fearsome than an owl.

Something brushed against her leg and with a startled squeal, she bolted for the church door. Pulling it roughly open, she tumbled inside, pushing it quickly shut behind her.

Voirrey dragged in a shaky breath and felt her heart beating in her throat. Nothing tried to follow her in, so after a few moments, she made her way down to the storeroom. Closing the door behind her, she stood with her back against it. 'Kurt?'

'Voirrey?' The voice came from the far end of the room. 'Why are you back? What was all that noise?'

'I've brought you some dry clothes. Something scared me, but it was only an owl. It's gone now.'

'You're a wonderful friend. Many thanks.' There was a shuffling and bumping, a few muttered curses, then he was at her side, gratefully taking the clothes from her trembling hands. 'It is hard to see in this darkness, but I've found the curtains you spoke of. I found, also, a settee of some sort, on which I can lie to sleep.'

'Good. Now I must go home. I'll try to bring you some more food tomorrow. An' a candle to see by.'

Kurt's gaze was soft as he looked into her eyes. 'I thank you so deeply, my little love.'

Reaching behind her, she opened the door, slipped through it and hurried up the stairs.

At the gate, Voirrey stopped to glance up the road, stiffening in terror. Not two yards away, silhouetted against the floodlights, a large figure stood, his back toward her, surveying the camp.

With an almost inaudible gasp, she ducked back through the

· CHAPTER 16 ·

gateway, crawled behind the pillar and crouched there, trembling. Pressing her forefinger against her top lip, she curled her thumb tight under her chin to stop her teeth chattering.

The unmistakable aroma of Caesar's cigar wafted to her on the night air. After what felt like a nightmare lifetime, Voirrey heard his footsteps moving away and wondered how he had failed to hear her drumming heart.

Watching from the protective shadows of the gateway, she waited until Caesar turned the corner, then bolted for home.

Once back in the safety of her bedroom, she leaned weakly against the door and heaved a shaky sigh of relief.

CHAPTER 17

In the morning Voirrey was wakened early by Eleanor calling angrily from the foot of the stairs. 'Voirrey Kelly — you get down here right this minute!'

Heart pumping painfully slowly, she leapt out of bed and ran downstairs. What had happened? Had she been seen last night? What had been discovered? Had Kurt been found — and wearing Uncle Edward's clothes? Would he have told how he'd come by them? Surely not! A guilty conscience tossed all sorts of frightening thoughts around in her head.

Pausing at the door only long enough to take a deep breath, she walked fearfully into the kitchen.

Eleanor pointed darkly to a point near the crocks. 'Look at that floor, girl!' she said furiously. 'That's your doing. You know you must always put a cover over the pail!'

Voirrey, looking to the floor, had to clamp her lips tight together to stop herself laughing. The flithers, having been spared the cooking pot the previous night, had climbed out of the bucket, and spread themselves around the slate flagstones.

'Sorry, Granny. I'll put them back in the pail. Bending, she took the shell between her fingers, to find the limpet had attached itself firmly to the floor. The others had all done likewise.

· CHAPTER 17 ·

Henry, who had rushed downstairs to find out what all the commotion was about, stood roaring with laughter. Handing Voirrey his pen-knife, he said, 'Here, lass, it will take this to shift them devils. I'll fetch the hammer.'

Eleanor watched apprehensively when Voirrey set about the shells with the knife and hammer.

'You mind you don't take pieces out o' the floor. An' take care of your fingers. When you're done wi' that you can bring in the eggs before you take the cows to the lhergy.'

The flithers all safely back in the bucket, Voirrey put a cover over it and moved on to her next chore.

Placing the last egg in the basket, she was about to rush indoors with the exciting news that there were ten this morning. Then she remembered Kurt. Glancing back and seeing no one at the kitchen window, she quickly pushed two of the eggs amongst the parsley, arranging the plants to hide the treasure.

Dog watched curiously, his head on one side, tail thumping the ground. Voirrey put a finger to her lips. 'Don't you tell!' she warned ferociously. 'An' don't touch!'

The rounds of Sunday School and church were more tedious than normal that day. Voirrey worried throughout that someone, for some reason, should go to the cellar. Her only consolation was that, being in the church, she was close to Kurt. She found herself constantly gazing at the floor.

After dinner, while the grown-ups relaxed in the parlour, Voirrey made a careful, guilty search of the kitchen. Finding four candles, she slipped one up her sleeve. Taking, also, some matches from the box, she placed them in her pinafore pocket. With them was the oatcake she had managed to secrete.

'I might take a walk an' pick some blackberries before Sunday

School,' she said strolling into the parlour, bowl in hand. 'Will you make a pie for tea, please, Granny?'

'Yes. If you get enough. That would be nice.'

Henry opened his eyes, raising his chin from his chest. 'Would you like me to come wi' you, girlie?' He asked sleepily.

Voirrey started guiltily. 'Oh no! I mean, no thank you, Daa. You're tired. Stay an' doze.'

Henry nodded contentedly and let his head droop again.

Backing quickly from the room, Voirrey took in a deep breath, held it for a moment and let it hiss quietly through clenched teeth. Quickly retrieving the two eggs, she left hurriedly.

There were blackberries aplenty and she soon had the bowl fairly full. For a change of flavour, she topped it up with wild rose hips, working her way back toward the church.

Strolling innocently through the churchyard, she stopped by the back door, checking warily to ensure that there was no one to see her.

The camp was a bit of worry during daylight, the back of the church being clearly visible from the compounds. She watched the afternoon sun struggle in the gathering wind, trying frantically to disentangle itself from the branches of a giant sycamore. She could see, beyond the tree, a group of prisoners standing in the exercise yard. Their backs were toward her and she felt sure they were too far off to present any danger.

With a final glance around the churchyard, she let herself into the church, hurrying down the stairs. Once inside the store-room, with the door safely shut behind her, she took the candle from her sleeve, lighting it with a match struck against the stone wall.

Kurt rose from behind a pile of old church pews a moment after she let herself into the cellar.

Together they gazed around the room, piled high with old,

CHAPTER 17

unused church furnishings. Pews, mostly broken; tattered, faded clothes and curtains; the scenery for the annual nativity play. Boxes upon boxes of goodness only knew what! Probably much of it had been there since the church was young. The accumulated clutter of many, many years.

The floor, Voirrey noticed, was liberally littered with dark, dry pellets of rat dung. Horrified, she pulled a face.

Following her gaze, Kurt smiled, saying, 'It is better than a cold, damp cave.'

'Why did you run away?' Voirrey shook her head slowly. 'To put yourself through this misery when you had the comforts of the camp.'

'It was something I did just on the spur of the moment when the storm put the floodlights out. I had a letter that day to tell me my Catherine's illness is much worse. She has tuberculosis.'

'Oh! I'm so sorry!' Voirrey felt a tear press sorely behind her eye.

'Then the lights went out and I thought, 'If I can get away from here, then perhaps I can find a way off the Island to be with my Catherine.' It is likely she will not live and I *must* be with her when the end comes. I *have* to be!' There was a note of desperation in his voice.

Voirrey studied him sadly, her heart heavy.

His eyes seemed to sink ever more deeply into his face. Those brown eyes of his, usually so warm and friendly, had become quite fixed and hollow.

'I wanted to reach Peel or Douglas. I thought I might try to take a boat. But there were too many searchers. Everyone was looking for me. I had to keep moving about, dodging people. Hiding in hollows under the gorse bushes — until I found that cave. It was cold and damp, but at least it was out of the wind and rain. I just seemed to grow so numb with cold, fatigue and hunger that I could think of no way out of the quandary I was in.' Kurt raised his shoulders and flapped his hands slightly in a gesture of hopeless resignation.

'I'll try to think of a way. I'll see if I can find a boat you can take. Now I must leave or I'll be late for Sunday School.' Voirrey gave him the biscuit and rose hips from her pocket. Digging under the blackberries, she found the eggs and handed those to him along with a handful of berries.

'I'll come back when I can.'

Voirrey opened the door a crack, peeping out to make sure the coast was clear before stepping outside.

Hurrying around the corner of the church, she was startled to collide, almost, with Caesar. With a frightened, guilty squeal, she clasped a hand to her mouth, almost dropping the bowl of berries.

'Voirrey? What are you doing here at this time?' Caesar seemed almost as startled as she.

'Oh! Um! Gathering blackberries!' She held the bowl toward him as proof.

'In the church?'

'I thought there might be some in the old graveyard.'

Caesar frowned disapprovingly. 'I don't really feel it's proper to walk over graves for such a purpose, do you?'

'I didn't walk on the graves!' Voirrey protested in righteous indignation.

'In the future, I think it'd be best if you found your fruit elsewhere. I'm sure your grandmother wouldn't approve o' this.'

'No, Mr Quine.' With a sigh of relief, Voirrey side-stepped past the policeman and hurried off home.

The escapee now being considered well gone, Henry felt there was no longer a need for him to accompany the girls to Peel.

· CHAPTER 17 ·

Emily met Voirrey at the camp gate the following morning with the news that Lily had a severe cold, so would be staying home from school for a few days.

Having said how sorry she was, Voirrey hurried toward Peel with a thoughtful smile. Being free of Lily would give her the chance to have a good look around the harbour and find if there was a boat that Kurt might easily 'borrow'.

The day seemed to grind through exceedingly slowly. Finding it hard to concentrate on schoolwork, Voirrey let her mind wander. Endless times she was scolded for inattentiveness.

When school ended for the day, she hurried to the station. It did cross her mind to wonder why she was hurrying, for that would not bring the train any earlier, but that thought didn't slow her.

The train had not properly stopped in Peel when she jumped off, curls flying, excitement fluttering her heart.

She strode quite briskly along the harbour-side, eagerly studying the boats docked there. As she came towards the end, without finding a boat small enough for one man to handle, despondency took her. So confident she had been of being able to take the news to Kurt that she had found him a boat!

While she walked home to Patrick the last of the light was draining away, turning the sky sooty. Drowning in disappointment, she felt as though everything around belonged to the darkness and that she would be sucked into it too. The trees of the roadside woodland loomed over her threateningly. Wind arched silver birches that straggled by the stream, thrashing their slender branches in whispering protest. Voirrey felt they could reach out and snatch her and no one would ever know to where she had vanished. Fear speeded her pace.

Caesar stood outside the pub, keeping watch as ever. 'You come home alone tonight, Voirrey?'

'Aye. Lily's sick. Didn't go to school today.'

'Well, you hurry on home. 'Tis gettin' a mite dark for you to be out alone.'

'Yes, Mr Quine,' Voirrey said meekly. She hurried past him and down the road. Stopping at the church gate she turned to check Caesar was not watching from the corner and, slipping into the churchyard, she moved carefully toward the back door, creeping nervously on tip-toe.

An owl hooted on the church roof and she heard the strange chattering noise of bats.

Spiders' webs fanned out between the gravestones, holding droplets of evening mist, like diamonds glittering in the moonlight.

A shadow moved beside a stone, detached itself from it, came towards Voirrey.

With a squeal, she turned to take flight, but a strong hand caught her arm. Panicking, she struggled to free herself.

'Don't be frightened, Voirrey. It's only me!' Kurt's voice sounded urgent in her ear.

'Oh, Kurt!' She gasped shakily. 'Why are you out here?'

'I must get some fresh air sometimes.'

'I couldn't get much food for you today. I saved some of my sandwiches and there are the crusts one girl threw away for the birds. I picked them up after she'd gone.'

'Thank you.' Kurt took the paltry scraps, ravenously shoving them into his mouth. 'I need water, too, if you could bring me some.'

'Perhaps you can find a bowl in your room somewhere. If not, I'll bring you one. Then you can fetch water from the ditch. Tonight I looked to see if there was a boat in Peel, but there was none small enough for you to sail alone. I'll keep watchin'. Now I must go or they'll start to worry at home.'

· CHAPTER 17 ·

'You're late!' Eleanor glared as she slipped in through the kitchen door.

'Sorry. I was talkin' to Mr Quine.'

'Has Caesar any news of interest?' Henry looked up questioningly from the peas he was shelling.

'Not really. He was just sayin' again how bad it is to have the camp so near the village.'

Henry nodded, smiling quietly to himself.

It was with a soaring feeling of joy and goodwill Voirrey scraped the leftovers into a bowl after tea. There were potato, a little herring and — Henry having acquired a turnip from a nearby field that day — a goodly amount of that.

'I'll take the scraps to the hens,' she offered cheerfully.

In the garden, out of sight of the kitchen window, she placed the bowl on the ground, carefully covering it with a piece of wood to keep out any slugs, rats or birds.

When everyone was settled in the parlour for the evening, Henry dozing with his pipe, Eleanor and Margaret busy with their mending, Voirrey slipped quietly away.

In her pocket, as she ran over to the church with the bowl of scraps, was a piece of dry bread she had secreted and a lump of bonnag she'd pinched from the larder.

Kurt was back in his hiding place and he lit the candle when Voirrey announced herself.

'I've brought you a bowl an' some more food.'

'Many thanks. Some day you'll find your reward in heaven,' he promised with great sincerity.

'Not too soon, I hope', Voirrey replied cheerfully. 'Now I must leave before I'm missed. Keep the bowl for water.' With that she was off, disappearing more quickly than she'd come.

At the gate, she paused to look up the road. The light from

the chip shop window shone out, warming the evening. Every now and then, when someone opened the door, a burst of voices came out on a cloud of steam which hung suspended on the cold night air.

Silhouetted against the floodlights, Caesar stood on the corner, his back turned to her.

Keeping as close as she could against the hedge, Voirrey hurried down the hill. Glancing back up the road, she saw to her horror that Caesar had seen her and was advancing quickly.

'Hey, you!' came his shout.

Heart lurching, Voirrey bolted across the road and up the garden path. Closing the kitchen door quietly, she hurried to her room, taking the stairs as quickly and silently as possible and avoiding the sixth from the top.

Before she had reached the top, there came a thundering on the front door.

Throwing off her coat, Voirrey swiftly lit a candle, spread her books on her bed and lay on her stomach beside them. There was a rumble of voices, then Henry's calling to her. Picking up the candle she went to her door, leaning over the bannister rail to look down, her heart thundering against her ribs.

Henry was at the first landing, the oil-lamp held aloft, peering anxiously upward.

'What's wrong, Daa?'

'You're here safe are you?'

'Aye. I'm doin' my homework. Where did you think I was? What's wrong?'

'Jus' Caesar Quine thought he saw someone run into our garden. You carry on wi' your work, lass .' Turning, he spoke downward. 'We'd better take a lamp an' check outside, Caesar, jus' in case there's someone up to no good out there.'

Voirrey set her teeth, swallowing the saliva which unbidden

CHAPTER 17

had filled her mouth. Returning to her room she heaved a sigh of relief and flopped, shaken to the bed. That had been too close for comfort. She must be more careful in future.

Though Voirrey saved parts of her sandwiches, picked up scraps dropped by the other children at school, and lovingly hid away the few leftovers at home, she was given no opportunity to go to Kurt in the following two days.

Each day, when returning from school, she quickly scoured Peel Harbour for a suitably small boat, but to no avail. At Patrick, Caesar was standing by the chip shop. He gave her a curt nod and she fancied he eyed her suspiciously. Whenever she reached the gate, she glanced over her shoulder and would find him always still watching.

Later in the evenings, when she sneaked to the gate with her meagre bundles of food, he was on the corner, ever watchful. Knowing she must not be caught, she was forced to neglect Kurt.

Did the policeman never sleep, she wondered. No matter what the time, he seemed to be there watching — always watching.

On the third night, concern for Kurt eating at her innards, she determined that, no matter what, she must get to him that night. The collection of food hidden in her drawer grew larger and ever more stale, but meanwhile, Kurt was starving.

Voirrey lay awake listening until the music stopped and the last post was played. Then she stayed, lying motionless, until long after the house was well asleep.

A rogue gust of wind threw a noisy smattering of raindrops on the roof. Close on its tail, a sudden storm beat the house. Unmerciful rains clawed at the attic window. To Voirrey it was like the grinding teeth of some vicious, vengeful beast. She snuggled deeper under the blankets, knowing she could not go out in such awful weather. There would be no satisfactory way to explain the wet clothes to her mother. Finally, she drifted into a restless sleep.

Late in the night, or well on toward morning, the storm abated. Waking, Voirrey slipped out of bed and pulled on her boots and coat. Taking the food from the drawer, she crept downstairs. From the kitchen, she took two herring, a candle and a slice of turnip, before hurrying across to the church.

A puff of wind in the treetops shook a flurry of raindrops from overhead. Voirrey almost cried out at the unexpected soft slap against her face.

Once she thought she heard the sound of a voice — a moan or a whisper — and stopped, startled, her heart throbbing noisily in the night. *'It must have been an animal,'* she thought. *'The woods will be full of them.'*

It came again, human — yet not human. Crouching, she felt the hairs march upright from the nape of her neck to the crown of her head.

It was a sound full of agony and strain. A soul in torment! Terrified, she turned her head, striving to identify it.

Poised for flight she listened, paralysed, horribly afraid, yet held against all her will and inclination. A ghost? A banshee? Was it maybe the hearse of ghosts they'd all heard so much about?

There was something familiar in it. Something she recognised.

With a tremendous sigh of relief, she remembered. Old Mac! Of course!

The dog from the farm. He always bayed at a full moon.

At last, her heart stopped thudding. She stood her ground for a moment, gritting her teeth, sweating. It took a supreme effort to force her legs to take another step forward. Once in the sanctuary of the church, she stood for a moment to regain her composure before going down to Kurt.

CHAPTER 17

Kurt's welcome was overwhelming. The joy he showed was for her company, though he was thankful also for the food she brought.

Kurt drew her to him. It was a gentle, confident movement and when he began to stroke her hair, more than ever it felt like her father.

The tenderness of his unconscious action caused the tears to prick at the back of her eyes. She wanted to lay her head against his shoulder and sob out the misery of the last years.

Voirrey's fingers gripped his sleeve tightly and the world seemed to wheel about her.

For a long time, he held her, swaying gently, rocking her. Voirrey could feel the strong, regular beat of his heart against her cheek as she clung to him. Kurt's love flowed through to her and she revelled in the warmth of it, her own heart soaring with pleasure. It was an affectionate contact they both desperately needed.

'It's very hard to come here,' She apologised at last. 'I think Mr Quine — the policeman — is suspicious. He keeps watchin' me.'

'Well, don't risk being caught. I don't want you to get into trouble on my account.'

'I won't. But I'd better go now. I'll come back as soon as I can.'

'Be careful.'

Voirrey nodded and slipped out. Opening the outside door just a crack, she peeped out. The light coming through the chink was tinged with the faint rose glow of sunrise. Already the threat of dawn was beginning to burn the edges of clouds piled high along the hilltops.

With a gasp of dismay, Voirrey stepped out into the graveyard. She must have spent longer with Kurt than she realised. Moving quickly, keeping to the darkest shadows, she reached the church gate and, finding the roadway clear, ran home.

Thankfully she climbed the last few steps to her room forgetting, in her relief, the sixth from the top, which groaned fit to wake the dead. Freezing, with her weight full on it, Voirrey listened.

'Who's there?' Margaret's sleepy voice drifted up to her.

Voirrey bit her lip. If there was no answer someone would come looking. 'It's me,' she replied tentatively.

'What're you doin' out o' bed? Where're you goin'?'

Voirrey thought quickly. 'I've been out to the closet.'

'You shouldn't go out in the middle o' the night. That's why you have a pofor.'

'I don't like usin' it. It makes my room smell!' She crept up the last few steps to her door.

'Alright. Get back to bed now.'

'Yes, Mammy.'

With a huge, shaky sigh Voirrey collapsed thankfully into bed, shivering with a combination of cold and fright. This had been a night she knew she would never forget.

In the morning Henry gave her a very severe scolding for leaving the house in the night. 'You don't know what sort of brigands may be waitin' out there. There might be other prisoners escaped who may attack you. Don't ever go outside again at night.'

'No, Daa.' Voirrey looked suitably repentant.

Lily was still not well enough to return to school the following day, Friday, but Emily hoped that by Monday she would be recovered again.

Though missing her friend, Voirrey was pleased with the freedom it gave her to search, albeit fruitlessly, for a boat.

Walking home alone from Peel that night her mind worked furiously on the problem of Kurt. He could not be kept long in

· CHAPTER 17 ·

the church. People, she felt, were becoming wary of her, suspecting her of some mischief. She sensed she was being watched more closely now.

And there was Kurt too. He had a desperate need to be gone, to reach England and his daughter. Hidden in the church he had less news of Catherine than when he was locked in the camp. Each time Voirrey set eyes on him he seemed to have failed even more. Now only a shell of the man was left. In the light of the candle, his face was no more than a skull.

Voirrey marched grimly, thoughtfully on toward Patrick. The scents of the day were still there, drifting unanchored. The smoke from the kipper houses and the cottages burning logs in their fireplaces.

At first, she was unaware of the bite of the wind, but then she felt it keenly. The roadside trees had tried to hold their last green leaves, but these were drying, shrivelling, and many had fallen. Now the ageing giants stretched their lonely arms to the sky, becoming ever more barren.

Voirrey trudged onwards through the cold evening. Before her, the lights of the camp cut into the gathering dusk.

Caesar was waiting at the corner. 'Evenin' Voirrey.'

'Good evenin' Mr Quine.' Voirrey passed by, head lowered, without slowing her pace.

'I'd like a word wi' you, lass!'

Voirrey stopped, turning apprehensively. 'Yes, Mister Quine?'

'What mischief are you up to?'

'Mischief?'

'Aye. Sneakin' around' in the dark!'

'I'm jus' goin' home from school.' She gazed up at him in wide-eyed innocence.

'I don't mean jus' now — as you well know. I mean the other

night – late when I chased you home.' He leaned so close she could see the network of broken veins across his cheeks.

"Twasn't me that night, Mr Quine. I was in my room doin' my homework.'

'You was by the time I got there. But it was you I chased. You sneakin' out to meet a lad?'

'No! I don't even like boys!' Voirrey was indignant, though thankful to be able to give a semi-truthful reply.

'Jus' don't do it again then!' Caesar pushed his face even closer and Voirrey stared in fascination at the pulse she saw throbbing in his temple. 'Jus' remember I'll be watching you!'

Suddenly there was an awful, terrified screaming.

Caesar turned, running toward the sound. Voirrey sped close on his heels. They reached the cottage gate just as Henry, Margaret and Eleanor rushed out.

'What's to do?' Henry called to Caesar's back.

Voirrey stopped beside them and Henry hurried through the gateway to stand by her. 'What's happening?' he asked.

'I don't know. I was talkin' to Mr Quine an' we suddenly heard this commotion.'

A woman came running, stumbling around the corner, making the most awful wailing and sobbing. Putting his arm around her, Caesar helped her, half-fainting, towards the cottage.

'Why 'tis Mabel Clucas!' Margaret pushed past her father and daughter and rushed to help.

Moments later Mabel was huddled in a chair close up to the kitchen fire, a shaking, sobbing mess.

'Whenever you feel up to it you must tell us what happened,' Caesar encouraged.

Eleanor dropped four spoonfuls of their precious sugar into the mug of thick black tea, stirred it well and handed it to Mabel, who gratefully took it in trembling hands.

CHAPTER 17

Mabel took a deep swig of the tea, wincing as it burned her throat. 'I saw the hearse!' She rasped.

The others all exchanged fearful looks.

'Three times, I saw it! The hearse of ghosses. Three times! First at the corner. Then it was waiting for me at the Vicarage! An' again at Barnell! It was then I knew!' Mabel burst into tears, sobbing uncontrollably.

Margaret sat on the chair arm, placing her arm around the older woman's shaking shoulders. 'Knew what?' she asked quietly, though she knew the answer.

Mabel swallowed a few deep, sobbing breaths. 'My Stanley's dead! That's what they come to tell me!'

'Who told you?' Caesar frowned, uncomprehending.

'The ghosses. In the hearse. They come when a Manxman has died. 'Tis my Stanley this time. I know it is, else they wouldn't ha' come to me. Oh' I should never ha' signed for him to go. But he wanted to — so much he wanted to go.' Mabel broke down into incoherent weeping.

'Hush now,' Margaret consoled. 'You don't know for sure 'tis Stanley. It may not be anybody dead.'

'It is! It is! The hearse only ever comes when a Manxman has died. His ghos' comes to tell us!'

When Mabel had calmed enough Caesar took her home.

'Do you think there's truth to it?' Eleanor asked fearfully.

'Aye.' Henry nodded sombrely. 'Every time the hearse has been seen there's been news later of a soldier dead in the family what saw it!'

'Pity if it is young Stanley. He's only a boy. Not had time to live yet.'

'Well, it was her what signed for him to go. Lied about his age. Weren't for that he'd be here safe,' Eleanor condemned.

'Mabel can hardly be blamed. He wanted to go. She didn'

make him — jus' helped. Wi' eleven children an' no man, 'tis hard to feed all those mouths.' Margaret argued.

'Aye. True, I suppose. I had eleven, but I had a man to provide for me.' She looked fondly at Henry. 'A pity Mabel's man's fishin' boat sank before the war started. Likely he wouldn't ha' let Stanley go.'

Voirrey shook and felt the bile rise in her throat. Stanley dead? How awful She had never really liked him much. Too rough. Bit of a show-off. But dead? He didn't deserve to die. She didn't doubt Mabel was right about the hearse. A mother would know!

'Please, God, look after Daddy,' she prayed that night. 'Daddy tried to look after Stanley. I know he did. Please look after him for me. An' if Stanley's wi' you, look after his soul too.' Voirrey knelt shivering by her bed, praying for hours.

In the melee of emotions, Kurt had been pushed from her mind and when, finally, she fell into a troubled sleep, it was to dream of flooded trenches and dead, rotting bodies.

CHAPTER 18

Voirrey's eyes snapped open, her waking thoughts of Kurt. Today she must find him as much food as possible, enough to last him most of the week. She might even, she thought, sneak to Peel to check the harbour.

Sliding quickly out of bed, she pulled on her chemise and bloomers, tucking her black stockings under their elastic at the knees. Having pulled the two flannelette petticoats over her head, she covered them with the pretty cotton cambric one her mother insisted she must wear 'in case her skirt blew up'. Then came the grey woollen dress, topped by her bright pinafore. Pushing her feet into her boots, she impatiently hooked the laces over the buttons.

Why, Voirrey often wondered, did she have to wear so many clothes. They made her so hot on all but the coldest winter's day — and itchy sometimes. In summer they were all quite unbearable.

Dragging a comb through her tangle of unruly curls, she ran downstairs to arrive breathless, in the kitchen.

Eleanor looked up from the pot she was stirring, frowning at Voirrey's noisy entrance. 'Young ladies do *not run*.' she said shortly. 'Sit yourself down child, the porridge is near ready.'

Voirrey sank into the nearest chair. 'I was thinkin' I might go to Traie Cabbag to-day an' see if I can dig some gibbins'.' She shuddered at the thought of the slimy little sand eels slithering in her fingers, but it was the only good reason she could think of to escape from home. Fingers crossed, she hopefully watched her grandmother.

Eleanor frowned, lifting the heavy black pot from the hob. 'You aren't usually so keen. Are you up to some mischief?'

Voirrey looked up in wide-eyed innocence. 'Oh, no!' she replied vehemently. 'It's just such a nice mornin' 'an' I thought gibbins would be a nice change from herrin'. I thought I might try to catch some crabs too.'

Not convinced, Eleanor grunted suspiciously. As she ladled porridge into bowls, she reflected on what she regarded as the depravity of today's young people. 'We shall have to see what your grandfather an' Mammy have to say about it. Go now an' tell Daa his breakfast is on the table.'

Hearing her grandfather chopping sticks in the back yard, Voirrey rose, strolling out to find him. 'Daa, Granny says to come for your porridge.'

Henry looked up sharply. 'You startled me, child. I didn't hear you comin'. What has brought you about so early?'

'It seemed such a nice, sunny mornin', I thought I might dig some gibbins.' She gave him her sweetest smile and hoped he would be too busy to think of coming with her.

Crow's feet crinkled the corners of Henry's blue eyes as he smiled down at his granddaughter. 'That would be good. Very nice indeed. Yes, you do that.'

Voirrey joyfully clutched his hand and they went indoors together.

'Mornin' Mammy.' Voirrey grimaced as she watched her mother pour buttermilk on the porridge.

'Mornin.' Your Granny tells me you wish to go to Traie Cabbag.'

Voirrey nodded. 'Please, Mammy.' Pushing the food around the bowl, she screwed her nose in distaste at the buttermilk, curdled and yellowing, mingled with the grey porridge.

'I think she should not go alone!' Eleanor said acidly. 'The child is at an age now when she might get into all sorts of mischief. At her age, she should be giving more help in the house.'

Margaret looked thoughtful. 'Eels would be a nice change of taste. We haven't had any for a while. But perhaps it might be unsafe for a girl alone, in case this desperate prisoner is still near.'

'He'll be gone a long way from here by now,' Voirrey said quickly. 'I heard the guards say he'd probably drowned trying to get off the Island.'

'What do you think, father?' Margaret passed the buck.

All eyes fixed on Henry, who looked thoughtfully at his granddaughter's eager young face.

'I think the child is right. If the fellow was still about here he would have been caught long since.' Looking intensely at the girl, he said, 'Once you've finished your chores you may go. I am trustin' you will get up to no mischief.'

He had sensed a difference about the child recently, a sort of excitement and a hitherto unseen keenness to work. Probably it was just her age — she certainly was growing up. This war had most likely made her grow up faster than she should. Two of the people she cared most about in the world had quite suddenly been torn from her life. Yes, that *would* make her grow up faster.

'Oh, no, I won't, Daa. I promise.' Voirrey fought not to make her joy too obvious.

'Well I don't approve,' Eleanor said sourly. 'There is work to be done here.'

'Not too much for the two of us,' Margaret said quietly.

'If the ladies come from the camp wantin' tea---!'

'Then we shall manage, as we do when Voirrey is at school.'

Eleanor snorted indignantly and determined she would have the last word. 'Well, eat up your porridge, girl. You'll go nowhere until it's finished and the cows are in the lhergy!'

Voirrey raised her head to protest but caught the eye of her grandfather. With a wink and an almost imperceptible shake of his head, he silenced her. Without a word, she settled to eat the grey and yellow gruel.

'I think I may go to see how Lily is,' Voirrey said as Henry walked to the gate with her. 'If she is well enough she might come wi' me.'

'I doubt if her mother will allow her out on this cold day after such an illness.'

Voirrey shrugged. 'I'll go anyway an' see.'

When she reached the corner, Henry was still at the gate watching. With a cheery wave, she turned toward Peel. To her chagrin, Caesar was just beyond the bend.

'Where you bound' for, lass?'

'Goin' to see how Lily is,' she called without stopping.

He was still eyeing her when she reached the Knockaloe track, so she had no alternative but to go to call on Lily. Her friend was still confined to bed but, Voirrey guessed from her exuberance, putting on a bit of an act to avoid having to go to school.

Voirrey stayed for a respectable time to play some board games, then excused herself to go crabbing.

At the camp gateway, she stopped to check, relieved to find Caesar was nowhere in sight. Swiftly she pumped her pedals and set off towards Peel. Three times, in the distance, she saw

CHAPTER 18

people coming, so lifted her bike over the hedge, hiding until they were safely past.

In Peel she had to risk being seen, resolving that her tale would be she had come to dig for gibbins in the sand. Luck being with her for once, she saw no one she knew.

As she neared the harbour mouth, her heart stopped for a moment, then leapt to her throat and stayed fluttering there. Chugging slowly toward the quay came a small boat. Not too small, but all right for one man to handle.

Sitting on a bollard, she watched until the boat was moored. Somehow she must find a way of getting Kurt to Peel this night.

There was a risk, she realized, that the boat might only be making a short stay and could be gone by night. But with luck, it might still be here and it was the only boat she had seen that was small enough for one man to handle. She just hoped Kurt knew enough about sailing.

Thankfully, Caesar was not in sight when she reached Patrick. Rushing through the village, she pedalled furiously to Traie Cabbag. Hurriedly and carelessly she knocked a collection of flithers from the rocks and poked a stick into rock crevices to chase out a few crabs. With enough only to make one reasonable meal, she sped home to think about what she must do tonight.

'I thought you went for gibbins? An' you didn't even get many flithers,' Eleanor grumbled, looking into the bucket.

'Sorry. But Lily was still abed an' weary o' her own company, so I stayed too long playin' games wi' her.'

After a long, slow evening, Voirrey waited tensely in bed until very long after the house had fallen silent, then dressed completely. For a trip to Peel, there could be no going with a coat over her nightdress. The hands which buttoned her boots were shaking uncontrollably.

More carefully than ever, she crept downstairs, pausing for a long time at the kitchen door before she dared go any further. She was sure the staccato crashing of her heart must wake the whole household.

At the gate, again, she waited an interminable time. This night, of all nights, she must not be caught. Satisfied there was no one around, she ran to the church. Letting herself in through the creaking gate she deliberately left it wide open. Again she paused until she was certain she had disturbed no one.

There was a need for caution, but also for speed. There was no knowing if the little boat might sail again before Kurt had his chance of it. Voirrey was well aware of this, and of fear only half-conquered, as she moved quickly forward. Speeding past the ghostly tombstones and the dark squat church, she made hurriedly for the rear door.

Downstairs, in the musty darkness of the store-room, she whispered, 'Kurt?'

'I'm here, Voirrey.' There was a rasping sound and a sudden bright flare as the match struck. He lit the candle and moved toward her.

'I've found a boat!' she said eagerly. 'In Peel. We'll have to go tonight. Now! In case it sails again.'

'Good! Wonderful!' Kurt's face lit up. 'I should change into my own clothes first. Leave your uncle's for you to return.'

Voirrey thought about it for a moment, remembering his city-looking clothes. 'No. Best you keep them. You'll look more like a fisherman. Less con — con — whatever it is.'

'Conspicuous,' he finished for her.

Voirrey nodded.

Taking Kurt's hand, she led him up the steps and to the church gate. Looking up toward the Peel Road, she hesitated. They could not go that way, with the camp lights glaring.

· CHAPTER 18 ·

'We must go down this way, then across the lhergy once we are out of view from the camp.'

For a moment her knees turned to water and heart cringed faintly at the reality of what she was about to do.

Suppose their venture was successful and Kurt escaped on the boat? What then? Well, she would have to get home, so she would have to travel back from Peel alone!' She shuddered at the thought and for a moment wondered if she should send him to Peel alone. But he wouldn't know where to look, would he? And what if the boat was gone?

'Are you all right, Voirrey?'

She nodded, taking a tentative step to see if the weakness had gone from her knees. 'Come on.'

They walked on the grass verge, half bent below the overhanging hedges. Passing the cottage, Voirrey several times glanced across the road, but there were no lights. So far her family were all still asleep.

Down to the corner past the vicarage, they crept, with Voirrey watching fearfully for the hearse. But it did not come. It had paid its visit last night. Then they turned left and stumbled over a stile and across a wet field to the Peel road. With a sigh of relief, Voirrey climbed through the hedge onto the road.

Kurt was in high spirits, excited to be on his way. Thrilling at the prospect of soon being at his Catherine's bedside.

They were pleased to meet no one on the journey, save a black and white collie which ran out barking and snapping at their ankles.

'Stop it Mac!' Voirrey commanded. The dog stopped, studying her in puzzlement. Then, recognising her as a friend, he bounced around, woofing excitedly.

'Don't be silly. Be quiet and go home.' The girl chastised,

pointing back up the farm track from whence he had come. 'Go!' she insisted when he was reluctant to obey.

Mac put his tail between his legs and slunk miserably homeward, bewildered that a friend who usually made such a fuss of him had so summarily dismissed him.

Kurt let out his breath in a sigh. 'I thought for a moment he was going to eat us.'

Voirrey giggled quietly.

Striding down through the narrow, winding streets of Peel with her heart in her mouth, Voirrey linked her arm through Kurt's, hoping they would look, to anyone who might see them, like father and daughter.

Just ahead of them Charles Christian, the painter from the nearest cottage on the Peel side of Patrick, stumbled from the tavern, looking back over his shoulder to call out to someone inside. A gusting roar of raucous laughter was snuffed as the door swung shut behind him.

In fear of being recognised, Voirrey turned in toward Kurt, pulling him around to face the shop window. When Charles Christian was out of sight they continued their journey.

Voirrey pointed to a mast much shorter than the others below the harbour wall. 'There 'tis!' she whispered excitedly. ''Tis still there.'

Kurt's face lit up and the tip of his tongue came out to wet dry lips. 'Let's take a look at it.'

The girl felt his tremor in the arm she was holding. Sticking together as though glued, they strolled slowly across the street. While they stood on the quayside looking down into the boat, they heard an occasional burst of drunken merriment from the tavern.

'It looks a sturdy enough craft,' Kurt enthused.

· CHAPTER 18 ·

'Are you goin' to go then?'
Kurt nodded. 'I must try.'
Voirrey bit her lip and nodded sadly. 'Straight out from here,' she told him, 'is the Mull o' Galloway. But you're best not to land there, 'cos then you have to find your way all around Luce Bay an' the Solway. Better to follow the coast up, then turn east past the Point of Ayre. If you keep due east from there you should come to land somewhere near St Bee's Head. Or if you turn left out o' the harbour an' sail straight across you'll be in Ireland.'
'Thank you, Voirrey. *No* thanks can be enough for all you have done to help me. I hope all goes well with your father and uncle in the future. I shall pray the war ends soon for you. You deserve only the greatest happiness.' He put his arms around her, holding her very tightly.
Voirrey clung to him, sobbing. 'I wish you weren't going,' she sobbed, a part of her wishing she had not started this adventure.
Kurt squeezed her a bit tighter. 'Will you be safe going home, little one?'
She nodded mutely, sniffing back he tears.
'Then go now. I want you gone from here before I leave.' He kissed her cheek, then breaking her grip, pushed her gently away from him. 'Go, please. Take care.'
Voirrey lunged at him. Locking her arms tightly around his neck, she pressed her wet face to his. Kissing his cheek suddenly, she broke her grip and pulled away.
'Good luck. God go with you,' she sobbed. Turning, she stumbled across the road, blinded by stinging tears.
When she turned to look again, she saw his head and shoulders just disappearing below the harbour wall. Moving deep into the shadow of a doorway, she waited to keep watch.
It was a calm night now, she noticed, with only a slight swell running. In the light of the moon, the water of the harbour

was like a spread of silver, shimmering with the movement of myriad insects.

Voirrey held her breath, fascinated, as the mast of the little boat drifted soundlessly away from the wall of the quay. Then the sail was hoist and the craft moved toward the harbour mouth.

'He's goin' to make it,' she whispered to the night. A swell of unutterable joy clutched at her throat.

Suddenly a man staggered from the tavern, glanced toward the sea, then straightened, staring bemusedly. With a cry, he turned and bolted back inside. 'Some bugger 's stole my boat!' Voirrey heard him shout.

Cringing into the blackness of the doorway, she watched a dozen or so men rush from the inn to their boats. There was a general melee as they scrambled down ladders. Suddenly a shot rang out from the harbour mouth. Voirrey gasped in horror as she saw an armed guard poised, ready to fire again.

The little boat faltered, then wheeled about.

In a very short amount of time, the boat was brought back. Its occupant was bound and dragged roughly up the ladder and marched into the tavern.

'Go get the constable,' a voice said. 'He'll know what to do with this thieving bastard.'

Even from that distance, Voirrey could see the dismal dejection in the hang of Kurt's head and the slump of his shoulders.

Devastated, Voirrey staggered, weeping, from the doorway and hurried, half stumbling half running up the hill and away from Peel.

The wind, quite suddenly, was sharper and cooler, heralding a storm. The first icy rain came quickly. It swept into her face, making her gasp and twist her face away from it.

CHAPTER 18

Beginning to run, she was unable to shake off a fear she may have been seen and followed. Desperately she tried to ignore the continual urge to look behind, to put from her mind her utter defencelessness if she were caught. Gradually her steps slowed again because the rising wind had tired her, taken her breath away. Because, too, each step and each minute took her farther away from Kurt.

Voirrey had tried her hardest. Had done her best for him. But it had not been enough. Now he was beyond her help.

A curtain of rain dropped, cutting out all other sounds, then a long, brilliant flash of lightning revealed, for a moment, a torrent of grey-brown water running in the gutter.

The storm did not last long. It moved on as abruptly as it had come, leaving Voirrey frightened and completely sodden.

The wind dropped suddenly and in the lull, she picked up the sound of horse's hooves and wheels rumbling on the road behind. For an instant, she stood still, terrified. They were close, frighteningly so, but the storm had prevented her hearing sooner. After a moment's fearful wonder, she began looking around desperately for cover. At that point, the road was treeless and bare. A ditch running with turgid grey water bounded her side of the road, a thick high hedge, the other. The dark of the night itself was her only offer of shelter.

Glancing fearfully over her shoulder, she saw the cart's swinging light coming rapidly closer. Turning toward the ditch in a panic she flung herself full length on its bank, praying the bitter coldness of the rain would have numbed the driver's watchfulness.

With her face turned away from the road, her cheek pressed hard into the grass, she felt the ground throb beneath her in response to the beat of the horse's hooves.

Waves of agonised terror swept over her while the horse drew level. She knew her prostrate body was exposed to the swinging light, albeit dim, and she waited for a cry from the driver. Thankfully it did not come!

Voirrey felt the tremor through the ground as the cart drew level. Then it was past and blessed darkness fell over her again. For a while she lay still, relief breaking over her as she heard the cart pull further away. A tremulous sigh escaped her as the distance increased until at last, she dared raise her head slightly to watch the diminishing light disappear entirely round the next bend.

Slowly she picked herself up, stumbling in the ruts, shivering with a mixture of fear and cold. Her clothing, clinging to her like a cold, wet plaster, made walking difficult.

In her heart, Voirrey knew Kurt was in that cart, being returned to Knockaloe.

In vain! It had all been in vain! Hurrying home, her insides twisted bitterly. It had been so close! If they had got there five minutes earlier. If the boat's owner had stayed in the tavern five minutes longer. But they had not, and he had not, so Kurt was once again a prisoner, unable to go to his daughter.

Before the corner, she climbed through the hedge, wading across the sodden field, and out into the St John's Road.

The trees at the Vicarage stood over her, gaunt and menacing, their blackened, leafless trunks and branches leaning toward each other like bars in a cage. She looked up fearfully as she moved forward between the trees. The shadows closed about her like a trap. Now and again she put up a hand to wipe away the moisture that dripped from the trees and ran down onto her forehead.

Suddenly a twig snapped, followed by the sound of something falling in the trees. She started violently.

What was that? A buggane? With a terrified squeal, she picked up her skirts and bolted like a young filly from a snake.

· CHAPTER 18 ·

Only when she reached the sanctuary of the kitchen did she pause for caution.

A scent of woodsmoke greeted her. Embers still glowed beneath the hob and she drew close to the fire, revelling in the warm flush that embraced her. Finally, she forced herself to move away, knowing it was getting on toward morning and that her folk would not be sleeping quite so soundly now.

Cautiously, stepping flat-footed, she climbed one slow step at a time. With great care, she avoided the sixth from the top and made it to her room undiscovered.

Thankfully she peeled the cold, wet clothes from her body, but could not think what to do with them. How could she explain their condition?

That was a problem for the morning. Right now she was too exhausted and too cold to think. Rolling them in a bundle she pushed them under the bed, then taking the tiny bone rose from the back of her drawer she held it tightly in her palm as she climbed into bed. She was asleep almost before her head touched the pillow.

After dinner the next day, when the grown-ups were in the parlour, Voirrey filled the tub in the kitchen and put her clothes in to soak. Trotting into the parlour she announced, 'I'm just going to wash some clothes. Have you any you want me to do Granny?'

Eleanor looked up, startled, from her sewing and eyed her suspiciously. 'Washin'? No! Just leave it, I'll do it tomorrow.'

'I've already put it to soak in the tub.'

'Oh! Well! You'd better wash it then.' Eleanor frowned at the doorway when she'd gone. 'That girl gets stranger every day! Washin' indeed! An' on a Sunday! She's up to some mischief — you just mark my words.'

CHAPTER 19

Lily returned to school the following day, which Voirrey was glad about, for the road to Peel had too many awful memories for her to face alone.

'They caught that prisoner!' Lily said excitedly, as soon as she met Voirrey at the gate.

Voirrey stared dully and frowned. 'What prisoner?'

'The one who escaped ages ago!'

'Oh! him? Where was he?' Not wishing to discuss it, Voirrey tried to sound disinterested.

'They found him on a boat in Peel Harbour. He nearly got away. Daddy says someone must have hidden him because he had different clothes on. Won't say where he got them though. Says he pinched them.'

'He probably did.' Voirrey sighed then drew a deep breath as she struggled to look composed.

School itself was a blessing. It helped to fill the raw, aching, void that kept her stomach clenched.

Passing the camp on her way home, she found herself eagerly studying the prisoners. But Kurt wasn't there. Of course, he wasn't there. They would probably lock him up for a while — a long while — she realised. They would want to punish him.

CHAPTER 19

But wasn't it punishment enough to keep him away from his very sick daughter?

Voirrey fancied Caesar watched her closely as she passed but he said nothing.

When she arrived home Margaret nodded towards the envelope on the table. 'A letter came from your Daddy today.'

Voirrey's day brightened suddenly. 'Is he well?'

'He's recovered from his illness.' Margaret's face shadowed. 'But now he's been sent back into the war.' She held out the letter.

Taking it, Voirrey turned it over uncertainly, not sure if she dared to read it.

'It isn't as bad as the last one,' Margaret said gently.

Drawing a deep, tremulous breath, Voirrey took it from the envelope, smoothed it out and carried it to the window.

My dearest family,

It pleases me to tell you I am now fully recovered from my illness and have returned to the battlefront. Stanley is well again and with me. I try my best to keep an eye on him, but there is only so much I can do.

The weather has been unbearably hot and the stench and flies as bad as ever, but the fighting has not been so fierce and we have gained some ground. We are near Lozista, high in the hills bordering the Struma Valley.

The mosquitoes here, thank God, are much less troublesome than when we were in the Marshlands.

We had some excitement here last week. We were camped on the hillside when three enemy planes flew in low over the crest and started strafing us with gunfire. We all dived for cover, into the trenches, or under anything solid we could find, and were sure that our end had come.

Without warning, some of our fighters dived from the clouds and in the following dogfight two of the enemy planes were shot down in flames.

We were all cheering from the trenches when the remaining rogue plane swooped right down, machine-gunning the trenches and lorries. Men were dying and injured and screaming all around.

Then three of our fighters set on him. He had one above and one on each side, chasing him. The whole mob roared over a hedge quite close to us, then we saw the German's tail shot off. He cartwheeled into the ground and disintegrated in flames.

Then our planes soared up, waggled their wings and made off.

Young Stanley was very excited and says he wants to be a pilot now. It is strange how war and suffering changes a person's feelings and outlook. The injuries I have seen and the awful conditions I have endured have served to harden my heart. They have taught me to clamp down on my emotions.

A shattered, dead body I no longer see as a ghastly tragedy. It is merely a useless shell from which the soul, mercifully, has departed.

I am writing this just before dawn, which may seem strange, but time really gets to have little meaning here. The fighting and shelling goes on twenty-four hours a day. We can only snatch a little sleep now and again when things go quiet for a while.

It is quiet now, but less than an hour ago, without warning, our gun position was hit. The first two shells scored direct hits on our sandbag shelters, both of which were full of men at the time and were completely blown to pieces. I was lucky enough to escape uninjured, as was Stanley, but eleven men were killed and many others injured.

The dead and injured have all been cleared away now, thank God.

CHAPTER 19

I can think of little else to write now. I must try to sleep while I can.

My love to you all, John.

Voirrey stared at the letter for a long time, frowning in dismay. 'He sounds so cold. So uncaring and cold. Writing about eleven men dying as if it doesn't matter. He doesn't sound like my Daddy at all. He seems like a different person.'

Margaret nodded sadly. 'It does sound like a letter from a stranger.'

'Well, at least we know Mrs. Clucas was wrong.' Voirrey brightened. 'Daddy says Stanley is still alive and well again.'

'We know no such thing, I'm afraid!' Henry shook his head sadly. 'Look at the date on the letter, lass. We only know he was alive then!'

Voirrey picked up the paper again. It was dated 27th of July. Almost two months before Mabel had seen the hearse! And with a shock that shook her to the soles of her feet, she realised the letter was no proof even that her father was still alive! A tear stung her eye and she choked back a sob.

'And Daddy ---?'

'Now don't be thinking the worst, girl,' Henry said quietly. 'If anything had happened to your Daddy, we would ha' got a telegraph.'

'But the hearse ---.'

'Is just a bit of superstition. You know that as well as I do.'

Voirrey knew no such thing, but realized there was no point in arguing with her Daa.'

A deep, black trough of despondency opened before Voirrey and, in the days following Kurt's recapture, she slid ever more deeply into it. Try as she would she could not pull herself out of it. It was like a thick, sticky quagmire, dragging her down into endless misery.

Lily told her stories which normally would have set her giggling, but now, if they brought any reaction at all, it was merely a polite smile.

Often she caught her mother watching her worriedly. Once she asked, 'Are you ill?'

Voirrey shook her head. 'It's just this war. It goes on forever.'

'The lass misses her Daddy an' Edward,' Eleanor said knowingly.

And Kurt! Voirrey thought, smiling weakly. It seemed when she grew to love a man he must be taken away from her. Would it always be like that?

While they waited in Douglas station for the train home, Lily chattered animatedly about the new boy in their class. He had only started on Monday, but already, just two days later, Lily was head over heels in love.

'He's so handsome, don't you think?'

Voirrey tried to listen, but it all seemed so petty compared with what she knew Kurt was going through! And Daddy! And Uncle Edward! How could Lily find any boy so exciting? How could she find *anything* exciting?

'Voirrey! Are you listening?'

She shook herself, looking blankly at Lily — like a sleepwalker just awakened. 'Sorry. I was thinking of something else.'

'I could tell that. What were you thinking about? You seem to have been in a daze this past week and a half. And you seem to find no fun in life any more.' Suddenly she looked past Voirrey, her eyes widening. Her fingers fluttered to her mouth.

At the same moment, a hand descended on Voirrey's shoulder, gripping it firmly.

· CHAPTER 19 ·

Startled, she spun around and her jaw dropped.

'Uncle Edward!' she mouthed, but the words didn't come. Her heart did a strange dance just before her arms entwined him. Closing her eyes to shut in the threatening tears, she tipped her head back.

So tall she has she grown, Edward thought. He only had to bend a little to lay his cheek against hers.

Slowly, as he straightened, lifting her with him, she could feel the tears on their faces but knew not whose they were.

Suddenly, with a loud whoop, he spun her round and round until dizziness caught him and, staggering, he had to return her to the ground. Then he stood rocking her until his balance was recovered.

Voirrey's heart soared with joy and she could not let him go. Would not let him go — ever again. He was home! God was starting to answer her prayers. So maybe there was God in Heaven after all! First Uncle Edward. Soon it would be Daddy. Then Kurt would be free to return to his Catherine.

At last, she found her voice. 'Is the war over? Are you home to stay this time? Please say you are! Oh, please tell me you won't be goin' away again.'

Edward, looking into the crystal blue eyes, saw the pleading there. He read the hope, and behind it the awful loneliness, and his face clouded.

'I wish with all my heart I could honestly say what you want to hear. But I'm sorry. No, the war isn't over yet. And, yes, I do have to go back again. My ship's docked in Douglas until Sunday, so I have three days leave.'

Three days? Only three days! Voirrey felt the misery knot up her stomach. Again she lost her footing on the edge of the slippery trough and felt herself sinking into despair. Hot tears burned a course down her cheeks.

'Come on, love. Don't take on so. We have three days together. Let's enjoy 'em an' make 'em happy days to remember.'

'Laugh, drink an' be merry,' Voirrey mumbled, carefully not thinking of the next line.

'Yes, exactly,' Edward agreed.

Voirrey sat, pressed close against him on the train, making her body almost a part of his, savouring every moment of his presence. Gradually she relaxed, hurt faded and waves of ecstasy swept over her. Three days! Well, that wasn't so bad, was it? It was three days more than she had expected.

Edward walked between the girls on the long walk from Peel. Holding hands, they swung their arms joyfully, singing as they marched along. A line at a time, they taught Lily the Manx Anthem, until she was word perfect.

Voirrey had to stifle a little pang of jealousy, for really she wanted Edward to herself!

Lily reluctantly left them at the camp gate.

Clinging to Edward, Voirrey could sense the ripple of wonder run amongst the people as they walked together through the village. One of their sons was home! Did this mean the end of this dreadful killing was in sight?

Mabel Clucas was in her doorway, garbed pathetically in black mourning dress. 'Have you bin out where my Stanley was fightin'?' Her dead, sunken eyes lit up in a brief moment of hope.

Edward shook his head. 'Sorry. No. We bin patrollin' the Irish Sea lookin' for enemy submarines.'

Mabel nodded mutely, her lips trembling. Eyes returning to the grave, she backed inside, closing the door softly to shut the cruel world out again.

'Has someone died?' Edward was puzzled.

· CHAPTER 19 ·

'She saw the hearse. About two weeks ago, it was. She's sure it was Stanley come to tell her he was dead.'

'Hearse? What hearse? I don't understand.'

'There's a hearse. Full o' ghosses. It comes whenever a Manxman dies!'

'An' Mrs Clucas saw it?'

'Aye.'

Edward shook his head sadly and gnawed on his lip.

Caesar was on his corner as usual. He pumped Edward's hand enthusiastically, thumping him heartily between the shoulder blades.

'Home is the sailor!' he roared. 'Good to see you, lad! Home to stay are you?'

Edward laughed. 'Not this time, Caesar. But it won't be long now.

'They'll give up soon I expect.'

'Aye.'

The excitement in the cottage bordered on the hysterical when they arrived. There was a babble of voices, growing constantly louder as everyone spoke at once, then each raised his voice to ensure his would be the one to be heard.

Then it would go suddenly quiet and they all would laugh a little selfconsciously.

Voirrey clung to Edward as the escaped flithers had clung to the smooth, slate floor.

He walked to Peel with her and Lily in the morning and when the train came it almost needed the same knife and hammer to separate her from his arm.

If only she wasn't so healthy, she thought, she could feign sickness to stay home with him. She thought about trying but knew she wouldn't get away with it.

'Go on, love.' Edward disentangled her fingers from his arm, pushing her gently towards the train. 'I'll still be here when you get back.'

Thursday and Friday trailed frustratingly past, with school and homework taking up far too much of the time she so desperately longed to spend with Edward. But Saturday would be her day, she determined. Edward promised to spend it with her alone, though he warned her he must leave right after tea-time, for his ship was to sail the following morning.

'We'll go out in the mornin' early. Maybe on your bike, so we can go further. We can take some sandwiches an' have the full day together.'

'Jus' the two of us?'

'Aye. Jus' the two of us.'

Awakening on the following morning, Voirrey's eyes flew straight to the skylight window. Blue sky! Brilliant sunshine! Not a single cloud drifted across the small square of light.

Margaret looked up, smiling, as Voirrey entered the kitchen. 'I've made you some cheese an' some honey sandwiches for your picnic.' She nodded toward the brown paper package on the table.

'Thank you, Mammy. Is Uncle Edward awake?'

'Yes. He's bin up a long time. Had his breakfast an' he's outside now checkin' all's well wi' the bike. It hasn't bin rode for a while.'

Voirrey rushed through her porridge. 'I'll take the cows to the lhergy,' she offered, unbidden.

A smile hovered on Eleanor's lips. 'Surprisin' how eager you are when there's somethin' excitin' you want to do after,' she said teasingly. It warmed her heart to see how Edward had brought the child back to life.

Edward came with Voirrey to the lhergy, so she felt no great need to hurry. They were together and alone to talk. Dog did the herding, while they strolled slowly behind.

CHAPTER 19

'Well, where shall we go?' Edward asked when they were ready to leave for their picnic. He held the bike, Voirrey the sandwiches.

'Somewhere where there's water. A lake! A picnic's always more fun if there's water.'

'You can't swim today. 'Tis too cold.'

Voirrey pulled a face and hunched her shoulders, giving an exaggerated mock shiver. 'Don't want to swim in it. Jus' sit by it. Let's decide an' go quickly, though, lest Lily comes and' wants to go wi' us.'

'All right! I've decided! We'll go to the Eairy Dam, beyond Foxdale.'

Henry frowned. "Tis a long way!'

'Oh, not too far, Daa. Anyway, we have all day.'

Edward threw his leg over the bike. 'C'mon lass.' He patted the crossbar.

Voirrey grimaced, remembering the bruises she had suffered when she had ridden the crossbar with Daa. *The day she found the dead man on the beach,* she remembered with a shudder.

'Give those here.' Edward took the package of sandwiches, cramming it inside his coat. 'Now hold your frock out the way so it doesn't catch in the wheels or chain.'

The ride was far from gentle, with Voirrey bouncing painfully on the bar, while Edward pedalled rather too quickly, singing and laughing, enjoying every moment of the day.

The sun glistened on their golden hair. Birds stilled their song, watchfully amazed at the strange behaviour of the noisy humans.

Nearing St John's, they met Joseph Callow, his cart piled high with herring.

'I think Mammy wants some herrin',' Edward called, waving gaily and startling Ned, who laid his ears back and jigged nervously.

'You home to stay?' Joseph called to their backs.

'Only until tonight!'

Voirrey's heart lurched. She didn't want to think of that. Not yet! Not now! This was a day to forget the war and be happy.

The last steep track down the hillside to the Eairy Dam was quite frightening. Voirrey wanted to get down and walk, but Edward wouldn't stop.

'You're comin' all the way on the bike!' He roared with laughter at her squeals.

'It hurts my bottom!' she yelled, tightening her grip as the bike hit yet another bump and slid sideways from the latest rock.

Relieved, yet glowing with excitement, exhilaration and the cool of the wind, she dismounted near the water.

'I'm covered in bruises !' she remonstrated.

Edward laughed. 'You'll have twice as many by tea-time!' He was breathless from his exertions.

'Isn't it beautiful here?' Voirrey spun slowly, absorbing the full spectrum of her surroundings. 'Look how still the water is. How perfect the reflections of the hills an' trees.'

Edward gazed about him, enraptured. 'Aye, 'tis peaceful.'

Voirrey strolled toward the water's edge. Edward followed, laying his arm across her shoulders. She glanced up at him briefly, smiled then tilted her head against him. Together, blended as one, they stared out across the water, watching the slow-moving reflections; the birds flitting from tree to tree, singing as though their lives depended on it.

'Let's eat!' Edward broke the spell a long time later. I'm starvin' after that long ride.'

It was a happy meal. Full of laughter and chatter and teasing. The best Voirrey could remember. Here, with Edward, in such peace, it was hard to remember there was a war raging

· CHAPTER 19 ·

in the rest of the world. Easy to believe it had all been just a bad dream. The world could not be at war when there was this beauty all around.

Sitting on a rock by the water's edge, well into the afternoon, she gazed down through the green depths of the lake. Down to the lances of reeds laid flat by the current. Images of fluffy white clouds scudded across her vision. Occasionally she tossed a little pebble, watching curiously as its ripples broke her images.

'I'd give a penny for your thoughts.' Edward lowered himself to the rock beside her.

'I was jus' thinkin' o' the war an' how unreal it seems.'

Edward gazed mistily across the lake. 'Oh, 'tis real a'right.' He said quietly. 'I've seen too many die, not to know how real it is.'

Voirrey shuddered involuntarily. A dark cloud passed between the sun and her mind.

'I don't want you to die, Uncle Edward.' Her voice was distorted, cracking with the pain and fear in her heart.

He looked at her sharply, tightening his embrace. 'I'm not goin' to die,' he said, trying to sound cheerful. 'They've tried an' failed to kill me for over three years. They won't get me in what little's left o' the war now.'

Voirrey looked up hopefully. 'Is it really almost over?'

'Aye. Jus' a few more months should do it.'

'You said before you went the first time, it would only take a few months.'

'Aye.' Edward sighed. 'We were wrong. But we didn't know much about it — about the enemy — then. They're weary o' it all now. We've got them on the run an' they're ready to give up. To surrender. They won't take another Christmas o' it.'

'Christmas?' Voirrey pounced on it. 'Will it really be over by Christmas?'

'Nothin' surer! Maybe sooner. Certainly no later.' Edward's voice was full of confident conviction.

Christmas! Voirrey's heart soared. She could feel it trying to burst from her chest with joy. Christmas! No later!

'You promise, Uncle Edward? No later than Christmas.'

'I promise.'

'An you 'll come home straight after? As soon as the 'war ends? You'll be home for Christmas?'

'I can't promise that. Not this year. They can't jus' let us all go at once. It has to be done a bit at a time.'

'But the fightin' will all be over? Definitely?'

'Aye. An' when I'm home to stay I thought I might buy one o' these motor-bike things. They're truly wondrous machines.'

'A motor-bike? You? Like the ones we saw racin' at Ballacraine jus' before the war started?' Voirrey's eyes widened.

A family of mallards drifted curiously across the lake. They stayed by the shore for a moment, then waddled up to see if their visitors had dropped any crumbs.

'Aye.' Edward agreed. 'I even thought I might try my hand at racin''

'Isn't it very dangerous?'

'Not like the las' three years ha' bin. They've bin the real danger.'

Voirrey found a few crumbs and threw them to the ducks. They gobbled them and came closer, hoping for more. Some climbed up out of the water and waddled hopefully toward them.

'Mostly I want it so I — we — can travel further. We could go to Ramsey and home in a day. Or Castletown. Port Erin or even right up to the Point of Ayre if we wanted.'

'An' you'll take me wi' you?'

'Aye. I wouldn't want to go all that way alone.'

· CHAPTER 19 ·

The ducks gave up hope and swam away. No more crumbs today.

Voirrey's heart was singing, soaring to the sky, like the lark above the hill. Christmas! No later!

The sun was slowly sinking. Golden coins of light dropped from between the high branches of the trees, dazzling, dappling, shimmering on the surface of the water. It was like some beautiful magic. Perfection!

"Tis time we left, Voirrey', Edward said, after a while. 'If I'm to have my tea an' catch the train.'

Even this could not destroy Voirrey's mood. Only a few more weeks, then the world would be at peace and her life returned to normal.

Edward left, alone by choice, to catch the train. He wanted no sad farewells at the railway station, so kissed his family goodbye on the doorstep.

Voirrey clung for an extra-long hug, then, kissing his cheek, she smiled up at him and asked, 'You promise? Christmas?'

His return smile was secretive as he nodded, whispering, 'Christmas!'

Voirrey watched from the gate, a quiet smile curling her lips until he turned the corner by the pub and was lost to sight.

Emily Beckinsale had offered to teach Voirrey tatting, so she spent the following day, with Lily to start learning. The delicate lace this new skill produced was quite beautiful. How pretty it would look sewn to the hem of her petticoats.

Happily, she prattled about her talk with Edward.

'He's quite right,' agreed Percy, inhaling a lungful of pipe smoke. 'The Germans won't want to be at it another Christmas. No more than our lads. It's my opinion we'll all be back in our own homes before we know it.'

CHAPTER 20

The girls stepped off the train at Peel two days later. The 9th October – a Tuesday — a day to be etched forever in Voirrey's mind.

There was an air, almost, of panic in the city.

People were rushing aimlessly. Heads were shaking as they huddled in sombre looking groups who hurried down the street with fear in their eyes.

Voirrey sensed the storm clouds gathering. Something dire must be happening in the city.

'What's going on?' she asked a porter.

'There's a boat been sunk off the west coast of the island somewhere. The lifeboat went out about one o'clock an' all the fishin' boats was asked to go out to the disaster.'

'What was the ship called?' she asked fearfully.

The man shrugged. 'Dunno. An English one it was, I think.'

'What happened to it?'

His shoulders twitched up again as he pulled the corners of his lips down.

'Is it bad? Was anyone killed?'

Again the shrug.

Voirrey gave an impatient sigh and, turning, ran toward the harbour.

· CHAPTER 20 ·

'Where are you going? Wait for me!' Lily wailed, then ran behind her.

A policeman stood, along towards the bridge a bit, trying to control an agitated crowd.

'Please,' Voirrey appealed to him, 'Can you tell me the name o' the ship that's been sunk?'

'Aye, Miss. A cruiser called 'Champagne'.'

Her heart turned to lead and plummeted to the soles of her boots, and her vision started to whirl. Taking a deep breath, she recovered her senses, forcing herself to ask, 'Is it bad?'

'I heard so. She was torpedoed by a German submarine.'

'Are there many dead?' Voirrey felt her fingernails digging into his hand, but to his credit, he did not jerk it away.

Gently easing her grip, he looked at her sympathetically. 'Got someone on her, have you? I'm sorry Miss, I don't know much about it. The lifeboat should be back soon. They'll be able to tell you more.'

Voirrey nodded mutely and mumbled her thanks. Turning away, her stomach knotted with fear, she looked fearfully toward the breakwater at the harbour mouth.

'We'd better go home and tell your family.' Lily put her arm around her, trying to guide her away, but Voirrey stood her ground, shaking her head vehemently.

'No. I'm stayin' here until I know something. You go home.'

Lily shook her head. 'I'm not leaving you here alone. I'm sure Edward will be all right.'

'I'm goin' to wait by the lifeboat station.'

'I'll come with you then.'

The two girls hurried, hand in hand to the other side of the harbour, by the castle. 'He'll be all right!' Voirrey spoke through clenched teeth. 'He will be! He promised he wouldn't die.'

Lily moved closer to her friend, concern clouding her dark eyes.

Voirrey stared toward the harbour mouth, embracing herself, her teeth chattering in the cold.

An ambulance stood, ominously, before the lifeboat shelter. Beside it lingered a man Voirrey recognised to be a doctor.

A sudden hum of voices started across the harbour, fingers pointed, then the bows of the lifeboat appeared.

The doctor moved toward the edge of the quay, the crowd pressing behind him.

Efficiently the boat sidled up to the dock wall and was moored. The doctor went swiftly down the rope ladder.

Looking down, Voirrey saw rows of gaunt faces. Men, grey and sunkeneyed with the horror they had endured. One by one, first the injured and walking wounded were carried up and taken off in the ambulance, then the uninjured climbed the ladder.

Voirrey anxiously scanned every face, but Edward's was not amongst them. Finally, she plucked at the sleeve of the last man.

'Are you all the survivors? Are there no more?' she asked tremulously.

'No, lass. A lot got away in the ship's lifeboats. Three boats got away that I saw. I think they might ha' gone further south. Maybe to Port Erin.'

'Do you know Edward Quilliam?'

'Aye.'

'Please, can you tell me if he's safe?'

The man shook his head. 'I don't know, lass. I honestly don't. In all the fright after the explosion 'twas hard to know who was who or where. He's likely in a boat gone south. A lot got away safe long before us.'

'Thank you.' Voirrey looked across the harbour through frightened, tear-filled eyes.

· CHAPTER 20 ·

The two girls stayed in Peel for a long time, until long after it was dark. Impotently they followed each fishing boat to its berth as it came in. Vainly they scanned the decks.

Finally, emptily, Voirrey submitted to Lily's urgings that they go home. She stumbled in a daze, with Lily holding her arm, up the hill from Peel.

'Would you girls like a ride home?'

Unnoticed, Joseph had drawn up alongside and he looked down on them now with sad, gentle, moist eyes.

'Thank you, Mr Callow.'

He handed them into the cart, where they all huddled together, miserably, on the seat.

'No sign o' Edward then?' Joseph asked quietly.

Voirrey shook her head mutely, tears aching at the backs of her eyes.

'Don't shed tears yet, lass,' Joseph said gently. 'Mos' of them was took to Port Erin an' Port St Mary. He might be already home by the time you get there.'

But he wasn't. The family — in fact, the whole village — had heard of the disaster. Guessing where Lily must be, Emily was waiting at the cottage when Joseph brought the girls home.

'There's no news then?' Joseph nervously twisted his cap in his hand.

Henry shook his head. 'If only I could get south. We might get news o' him there.'

'I'll take you. In the cart. I've allus bin fond o' young Edward. I want to know he's safe too,' Joseph offered eagerly.

'I'll get my coat!' Henry didn't hesitate.

'I'm comin' too!'

'No Voirrey!' Margaret protested. "Tis no mission for a girl.'

'Please, Mammy. I must be there! I must!' Voirrey's voice pitched higher as panic took her and tears came closer.

'Let her go!' Eleanor was calm and authoritative. Perhaps too calm. 'Better she's occupied. 'Twill do her no good to be sittin' here frettin'.'

Margaret bit her lip, nodding. 'Wrap up well then, love. Wear a warm hat an' gloves. There's no sayin' how long you'll be out.'

'Thank you.' Voirrey ran to hug her grandmother and could feel her suffering. Edward was her son. Her baby! Part of her body. Part of her very soul. Pressing her cheek to Eleanor's she vowed, 'We'll find him for you, Granny.'

Joseph slapped the reins against Ned's flanks, putting him straight away into a brisk trot.

Mile after endless mile passed beneath the wheels, the poor glow of the oil lamp swinging erratically. The cart swayed and bobbed, sliding from ridges into ruts, till Voirrey felt sure it would topple. Joseph paid it no heed and kept egging Ned to keep up his pace.

At the roadside, the dark bulk of the woodlands crouched, like animals waiting to pounce. The trees danced grotesque dances in the breeze, an occasional gust growling in their tops.

The last rise was topped, Port Erin in view, and Ned, sensing the urgency, broke into a canter.

Joseph leaned back on the reins. 'Slow down a bit boy or you'll have us all out,' he cajoled.

All was quiet in Port Erin. The excitement over, the people had settled into their routines. Most were already abed.

Henry knocked the policeman up, apologising profusely. 'My boy was on the Champagne. We've travelled from Patrick to seek him. Can you help?'

'I hope so. I have a list of the survivors who landed here.'

'You read it, girlie.' Henry pushed the paper toward her.

Over and over, one name at a time, she hopefully scanned

CHAPTER 20

the list, feeling the bile rise in her throat when she could not find it.

The policeman looked too, sadly shaking his head. 'Sorry.'

'These are all?' Henry asked despairingly.

'Aye. But only forty-seven landed here. Another one hundred and fifty or so put into Port St Mary, but I don't have their names.'

'I'll take you on there,' the herring man offered immediately.

'Many thanks, Joseph'

On the journey across the island, which seemed to last forever, Voirrey sat between the two men, her hands tormenting each other, lips gnawed almost raw.

'He's got to be there. One hundred and fifty more! He promised me he wouldn't die. He promised he would buy a motor-bike an' take me all over the Island!' Voirrey was trying to talk herself into hope.

As if sensing the urgency, Ned gamely cantered all the way on the rough track and Joseph let him run.

'Here's my list. That's all who landed here.' The policeman in Port St Mary handed them a few sheets of paper.

Voirrey scoured the list repeatedly. 'It must be here! I must just be missin' it,' she said the first few times. Then later, 'Are you sure you've got *all* of the names? Well, are you sure they're right?'

The policeman nodded grimly. 'Yes. We were careful not to miss any.'

'Well, I must have jus' missed it. Jus' let me look again. I'll find it this time.'

Henry gently prised the piece of paper from her fingers, handing it to the policeman.

'You're not goin' to find it, lass. You haven't missed it. It isn't there. We'd best go home.' His shoulders slumped and suddenly he looked twenty years older.

'Sit for a while an' I'll bring you a cup o' tea,' the policeman offered.

Henry nodded his thanks and took Voirrey's arm, guiding her to a chair.

A few minutes later the policeman came back with three cups of thick, black tea, well laced with sugar.

'Don't give up hope yet. There could well have been others landed around the coast. Maybe some picked up by fishin' vessels what haven't reported in yet.'

'Maybe we'd best get home,' Henry suggested quietly and Voirrey nodded mutely.

Black clouds obscured the moon and the darkness was absolute when they set off.

Ned was less eager on the return journey. Snorting he often turned to glare at Joseph on the long steep climb up through the hills.

To Voirrey it was just the worst part, so far, of a nightmare which had started over three years before. Huddled miserably between the two men, she stared, unseeing, at the ground behind Ned's hooves.

'Maybe he'll have found his way home by now.' Joseph tried to sound hopeful but merely sounded miserably unconvinced.

Henry just grunted and they covered the rest of the journey without conversation.

The sky began to lighten and, as they neared Patrick, Voirrey could see the vague, eerie shape of the hills through a morning haze, suffused with a rosy glow.

''Tis almost dawn,' Joseph said needlessly.

'Aye.' Henry grunted.

Voirrey chewed relentlessly on her lip, her stomach knotted, mouth too dry to speak.

On approaching the bend before the vicarage, Ned laid his

· CHAPTER 20 ·

ears back, snickering nervously. Then he stopped, pawing the ground with a forehoof and refused to go any further.

Joseph shouted and swore, but to no avail, so finally he had to dismount and lead him. Ned reluctantly allowed himself to be led, or dragged, dancing on tiptoe, rolling his eyes until the whites showed.

Raising her eyes, Voirrey gasped, clasping a hand to her mouth to stifle a scream. Clutching her grandfather's sleeve, her free hand pointed, trembling.

'Look, Daa!' she rasped.

Henry followed her horrified gaze, his face paling, eyes twitching. 'The hearse!' he whispered hoarsely.

The vision faded as they drew near, but it was waiting at the Vicarage and again at Barnell, gleaming in the moonlight, its brasses shining, black horses prancing restlessly.

'Edward's gone,' Henry muttered dully.

Margaret and Eleanor knew the awful news as soon as they arrived. Watching from the window, they saw the horror, defeat and emptiness in the three faces as they straggled miserably up the path, Voirrey half supported by Henry.

Eleanor drew the girl straight into her arms as she entered the dark hallway. Clinging together, the child now as tall as her grandmother, they let their grief flood out in a torrent of hot, gushing tears. The others stood around in shocked silence.

Voirrey sat on the cliff above Traie Cabbag Bay, alone except for Dog. He lay at her feet, pressed hard against her legs, as though to draw out some of the pain which was festering inside her. Her eyes, as had been their wont in the weeks since the Champagne disaster, constantly moved across the surface of the water.

A part of her refused, even yet, to accept the reality. She

spent many hours now, a solitary figure, scanning the ocean, her eyes never still; searching; always searching.

The family knew where she went, worried about her, but no longer tried to interfere.

'I don't like you going there alone,' Margaret had protested at first.

'I like to be alone,' she had replied flatly. 'Uncle Edward's in the sea there. I feel close to him. When I talk to him there he can hear me.'

Margaret shook her head. Unshed tears stung her eyes. 'It's too dangerous. Those cliffs are unsafe. Can't you go somewhere else to be alone?' her voice in high pitch.

Voirrey shrugged, her face expressionless.

Margaret had tossed her head in despair. The child's mind seemed to have moved away — somewhere out of reach.

'Best let her go,' Eleanor suggested quietly. 'She needs to work her grief out in her own way. She'll come back to us when she has.'

Voirrey absently caressed the collie's ear. It had been dark when she left the cottage, Dog faithfully tagging at her heels. The sky had gradually brightened and the light grew quite quickly now, reflected redly on the mirror of a calm sea.

The gulls had recently awakened, rising in their hundreds from the strong grey solidity of the cliffs. Now they glittered like snowflakes in the first early rays of the sun. Above the sea they wheeled, soaring and screaming overhead in a ceaseless search for food.

'He's really gone forever, hasn't he?'

Dog looked up at her and whimpered.

'Dead!' She spat the last word.

A tabby cat, a true Manx, stalked across the nearby heath. Hearing Dog's deep, throaty growl, it stopped on tip-toe, back arched, hackles raised, spitting.

CHAPTER 20

Dog half raised himself, stared at it for a moment, snorted, then decided it was not worth the effort and lay back down.

The cat warily continued its journey.

Grey, heavy clouds scudded across the leaden sky and the first few snowflakes fell.

Voirrey stood up, shivering. 'C'mon Dog, we'd better get home.'

Eleanor was up when they arrived, preparing the porridge for cooking.

She glanced up at Voirrey's entry. 'You all right, lass?'

Voirrey nodded noncommittally. She didn't feel as if she would ever really be all right again. Sagging into a chair, she said, 'Oh, Granny, I wish!'

Eleanor was immediately beside her, taking her hand. 'I know love, I wish too, but I'm afraid it doesn't do no good. If wishes were horses, you know, beggars would ride!'

'He shouldn't have gone an' died! He promised me he wouldn't! He promised! He was going to get a motor-bike an' take me all over the island!' Voirrey jumped to her feet banging her fist angrily on the table. 'He promised an' then he went an' died anyway!' she shouted.

Eleanor looked stricken. 'He didn't mean to die. He didn't want to. He would have fought to live. Likely God needed him in Heaven.'

'I hate God!' Voirrey screamed. 'I prayed an' prayed. I spend most of every Sunday in church. He should've listened to me. But He didn't! He killed Uncle Edward!' Scalding tears gushed down her cheeks to drip, unchecked, to her pinafore.

Henry rushed into the room to throw his arms around her. 'Hush, love, you'll be heard all over the village. God didn't kill Edward — the Germans did. It happens in war. Folk get hurt. Folk die. 'Twasn't Edward's fault — or God's. But they're together now an' Edward's not sufferin' no more. Try to see that, lass. He truly meant to keep his promise.'

Margaret appeared, flushed and anxious. Taking Voirrey's trembling body in her arms she rocked her as she had done when she was a small child. 'What's happened?'

Eleanor smiled quietly. 'She's come back to us — jus' like I said she would. She'll be all right now.'

Weeks passed, each much like the one before. Weeks in which Voirrey's life seemed to hold only travel, school, homework, Sunday school and church and the interminable task of taking the cows to the lhergy.

Life ground along, promising little of interest. Except for Saturday. Most of that day was spent with Lily playing board games, which absorbed her mind and anaesthetised the pain.

Christmas drew nearer and with it, the memory of Edward's promise that the war would be over by then. But still, it continued. Still, it was no nearer settlement.

Just another Christmas. Another of Edward's broken promises!

A week before Christmas another letter arrived from John.

'This one only took six weeks to come,' Voirrey said as she took it from the envelope.

Dear family,

Still, this awful war drags on.

We have had an eventful few weeks here. For a while, we were entrenched high in the hills, which was a great relief. We lost young Stanley up there, I'm afraid.

We had driven the Bulgars back and moved into their trenches, I was reloading my rifle, young Stanley beside me. He stood up to fire and I heard him let off a shot. He fell suddenly to the ground without ever making a sound and at first, I thought he had lost his footing. I reached down to help him up and found he had most of his face shot away.

I sat to see if there was anything I could do for him. There was nothing. He must have died the moment the bullet hit him. He could have felt nothing. Tell his mammy he didn't suffer — if it is any comfort to her.

I tried to look after him, but there is nothing you can do in this Hell. Stanley was a man when he died. Like a man, he died fighting. His mammy can feel proud of him.

It has made me more angry with the Bulgars. More keen to kill. I don't think I've killed enough of them yet!

We have recently moved back down to the plain and are finding the mosquitoes troublesome again. The only way we have been able to fully protect ourselves on patrol has been to cover our faces and necks with a foul-smelling mixture. We then wear a veil over our faces, fastened to our tunic below the neck. No part of our bodies must be left exposed, so we also have to wear mosquito gloves to half-way up our arms.

In the awful heat here these measures are unbearable but, unfortunately, necessary.

The Bulgars have been troublesome recently, causing us a great deal of patrol work.

However last week, the Cheshires penetrated the Bulgar outpost line at Butkova Dzuma. They circled behind the village, moving at dawn and driving the enemy out to where we had formed a flank line to prevent their escape.

It was a very successful and satisfying mission.

Our casualties are no longer being moved to Malta as the Germans are now sinking the hospital ships. New hospitals have had to be set up in several places to take all the sick and injured.

I must finish now.

John.

Voirrey shook her head sadly. Poor Stanley. How brave he had been. 'Should we tell Mrs Clucas?' she asked.

Henry sighed, 'I think we should tell her he died quickly and didn't suffer. Also that he died bravely. The letter from the Home Office only said he died in action an' she's been in agony imagining all sorts ever since. Best not to tell her his face was shot away. It would likely make her suffer more. You tell no one about that!' He glared ferociously at Voirrey.

Shaking her head soulfully she promised, 'I won't. We've all been hurt enough already.'

Christmas was a painful day. Voirrey, trying hard to feel excited and enjoy the day, felt only emptiness. Her thoughts kept straying back to her last happy Christmas. When was it? Two years ago? Yes, 1915. The Christmas her father had come home. Just before he had gone to Salonika. But even that Christmas had been spoiled a bit because she had known he was soon going off to fight.

No, the last *really* happy Christmas had been four years ago, when they had all been together. All alive and well. Before *it* had begun. She had never even heard the word *war* then.

All day she kept seeing a vision of Edward standing by the Eairy Dam. The wind blew his golden hair and he was smiling, saying, 'It'll all be over by Christmas!'

'Christmas!' Voirrey said suddenly during dinner.

Everyone stopped, startled, waiting for her to continue.

'What about it?' Henry asked eventually.

'Uncle Edward said the war would be over by now. It isn't ever goin' to be over, is it? It's just goin' to go on 'till there's no one left alive.'

Henry gripped her hand. 'It *will* finish, girlie. All wars come to an end some time.'

'What if we lose an' it's all been for nothin'?'

CHAPTER 20

'We won't lose, love.'

Voirrey snorted. 'Well, someone will lose, so how can you be sure it won't be us?'

The grown-ups around the table looked at each other in dismay, but no one knew how to answer.

CHAPTER 21

Months went by, fading greyly into the past. They were months of waiting — of pretence life. Waiting for an end. To what? It all seemed false to Voirrey. Life seemed false. The promises had all been empty. All lies!

An occasional letter came from John now, but even those didn't seem real any more. They were as though from a stranger.

One, which came in February, described their Christmas. It had been a happy time, John wrote, the happiest since the Christmas of 1915.

To everyone's' joy, their supplies had got through. The fighting had stopped for the day and they had been able to leave the trenches. About sixty of the men had formed themselves into a choir and, with the others joining in, had sung many of the favourite Manx National songs.

Then he went on to talk about the butchery, the carnage they had inflicted on the enemy.

So his letters continued, each one less personal than the one before.

To Voirrey's dismay, every one a was a journal of killing and his enjoyment of it.

In January they had taken part in another action at Butkova

· CHAPTER 21 ·

Dzuma and John related joyfully that sixty of the Bulgars had been killed.

Voirrey no longer liked to read his letters, nor, indeed, did she look forward to them coming. Missives from a stranger! They made her feel ill. The only pleasure she could feel in them was that they proved her father had still been alive at the time of writing.

Margaret now greeted them with despair, saying little, but her daughter sensed how much they made her suffer.

After a while, Voirrey found herself again scrutinising the prisoners, in a search for Kurt.

For a long time after Edward's death, she had blamed Kurt, as she had blamed everyone — even God and Edward himself. But, as acceptance had come, and the pain had dulled, she had placed the guilt squarely where it belonged — on the shoulders of the warmongers.

It was in April, on her way home from school, she finally saw the familiar figure near the wire. At first, in the early spring dusk, she was unsure. Then he turned and she saw his face properly, clean-shaven again now. Gaunt still, though looking better than when she had last seen him.

'Kurt.' She whispered, her heart quickening.

He saw her, smiled and moved closer to the wire.

'Voirrey. How are you? I have thought about you a lot and wondered how you were. Did you get home safely that dreadful night?'

'Yes, I got home. I was awful wet, though. I'm sorry you didn't get away. Where have you been all this time? I've looked for you.' She was aware of a simmering excitement in her voice.

'I have been kept in a cell ever since. I was only released today.'

'Oh. I'm sorry. How's Catherine? Have you been able to see her yet?'

Kurt's face shadowed, like a thundercloud crossing the sun. 'My Catherine died. Just before Christmas. I never managed to see her before!' His voice choked off in a sob.

Voirrey felt suddenly cold, as though the warmth of the sunlight had been shut out by a dark-boled palisade of trees. She shook her head in helpless frustration unable, for a moment, to speak.

'My uncle Edward died too.' She managed finally, her voice breaking. 'His ship was sunk by a German submarine. Just out there!' Her eyes looked, unseeing, toward the south-west.

'My poor little one,' Kurt said feelingly. 'How my countrymen have made you suffer. I would that I could change it all for you.'

Voirrey smiled. 'I feel happier now I've seen you.'

Walking home, she experienced a strange mixture of sadness and excitement.

Caesar leaned on the wall, watching while Voirrey helped Henry weed a flower bed.

'You should put it all to grass. Make a lot less work,' he advised.

Henry straightened, scratching his head and massaging his back. 'Aye. But I like to see a flower or two.'

'D'you hear about the bread subsidy?'

'No.'

'Well, I heard that at a meetin' at Tynwald two days ago Lord Raglan, the Governor, said the subsidy had to end.'

'How so?'

'Seems that when the United Kingdom Government granted the subsidy 'twas on condition the Island Government started takin' some income tax off us. The House o' Keys wouldn't let the bill pass to start the tax, so now the English Government says the subsidy has to stop.'

Henry whistled in a breath. 'That's bad. If we ha' t' pay any more we won't be able to buy much bread. We have little enough as 'tis.'

'The bakers say they will ha' t' charge at least a shillin' a loaf, else they'll lose money on it.'

'A shillin!' Henry shook his head in dismay. 'Up a whole thrupence! Not many'll afford that!'

'There'll be trouble over it!' Caesar concluded darkly.

Voirrey and Lily witnessed the trouble brewing and building as they travelled to and from school in Douglas. All conversations seemed to concern the price of bread.

Noisy, angry crowds roamed the streets of Douglas, finally holding a mass demonstration on the foreshore.

'It doesn't look good,' Caesar frowned. 'Lord Raglan has proclaimed a maximum charge o' tenpence ha'penny a loaf. The bakers say they'll lose money if they sell at that price. So, they're demandin' the subsidy be restored. An' they're closin' the bakehouses until it is.'

'There'll be no bread for a while then?' Henry shoved a wad of tobacco in his pipe and applied a match.

'What'll I have for sandwiches if there's no bread, then, Daa?' Voirrey did not much fancy missing her mid-day meal.

Henry glanced at her, laughing. 'Well, I guess your Mammy an' Granny'll think o' somethin'.'

'Anyway', continued Caesar, frowning at the interruptions to his story, 'There's to be a general strike on the fourth o' July. Everything's goin' to stop. Steamers an' all. An' the Tynwald Day Ceremony on the 5th has bin cancelled 'cos the Government fear a riot if there's a big crowd gathered.'

'No ceremony on Tynwald Day? That's a pity. I was goin' to take the girlie to the fair.'

Voirrey scowled. For weeks she had set her heart on going to the big fair that was always held on the green behind Tynwald Hill.

It all blew over of course. There were reports of a few outbreaks of rioting and violence, but in the end, Lord Raglan agreed to replace the subsidy, the Manx Government agreed to introduce a system of income tax, the first ever on the Island. And the price of a loaf of bread returned to ninepence!

School holidays began soon after, with the girls thrilled to be free of the daily drudgery of trailing to Douglas and back, whatever the weather, to sit in a classroom, often drenched right through to the skin.

'We'll have to find plenty to do,' Voirrey plotted. 'An' new places to go.'

'If we take picnics we can go for long rides.'

'Aye. I'd like to go to Eairy Dam, one day. I think I can remember the way. That's where Uncle Edward took me the day he went away.' Her blue eyes clouded.

Lily nodded sadly. 'I'd like to go there.'

Kurt spent a lot of time near the wire, Voirrey noticed, staring, dejectedly into the distance. Then he would spy her, his face would light up and he would wink. Whenever Caesar wasn't around she would stop and talk to him for a while.

'I used to have a garden,' he once said dreamily. 'A large garden with fruit trees and every kind of flower. There was a giant walnut tree with a large, spreading branch. I made Catherine a swing on this branch and used to spend hours with her on it. Near it was a corner with several different fuchsia bushes. They were Catherine's favourite.'

Voirrey looked around the camp at the plain wooden huts. The cindered compounds divided by high barbed-wire fences. Roads of railway sleepers. Brown and grey scenery, with brown and grey

CHAPTER 21

people, with the backdrop of green hills, beyond the wire being the only sign of colour and real life. Not a flower was in sight.

'I'll bring you a plant for your hut,' she promised. 'If you can find something to grow it in.'

'I will!' he vowed, his eyes lighting more than she had seen them do since that dreadful night in Peel.

The following day Voirrey tore a small branch from a wild Manx fuchsia at the roadside. With Lily acting as a lookout, she managed to pass it between the wires to Kurt's eager hands.

'If you plant it in a pot o' soil an' keep it well watered it should take root easily,' she instructed.

His eyes were moist and his lips trembled. 'I shall always treasure it,' he promised.

There was a loud thundering on the door. Before anyone could move to open it Caesar strode into the room, his bulk filling it.

'Have you heard the news?' he roared.

Henry stopped halfway out of his chair. 'What news is that Caesar?'

''Tis all over!'

'What is?' Henry asked as he tried to recover from his fright.

'The fightin'! 'Tis finished. The war is over!'

Henry slowly straightened and Margaret leapt to her feet.

'Are you sure, Caesar? There can be no mistake?'

'None! The enemy agreed to stop the fightin' and it ended at the eleventh hour this mornin'.'

'Over? Is it really? Will Daddy be home for Christmas?' Voirrey was on her feet, dancing. Her heart leaping out of control. All those years. All the waiting. The promises made then broken, re-made and re-broken. Uncle Edward dead! Stanley Clucas — dead! All the others. Hundreds! Thousands! The ghost hearse roaming at night with its ghastly messages!

Now, more suddenly than it had started, it was finished. Just like that! Without any warning. They had all seen sense — at last. The killing and the dying and the suffering were over. Now her father would be home. Soon he would be home. Soon their lives could get back to normal except — except that Uncle Edward would never come back!

Voirrey skipped from one grown-up to the other, hugging them and squealing excitedly, 'It's over! The war's really over! Can I go and tell Lily? Please, can I go and tell Lily?'

'Bless you, love. I'm sure she knows already!' Caesar laughed.

'I'd still like to go an' see her, just the same.'

'Go on then, but don't be too long, it's gettin' late.' Margaret's eyes were glowing, her heart dancing with joy.

Voirrey ran up the street, shouting to everyone she saw, 'The war 's over! It's over!'

Kurt was standing near the fence, smiling when he saw her coming.

'It's ended! The war is over!' she shouted, running straight to him without first checking for guards.

'I know. I heard. It's wonderful. We can all go home and start our lives again. Home!' His eyes, filled with tears, had a faraway look.

'I'll miss you.'

Kurt laughed. 'No you won't. You'll forget me once you have your father back.'

'Hey, you! Get away from there!'

Voirrey jumped away from the wire, waving to Kurt as she ran off. Waving to the guard who had shouted at her.

'Did you hear the war's over' she yelled as she passed the guard.

'Aye. It's great news,' the man called back.

Of course Lily, Emily and Percy knew — probably even before Voirrey.

CHAPTER 21

The girls hugged each other and danced around excitedly.

'Your father should be home soon,' Emily said kindly. 'Everyone will be sent home now. Us too,' she added with a smile.

Voirrey's spirits dropped momentarily, but that was a worry for another day. Nothing was going to mar this one.

'Listen to this!' Voirrey was reading, the following day, from a newspaper she had found on the train.

'It says: When the message came yesterday, by wireless, from the Eiffel Tower in Paris, that the Armistice had been signed, the Mayor of Douglas called a demonstration of thanksgiving in the Villa Marina. Oh, my goodness!'

'What's wrong?' Henry asked.

'Nothin'. It's jus' it says there was more than three thousand people there — in the Villa Marina — an' Lord Raglan. There was a famous author too — a Sir Hall Caine. He gave a long speech sayin', *'Some o' the best o' our young Manx manhood, the hope an' the pride an' the flower o' it, have fallen. It makes my heart bleed to think o' the Manx mothers an' fathers from whose life all brightness has gone'.'* Voirrey broke off, seeing the tears on her grandparents' faces.

They looked at her expectantly, waiting for more.

'Do you wish me to stop?' She asked in concern.

'No. Finish. Read it all. It's about our Edward too.' Henry leaned forward in his chair, listening eagerly.

'Right. Now, where was I? Oh, yes. *'If there are many such who are waterin' their pillows with their tears each night they have this one great consolation — that their loss is to the world's gain; that they have given their sons for the greatest battle for liberty and freedom that the world has yet fought. The world will never forget.'*

'Amen to that!' Eleanor said feelingly.

"Twas nice to hear,' Henry said quietly, gripping Eleanor's

hand. 'This is the fus' time I ha' felt Edward's death was not for nothin'. 'Tis a comfort to know the loss o' his life has benefitted the world.'

Voirrey handed the newspaper to her mother. 'There's lots more, but I thought that was the most important part.'

'I wish I'd bin at that meetin',' Margaret said, after reading the paper thoroughly. It would have bin very stirrin'.'

A letter that came from John a few days later told them his war had finished on the 30th of September, when the order had come at noon to cease firing. Hostilities had ended and the Manx Company were to take part in the occupation of Bulgaria.

Soon after, they started moving the internees out of Knockaloe.

A few times, the girls, walking to catch their train, would have to step onto the verge to make way for a large group of the men being marched briskly to Peel.

The prisoners, mostly happy and singing would wave and call out to the girls as they passed.

Voirrey always found herself studying the faces with mixed feelings. Part of her wanted Kurt to be amongst them, to be going home to his wife. But at the same time she was scared of him leaving; of losing yet another of her loved ones. It was with relief, however, she saw him each evening with his ready smile and wink.

Whenever she could, she talked to him, but even when she could not, she felt it a comfort to know he was there.

Each day she rushed home, praying that this would be the day her father would be there, waiting to hold her, swing her in his arms and tell there would never be another war. That he would never have to leave her again.

CHAPTER 21

At the weekends she spent much time at the gate, gazing longingly down the road.

'Come up and play with me. Or lets' go walking for a change,' Lily pleaded often.

Voirrey shook her head adamantly. 'If he comes at a weekend I must be here!' she insisted.

Christmas Day came, much like any other day. There were a few exciting minutes in the morning when she came down and found the little parcel on the table. From Daddy, Mammy, Granny and Daa, she read on the outside. With shaking fingers she carefully unwrapped it.

'It's wonderful,' She opened the little book of verse, a tear in her eye. 'Just what I wanted. You couldn't have given me a nicer present.'

Margaret smiled, satisfied, knowing her daughter was sincere. It had seemed so important, this year, to give Voirrey something really special. Then she had found the book, in such good condition, in a little secondhand shop in Peel and it had been all she could afford.

After breakfast, Voirrey sat on the floor, huddled close to the fire, reading and soaking in the beauty of the poems. *If only*, she thought, *If only Daddy had been here for me to read them to!* There was an awful, aching sadness; the disappointment of another Christmas spent without her father.

Later, after placing the treasured book in her drawer, she took out the bone rose, turning it lovingly, admiring the delicate petals. Poor Kurt, what a miserable Christmas it must be for him. Perhaps Catherine would be with Edward. He would look after her. She must tell Kurt next time she saw him! It would put his mind at rest a bit.

There was a nagging heaviness in her heart when she looked

at the sugar mouse. His gleaming white had greyed, just as life itself had dulled and darkened since that Christmas of 1915.

A flurry of snow blew against the attic window, catching and building around the edges to give the glass a white frame.

The camp floodlights were no less bright, though there were fewer prisoners to be watched. Those who did remain were unlikely to attempt an escape at this stage. Voirrey knew that in the internment history of the Island, not one of the prisoners who had escaped from camps had ever made it off the Island.

Caesar had related, with some amusement, the story of one escapee from the Cunningham's camp in Douglas. This poor fellow had swum out, with the idea of climbing aboard a steamer. Unfortunately, before he reached it, the ship had sailed and he had been forced to swim ashore. He was recaptured then, wet, shivering and half choked with seawater.

Listening to the sad story, Voirrey's heart went out to the poor man.

CHAPTER 22

Voirrey bounced in from school, throwing her school-bag on the floor. 'Guess what---?' she started. Suddenly she stopped short, her mouth open to speak. Taking a deep breath she mouthed, 'Daddy!'

He didn't move from his seat by the table; just sat there looking at her, his face empty and expressionless.

For quite a few moments she stood staring, unsure if it was really him. If it was, he had changed a lot. Older. Thinner. The warmth and sparkle were gone from his eyes. There was a hardness she had never seen before.

'Is it you, Daddy?' she asked timidly. Still, she was in doubt.

And still, he did not rise, but just nodded his head.

'Oh, Daddy!' Voirrey ran to him, choking for words. 'I've missed you so much. I'm glad you're home.' Tears of joy flooded down her cheeks.

Throwing her arms around him, she tried to cuddle up to him, but he made no attempt to push his chair away from the table to give her room.

Puzzled, she pulled back a little, studying him worriedly. In her dreams, she had imagined him rushing to crush her in his arms, lift her, swing her around, show endless love — as

Edward had done. Now here he was, suddenly, sitting uninterested, uncaring — like an empty shell.

John let his arms drop. Nudging her gently aside, he leaned his elbows on the table.

Stung, feeling as though her face had been slapped, Voirrey looked at the other grown-ups. In their eyes, she could see mirrored her own disappointment and fears.

'What's wrong, Daddy? Aren't you pleased to be home?'

John's head jerked up and he looked at her intently. 'Of course, I am! It's what I looked forward to through all the killin', the carnage, the holocaust. It will just take time to adjust.'

'Adjust to what?' Henry questioned. 'You're home now. Safe amongst people who love you. Back with your family. As soon as you're ready you can get back to your job an' settle back into your normal life.'

John shook his head. 'You make it sound so easy, Daa. It's not as simple as that, though. I don't know what normal is any more. Normal to me for the last years has been a muddy trench, death, smell, heat, cold, insects, killin', stayin' alive. An' fear! Most of all fear! I just don't know any more.'

'Why not? I don't understand!' There was a catch in Margaret's voice.

'Don't you see? Are you all so blind?'

'I can only see you are home. You are well. You are still whole. The war is ended an' life must go on — jus' as it did before.'

'It can not go on just as before. Life is different now. Everything is different now. The war has changed everything. I am not the same. I left here, but a poor farm worker over three years ago. Oh, I'd had an education — and done well — but I'd never had the chance to use it. Until the war, I'd only ever been off this Island for those few years at College. Never seen anything of the rest of the world. Never really known what life was all about!'

· CHAPTER 22 ·

'An' now you think you do?' Henry sighed deeply.

'I think so. There's more to life than will ever be found on this dreary little island!'

'For some, perhaps. Not for all. The war is ended now an', wi' it, all the adventure an' excitement o' that other life. Your rightful place now is here, being a husband to your wife an' a father to your daughter. The soldier ended along wi' the war. The farmer is home. Your duty now is here, caring for your family. After all, it is what you have here that you were fightin' to keep the world good for.'

'Duty?' John shook his head sadly. 'It'll take a while to adjust. But I will settle.'

Voirrey looked apprehensively from one face to the other. She could sense something going drastically wrong, but was at a loss to understand.

'I'm goin' for a walk!' John stood up so quickly the chair almost toppled over.

'Can I come wi' you?' Voirrey asked hopefully.

John scowled at her for a moment, then shrugged. 'I s'pose so.'

Voirrey ran behind as he strode to the door, pulling on her coat as she hurried out into the cold February night air. Pushing her hand into his, she gripped tightly but found him unresponsive. After a moment, he firmly extricated his hand, pushing it deep into his pocket.

Tears stung her eyes, but she stayed abreast of her father as he marched briskly towards Barnell.

At the road end, she hesitated nervously. 'This was the las' place the hearse was seen.'

John stopped in his tracks, frowning. 'What hearse?'

"Twas a ghos' hearse. Used to appear when someone from hereabouts was killed in the war. People said it brought the ghos' of the dead person to tell his kin.'

John snorted. 'Ghosses indeed! I've never heard such superstitious nonsense! There's no such things as ghosses. Jus' stories made up by ol' wives who got nothin' better to do wi' their time.' He spun on his heel and marched angrily up Barnell.

"Tis true! It came fus' on the corner, then at the Vicarage, then here.' She trotted after John, struggling to keep up.

'You saw it, you say?'

'Aye.'

'When?'

Voirrey felt her lips tremble. 'The night Uncle Edward died!' She caught hold of his arm. 'Please don't walk so fast, Daddy!'

John slackened his pace. 'Are you sure? Did you not just imagine it?'

'No. I really saw it. So did Daa an' Mr Callow. That was when I knew for sure he was dead!' Her voice hiccoughed in a sob. 'Mrs. Clucas saw it, too, the night Stanley died!'

John stopped, looking intensely into her eyes. 'When was that, then?'

Voirrey thought about it. So much had happened since then. 'Twould have bin late in September. Not las' year — the one before. Mrs Clucas saw the hearse an' she knew Stanley was dead then, but 'twas weeks before she got the letter tellin' her. About two weeks before Uncle Edward!'

'Aye.' John looked thoughtful. 'That'd be when it happened all right. He jus' stuck his head above the trench an' got it all but shot off!'

Voirrey shuddered and felt her stomach clench. It frightened her that he had sounded so dispassionate about it. 'It must've bin awful,' she whispered.

John shrugged almost nonchalantly. 'Not really. Jus' another body. You get used to it when you see it every day. At least he died quickly — without any pain. Some scream for hours! Days

CHAPTER 22

even! Often we heard men screamin' for help – out on no-man's land, but we couldn't reach them. We just had to listen until they finally died an' went quiet.' He reached the glen gate and leaned on it, looking absently towards the tholtans.

Voirrey climbed to sit atop the gate, studying his profile incredulously. 'How can you get used to watching people die or suffer? I could never get used to all that blood. I'd be sick!'

'You had to be able to take it. If you didn't you'd go mad — as many men did. To survive you had to get to like death — other people's; an' to enjoy killin''

Voirrey felt quite ill. 'You didn't, did you? Like killin', I mean?'

'Not at first. In the beginnin', whenever I fired a shot I felt quite sick, thinkin' I might ha' killed or maimed someone. Then after I'd watched many of my comrades suffer an' die I was glad to take my revenge on the Bulgars!'

'I was glad when you were in hospital in Malta an' I knew you was safe an' comfortable.'

John gave a snorting laugh. 'I wasn't! At first, when I was really ill an' weak I didn't mind. But after I recovered a bit I was impatient to be back in the action. One thing about young Stanley bein' shot was it made me keen to kill as many of the enemy as possible. It gave me pleasure to kill then. Every one o' them who died made Stanley's death more worthwhile!'

Voirrey was shivering uncontrollably. 'I'm cold, Daddy. Can we go home?'.

He continued, not hearing. 'I'll miss the war, girl. The excitement o' it. Life has been tedious since it ended an' it'll be even worse on this wearisome Island.'

'I'm goin' home!' Voirrey jumped from the gate, starting down the lane. After a moment's hesitation, John followed.

They walked home without speaking, the frosted grass and iced puddles crunching under their feet. The music from the prison drifted across to them. It was noticeably quieter now, with so many of the prisoners gone. How strange it would seem when the last of the men left and there was no longer music or floodlighting.

The city which had so suddenly sprouted, like a crop of mushrooms, on the fields of Knockaloe, was fading more rapidly than it had grown. Soon, now, the last prisoners would be gone. Knockaloe would be a ghost town. No more lights. No more music. No more, the enchanted orchestra that had brought so much magic to her life. Voirrey would no longer be the fairy princess in her castle of ice, listening to her musicians. Gone would be the Prima Ballerina and the greatest ice-skater the world would ever know!

Voirrey stood at her window that night, the frosty ferns on the pane distorting the floodlights. The dream — oftimes a nightmare — would be over soon and Patrick, once more, would be returned to being just another sleepy little village.

And Kurt would be gone too! A razor-sharp pain stabbed into her heart.

'Daddy looks the same — well almost,' Voirrey told Kurt a few weeks later. 'But he's not like the same person at all. He seems so harsh and cruel now.' She was thankful that, with the war over and the numbers of prisoners and guards reduced, the vigilance of the watch had been slackened. It was quite easy for her now to talk openly with Kurt.

'Well, you know,' Kurt replied sympathetically, 'He was away for a long time, fighting, killing, seeing his friends suffer and die. Living in fear for his own life. It could take a long time for him to hide it all away in the back of his mind. He could not possibly have returned unscarred and unchanged.'

A guard appeared from behind a hut and stood watching

them. Voirrey eyed him warily, but after a moment he smiled, shrugged, flapped a hand and turned away.

'But he has changed completely, Kurt. He told me he enjoyed killing and was sorry the war ended because now he can kill no more!'

Kurt shook his head sadly. 'I don't know what to say, Voirrey. I can only hope he will recover in the end. Just keep praying for him.'

'You say that as though he were ill.'

'Well of course he is. There are all sorts of illnesses, and his is one of the mind. Let's hope that time will heal.'

Time didn't heal!

John shut everyone out.

Promptly after his return, he went back to his pre-war job on the farm. Every evening he came home grumbling about the way the farm was being run and the work he was expected to do.

'Everyone here is so petty!' He exploded one night. 'This Island is so petty — and every person on it!'

'What on earth has angered you so?' Henry asked, startled at the sudden outburst.

Today Joshua was complainin' to me about how little there was to eat here during the war. *To me* — mark you! I told him, in no uncertain terms, how lucky he'd been. *We* had only two biscuits an' a tin o' corned beef each day. Tea was like liquid gold — we were lucky to get one cup of tea a week. We had to sleep in trenches full o' rain an' urine an' worse, wi' rottin' bodies on the ground around us. Rats crawlin' over us; biting at us! An' Joshua whines about how poor conditions were here!'

Voirrey's heart wrenched and she moved to comfort him, winding her arms around his chest.

Gripping her shoulders, he pushed her roughly away. 'For

God's sake, child, stop fawning over me all the time! Just give me space,' He snarled.

With a sob, she wheeled and ran weeping up the stairs.

Henry rounded on him. 'She's your daughter, for goodness sake! She loves you. Have you no idea how she longed for you to return? Prayed every night for just that. Do you think you're the only one who suffered? Voirrey suffered too — perhaps more than you in some ways. We *all* suffered!' he snarled.

The arguments raged on endlessly, through the long hours of darkness.

Voirrey lay on her side, weeping until she had no more tears to cry. She lay, staring sightlessly at the square of window. Night arched darkly above her, but she could not sleep. Her loneliness and emptiness were complete.

Less than a week later she arrived home from school to find herself in the midst of yet another row.

'But why did you hit him, for God's sake? You an' Joshua was always such good friends. He put another man out o' work to give you your job back!'

'I didn't ask him for the job, did I? I don't want his charity. Well, now he can give it back to the other poor fellow, for *I* don't want it!'

'Why John? You need that job. How are you goin' to get another now?'

'I'll get one. But it won't be tedious farm work. I didn't spend all those years goin' to school jus' to spend my life labourin' on some other bugger's farm. Nor will I work among people who spend their time tellin' me how hard they've had it! I'm goin' to get some rabbits!' Grabbing his gun from where it leaned against the table, John stormed out, pushing Voirrey roughly aside in the doorway.

CHAPTER 22

'Why does he always have to take that shotgun?' Margaret's eyes were tortured. 'He never does bring home a rabbit!'

'It's as though he's lived with a gun in his hand so long it's become a part o' him. An extension o' his body.' Henry spoke thoughtfully.

Voirrey listened, distraught, to the endless arguments which became longer and more intense with every passing day. At nights she put a pillow over her head, pressing it against her ear to shut out the angry words.

'You know you're very welcome here as often as you care to come and for as long as you need. I know it is very difficult for you at home just now.' Emily, full of gentle sympathy, encouraged Voirrey to spend as much time at their cottage as she could.

'Thank you. I wish I could stay here all the time, but Mammy needs me.'

'Perhaps you could spend next weekend with us. I'm sure your mother would be relieved to have you away from the arguements for a while.'

Voirrey felt a surge of warm pleasure. 'It would be nice to be out of it for a day or two. I'll ask Mammy tonight.'

Margaret's face lit with relief when Voirrey put it to her. 'Of course, you may, love. It would do you good. Emily has been such a good friend to us.' Her eyes clouded. 'Especially since your father came home so changed. I don't know how I could have survived these last weeks without her support.'

Voirrey knew Emily had been spending all her spare time at the cottage trying, with her gentle patience, to call a truce in John's mental war. Several times she had been forced to flee in terror when he had reared over her, calling her an interfering witch and ordering her from his home. Henry had intervened, pointing out that the cottage was, in fact, his and John only a lodger.

Voirrey let out a muffled cry, catching John's arm as he rounded on Henry, looking as though about to strike him. 'No, Daddy!' she screamed.

He shook her off angrily then, grabbing the gun, stormed out, slamming the door behind him.

Running through to the parlour, Voirrey stood watching him stride towards Barnell, his jaw set tight, the gun clamped firmly in his hand.

'Oh Daddy,' she whispered helplessly. Tears flowed unchecked, burning a channel down her face, past the corners of her mouth to drip on her pinafore.

An arm was laid gently along her shoulders. ''Tis a cross we're all goin' to have to bear for a while, child!' Eleanor said softly.

'It's as if he hates us!' Voirrey weepingly told Kurt one day.

'War teaches men to hate. He learned to enjoy the excitement of the kill. Like the gentry who mount their horses and follow the hounds to trap a fox. The thrill of the chase. It is in man's nature to be aggressive. I shall pray things come well for him soon.'

'But it's been over two months now since he came home an' he seems to get worse. He's causin' everyone so much pain. I see my mother growin' older too quickly.'

Kurt felt the aching frustration of being able to do little. He had watched Voirrey turn painfully from an innocent child to a young woman. He longed to take the girl in his arms, give her comfort, but between them, always, was the damnable hedge of thorns.

Voirrey straggled towards the cottage a few days later, dragging her heels. Arriving home nowadays was a dreaded experience. She remembered when she used to run home, full of excitement, to a house filled with love and happiness. Eager

CHAPTER 22

to tell of her day at school. To show off what she had learned. But that was years ago! A lifetime ago! Had it ever really been as she remembered? It was like a dream now.

Now even Lily wouldn't come to the cottage, so scared was she of John's violent outbursts.

Long before she reached the gate, Voirrey heard the voices raised in anger and was relieved Lily had not come home with her.

'That's eight jobs now! Eight you've lost! You'll find it hard to get another. People know about you now!' Henry shouted.

'Know what? What do people know about me?'

'That you cause trouble. Pick fights. Everyone has tried so hard. Given you jobs you don't deserve — or appreciate. They've made allowances because you were away in the war. And you thank them by makin' mischief. You accuse other people o' bein' petty an' complainin', but it seems to me you are the one doin' all the moanin'!'

John's face turned from red to purple. 'Well, no man need pity me nor condescend to give me a job again!' he roared, spittle splashing at the corner of his mouth.

Picking up a chair, he hurled it violently across the room. It flew, narrowly missing Henry, to crash into the large stone crocks. One of them shattered and Voirrey watched, spellbound, as in slow motion, the pieces. of clay flew in every direction. Salty water spurted from the holes, spreading quickly across the kitchen floor. With it slithered dozens of silvery herring, looking almost to be alive and swimming again.

Without another word, John snatched the gun and pounded from the house. The door crashed behind him, trembling on its hinges.

He left behind him a deathly, shocked hush.

Insides churning and hands trembling, Voirrey took a large

bowl from the larder and, without a word, began to rescue the fish from the floor.

Eleanor and Margaret resignedly set about mopping up the mess.

In the months that followed, John refused to attempt to find work. Withdrawing ever further inside himself, he spent his days aimlessly wandering the lanes and lhergies, gun in hand, ever on the alert. For what — no one knew. Occasionally, but not too often, he brought home a rabbit.

One evening John sat quietly in the kitchen. He seemed more at peace, Voirrey thought, than she had seen him since his return. His elbows rested on the table, thumbs supporting his chin and fingers tented over his lips. Unblinkingly, he contemplated the wall above the door.

Margaret and Eleanor moved quietly, preparing the meal, while Henry scraped mud from his boots. Voirrey tried to concentrate on homework, unsettled by the uneasy, unaccustomed silence.

John slowly picked up a newspaper from where it lay on the table. For a long time, he studied it, frowning, one fore-finger moving around the page as he read different areas of it.

Head lowered, Voirrey covertly watched him through her lashes, wishing she could read his mind.

Suddenly he snapped the paper viciously, bringing four pairs of eyes immediately to bear on him.

'I have made my decision!'

'Decision?' Margaret straightened from the soup she'd been stirring and stared uneasily at him.

'Yes. I'm leavin'!'

'Leavin'? Leavin' where?'

'Must you repeat everything I say? I'm leavin' this island. I can bear its smallness an' pettiness no longer!'

CHAPTER 22

Margaret gasped. Voirrey laid her pencil on the table, slowly closing her book. The ponderous ticking of the grandfather clock echoed through to them, the only sound in the room.

'When, Daddy?' Voirrey's mouth was unaccountably dry.

'Tomorra!'

'Tomorra? We can't be ready to leave so soon!' Margaret protested. 'Where shall we go? Where shall we live?'

John turned a cool, level gaze on her, the calmest he had been since his return. He smiled and for a heart-stopping moment, Voirrey saw the father she had known before this damnable war came to change him. Briefly, her hopes soared.

'I'm goin' alone!' He said it quietly, but it had all the impact of a sword slash.

'Alone? But what about Voirrey an' me? I don't understan'. Where are you goin'?'

'I don't know yet. Somewhere where I can get a decent job that I can use my brains and my education in. Maybe Australia, New Zealand, Canada or the Americas. I shall decide later. First I must get off this suffocating little Island as soon as possible.'

'What about us?' Margaret repeated.

'You?' John looked puzzled for a moment, then shrugged. 'I'll send for you when I'm settled. I'll write when 'tis time for you to come.'

He refused to enter into any further discussion. His mind was made up and would not be changed!

When Voirrey came for breakfast in the morning he was gone!

'He didn't even say goodbye!' she wept.

'Nor to any of us,' Eleanor consoled. 'All he would say was he'll send for you an' your Mammy when he's settled. 'Tis probably best you didn't see him go, the mood he was in.'

Voirrey found her mother at the bottom of the garden, gazing blindly into the stream where trout played and flitted happily amongst the reeds.

'If only *our* lives could be as free of cares as the fishes,' Margaret said quietly. 'Daddy will find somewhere soon an' send for us.'

'An' tear the family apart! Or would we all go?' Voirrey frowned, puzzled.

'You don't think your Granny or Daa would come, do you? They've never lived anywhere but this Island. They're too old to dash off halfway around the world now, on some whim of your father's. Nor would your father want them there!'

'But Daddy used to love them so!'

'Used to — yes. But he's a different man now!'

CHAPTER 23

The weeks stretched out darkly.

'I feel so torn,' Voirrey confessed to Lily on the long walk home from Peel. 'Every day I rush home, hoping there will be a letter from Daddy. But a part of me is relieved when there isn't. I don't want to leave the island an' I don't want to leave Granny and Daa. Neither does Mammy. We do want to be with Daddy, but only if he's like he was before he went away.'

'If he was he'd be here wouldn't he?'

Voirrey kicked viciously at a stone. 'That's what I'd really like,' she said sadly. 'Daddy back here and everythin' just the way it used to be.'

'Has there been a letter today?' she asked apprehensively, putting her schoolbag on the chair when she got home.

Eleanor looked up from the pudding she was mixing, shaking her head sadly. 'No love, nothing.'

'Do you think he'll ever write?'

'When he settles, he will.'

'Will he ever settle? I wish I knew where he was.'

Margaret shrugged helplessly. How she wished she had an answer for the girl. It tore her heart to watch her daughter pining.

Now the days were warming into summer, Voirrey spent long hours at her skylight window, listening to the orchestras. With so many of the musicians gone, it was quieter and seemed more distant. It was late before the camp floodlighting could take over from the natural light. She tried to imagine what it would be like when the camp was all gone. When Kurt was gone! The thought made her wince.

Voirrey, sitting by the parlour window, saw Lily approaching well before she reached the gate. Something in her friend's demeanour stirred a deep feeling of foreboding.

'What's wrong?' she asked when she met Lily at the door.

'Wrong?' Lily frowned, puzzled.

'I watched you coming, you looked upset.'

'Did I? Well, my feelings are mixed really. Partly I'm excited. But mostly I'm sad.' Lily tailed off, watchfully attempting to gauge her friend's reaction.

Voirrey looked at her apprehensively, her blue eyes moist. Mouth dry as chalk she asked, 'You're leavin', aren't you?'

Lily nodded wordlessly.

'When?'

'The twenty-eighth.'

'Of June?'

Another nod.

'That's only two weeks away!' Voirrey's eyes, riveted on Lily, were wide with horror.

'I know. It's a Saturday. Will you come to Douglas — to the boat with us?'

Voirrey nodded, her heart filled with emptiness. Just when the school holidays were about to start she was to lose her friend!

"I'll be alone all through the summer,' she said quietly, her

CHAPTER 23

insides knotted in a tight ball. 'There'll be no one here to talk to me or share my secrets.'

The hair on her neck crawled at the thought, her feeling of devastation was complete. A heavy, cloying feeling of sickness gripped her chest. First Edward, then her father, now Lily, whom she had grown to love more than a sister.

The pair clung together like Siamese twins for the next two weeks. Inseparable throughout their waking hours, they made the most of every moment they had left together.

On the Sunday before Lily's departure, they packed a picnic and walked (for Lily's bike had been sent on ahead, along with most of the Beckinsale's household effects) to the beach at Traie Cabbag.

'We've had a lot of fun here haven't we?' Lily was perched on a rock near the water's edge, scuffing the sand with her toes.

'Aye. Many good times,' Voirrey's eyes were misty. 'All the years we've been together an' now 'tis almost over. Only six days left!'

'Don't be too sad.' Concern cast a shadow over Lily's dark features. 'They've been good years. Our friendship has been one I wouldn't have missed for the world. All the fun we've had. The mischief we've made. The trouble you have got me into!'

Voirrey laughed, tossing a pebble into the waves. 'It took you less courage to do the deeds that frightened you than to admit you were afraid.'

'And you taunted me until I gave in and you got your own way every time!'

They sat there giggling and reminiscing throughout the day, eating their sandwiches when hunger pangs told them it was time. Though the morning had been cool, the afternoon warmed, dissolving the clouds and allowing in the sunshine that unexpectedly brought a real, balmy summer evening.

After sitting in silence for quite some time, enjoying the warmth, they rose and arm in arm, set off up the stony track toward home.

'That's the end of our last weekend together,' Voirrey said sadly as they approached the final corner.

'No, not the last ever. Just for a while. We'll visit each other when we can. Promise you'll write?'

'I promise. Of course I shall write.'

Saturday, June 28th dawned bright and clear.

Voirrey, wakened early by the sun through her skylight, dressed quickly and ran downstairs. Eleanor looked up from the porridge she was stirring on the hob.

'May I go to Lily's straight after breakfast?'

Eleanor chewed her lip doubtfully. 'Don't you think it might be a little early?'

Voirrey shook her head emphatically. 'They'll be about early today. Lily said they have much to do before they leave.'

'Then you'd likely be in the way.'

'I wouldn't! I promise! I'd help! Please, Granny.'

Eleanor softened. With a sigh, she said, 'Well, take the cows to the lhergy fus', then you can go.'

'Thank you.' Voirrey moved to hug her and realised suddenly that her grandmother was now much shorter than she.

'Aren't you tall now?' Eleanor smiled up at her.

Dog, his limbs now stiffening with age, limped more than ever as he helped Voirrey hurry the cattle along.

The Beckinsales' hut, when she arrived, was a bustling hive of activity. There was a simmering air of excitement in the home which, in spite of her sadness, infected Voirrey too.

A gentle tapping on the door, early in the afternoon, heralded

CHAPTER 23

the arrival of Eleanor and Margaret. 'We've just come to pay our respects an' say our farewells.'

'I'm pleased you did. We were just about to leave. There's a train to take us to Peel. Then we catch the normal service train from there to Douglas. The steamer sails at five o'clock.'

'It'll be a long journey. A lot o' travellin' for one day. You'll be late gettin' to Manchester tonight.'

Emily explained they were being met by friends in Liverpool with whom they were spending the night.

Then it was time for them to go.

'I'm glad you came,' Emily said, hugging Eleanor and Margaret in turn.

'We couldn't let you leave without sayin' good-bye. You've bin such good friends. I don't know how we'd ha' survived the war an' its aftermath wi'out you. We must keep in touch.'

Tears flowed freely both inside the train and out when it pulled away from the little station.

Looking out, Voirrey saw Kurt watching them, looking so small and forlorn and alone.

Conversation on the train was spasmodic and stilted. None seemed able to meet another's eye.

Voirrey gazed mistily at the moving world outside, not really conscious of the hedges, sheep and cattle flashing past. The monotonous droning rattle of the metal wheels against the rails had a mesmeric effect.

They straggled slowly to the harbour in Douglas, dragging rather too much luggage.

With every step she took, Voirrey's heart and spirits sank ever lower. It was really happening. Always, she had known this day would come, had dreaded it — at times had almost convinced herself it would never happen. Now it was here — their parting only minutes away as they wandered down the quay!

The steamer was waiting, straining at the hawsers, the gangway in place. Seamen bustled on the dock, making ready to sail.

Voirrey looked around without any real interest, her spirits sinking lower by the minute as she tried hard to think of something to say. In her misery, words would not come.

'I think we'd best go aboard,' Emily suggested quietly.

The girls embraced, clinging tightly, then when they parted Emily and Percy gave Voirrey a tender hug and kiss.

'I wish you every happiness in the future.' Emily stroked the backs of her fingers down Voirrey's stricken face.

Too overcome to trust her voice, Voirrey nodded mutely as she struggled to hold back the tears that stung her eyes.

'Don't forget to write!' Lily called from the far end of the gangway.

The darkness of the ship's interior swallowed them and quite suddenly they were lost from view. Lost from her life! Gone!

Voirrey's world suddenly had another gaping hole!

Within minutes the gangways were withdrawn and the giant hawsers dropped away from the bollards. White water churned in the rapidly increasing gap between the quay and the steamer's hull.

Voirrey desperately, vainly searched the faces along the deck as the boat reversed away toward the harbour mouth. Hot tears blinded her eyes, blurring everything.

Suddenly there was a thundering roar from somewhere further around the bay. She looked up, startled, searching for the source of the sound, wondering if the war had started again. Immediately it was repeated, followed by nineteen more.

Before the final rumble had died, all the steamers and many of the little boats in the harbour added the din of their sirens. Church bells sounded through the odd moments of silence.

· CHAPTER 23 ·

Bewildered and frightened, Voirrey approached a policeman. 'What's happened? Has the war started again?'

The man looked down at her, his eyes twinkling. 'Bless you child, just the opposite. Word has been received to-day that the German Empire has finally signed our Peace Treaty. They'll have learned their lesson now. There will never be another war!'

The ship in the bay disgorged a huge belch of black smoke, then surged forward to carry the Beckinsales to Liverpool.

Voirrey wandered morosely from the quay. With nearly two hours before her train was due, she strolled out along the promenade.

People were thronging out into the streets. The holidaymakers were back, Voirrey noticed, rushing down the steps from their boarding houses. They mingled, singing and cheering, with the townspeople who had filled the roadways, waving flags.

A group of young people converged on Voirrey, grabbing her arms, gigglingly involving her in a lively, ungainly dance.

In spite of herself, the excitement of the moment took its hold and she felt her spirits lifting. Laughing, she linked arms with other youngsters and threw herself wholeheartedly into the dance.

A motor lorry, the first Voirrey had ever seen, drove along the seafront, blasting a noisy horn at the pedestrians who wandered in its path. When it passed Voirrey saw it was decorated with many allied flags. A group of boy-scouts with bugles blew the 'All Clear.'

Carried along by the tidal wave of bodies, she found herself near the Council Chamber in Ridgeway Street, from where the Mayor of Douglas was making a victory speech. Bunting and flags flew from all the buildings and confetti fell like summer rain.

Still trembling with excitement, Voirrey jumped from the train before it was properly stopped in Peel station. Hurrying home, almost at a run, she heard the clink of horseshoes on the stones behind.

'You like a ride, girlie?'

She stopped, turning. 'Yes please, Mr Callow. Have you heard the news?'

'What news is that, lass?'

Pulling herself up to the seat at his side, she blurted, 'The Germans ha' finally signed the Peace Treaty today. There won't ever be a war again!'

Joseph's face lit up. 'That so? Then we'd better hurry an' let everybody know!' He gee'd Ned into a rhythmic canter.

The cart swayed and jolted across the ruts, sliding on the corners, its load of fish sloshing from side to side.

Voirrey clung for dear life to the seat, fearing she was going to be tipped to the ground at any moment.

Kurt was in the compound and when he saw her in the cart he moved closer to the wire, smiling.

'Stop here, please, Mr Callow,' Voirrey asked quietly.

Joseph leaned back on the reins and Ned managed to end his wild dash close to the shop, where Caesar stood, watching still.

Jumping down from the cart, Voirrey ran back to Kurt. 'Have you heard the news?' she asked excitedly.

'Yes. It came through a while ago.'

'Isn't it wonderful! There won't ever be another war, the policeman in Douglas told me! An' I'm sure they'll soon send you home now.'

'I hope so. I have doubts though.'

She noticed Caesar's eyes on her, but he made no unfriendly move.

'They no longer have any reason to keep you here now, do they?'

'Not here. But they may not send me home. Not to England, I mean!'

CHAPTER 23

'Where else *could* they send you?'

'Germany!'

'Germany? But why there?'

'They are deporting most of us to our countries of origin. Only about one man in six is being allowed to stay in Britain.'

Voirrey shook her head. What was the sense in that? Surely they could no longer be regarded as enemy aliens?

'Well I'm sure you'll be one of the ones who are allowed to stay in England,' she told him, trying to convey a confidence she did not feel. 'Now I must go an' tell the news to my family.'

Turning, she ran toward the corner. Joseph had moved on to spread his glad tidings, but Caesar still stood there.

'Isn't it excitin' news Mr Quine?'

'It is indeed, but you know, lass, I don't think you should spend so much time talkin' to the prisoners.'

Voirrey glanced back toward the camp. 'Just one prisoner, Mr Quine, an' he's very nice. He would never harm me.'

Caesar grunted but said no more.

Summer drifted into early autumn. Voirrey, empty and lost, was relieved when the time came to return to school.

Many a lonely hour the girl had spent wandering the country lanes, with Dog limping stiffly in her wake. His rheumatic old joints no longer allowed him to bound ahead chasing rabbits — or shadows — though he courageously followed her for hours.

Somehow, without Lily, the bike had lost its appeal and had lain unused throughout the school holidays.

"Tis like a different world altogether, Dog.' Voirrey caressed his silken ears. Lovingly he twisted his head to lick her wrist. Sitting high on the Creggans, she looked down on the camp. It was all still there. The huts. The wire-bounded compounds.

The railway sleeper roads. Even the railway was still there, now rarely used.

But the noise! The activity! The many thousands of people (Voirrey had heard there had been 28,000 in all, including the guards and their families) were no longer there. Only a few hundred men left now and soon they, too, would be gone. Most of the compounds were empty, deserted, weeds starting to poke their heads through the cinders of the exercise yards.

'It will be like a ghost town, Dog. Then I s'ppose they'll come an' take all the huts away, an' the barbed wire' an' turn it into a farm again. It will be like it was before. As though none o' it never happened. Except for all the men who went to war and never came home!'

Over to her left, the Three Legs of Man stood out on the hillside as clearly as they ever had.

Clear water gurgled up from a spring, to run away from her down the hill toward the camp.

A few prisoners strolled idly in a compound near the road.

'Let's go an' see if Kurt's there.'

When she rose, the birds, watchful for any sign of danger, ceased their song and for a moment all the natural sounds of the hillside were stilled.

Kurt was there, leaning on a post, kicking absently at a tuft of grass, his head hanging.

Voirrey approached him, a little concerned about his demeanour.

Starting, aware of her for the first time, his head shot up. His eyes, sparkling with an unshed tear and seemingly unable to meet hers, were fixed on the distant hills, where the wind blew a rainy mist across their peaks.

'I have had news,' He sighed.

'Not good news?'

· CHAPTER 23 ·

'Not good news at all.' His head shook slowly. 'I am to leave here next Friday.'

For a moment Voirrey's heart sank, then she felt for him and forced a smile to her face. 'Oh I am pleased. You'll be free at last. You can go home!'

Kurt shook his head again, more emphatically this time.

'No. You don't understand. I am not to be repatriated. They say I must be deported to Germany!'

'Oh, no!' Voirrey's horror reflected in her eyes. 'Not Germany? Why?'

'Because I was born there. So that makes me German. I know no one there. I have not lived there since I was three years old.'

'But what will you do there? What does your wife say?'

Kurt looked deep into her eyes and she could see the most awful, heart-wrenching pain behind his.

'My wife is British. She refuses to live with me in Germany. And I can't blame her for that, heartbreaking as it is.' His body sagged and suddenly he seemed to halve in size. 'So now, my little friend, I have nothing. This war I had no part in has left my life empty. My only child is dead. My wife has left me and I have no one to care.'

Voirrey pushed her fingers between the jagged wires and he forced his through to meet them.

'You have me. I will always love you. I'll always care.' Tears pressed, aching, behind her eyes.

'And I shall always remember and love you. How good a friend you have been. These years in Knockaloe would have been unbearable without your friendship.' He squeezed her hand too tightly, but she did not complain.

Voirrey stood by the camp gate with Henry, sadly watching them muster the last one hundred and seventy-five prisoners.

The awful day had finally arrived. It was the day she had dreaded, but she had forced herself to come. Somehow she had to manage to say a last farewell to Kurt.

With a terrible, aching emptiness, she watched as the prisoners were being lined up in the compound. Flanked by the guards, they were marched towards the gate.

Kurt's eyes, locked with her's, showed an agonised loneliness and suddenly she knew *his* pain was the greater. She had her mother and grandparents, he had no one — nothing — not even the country he had grown up in!

The column marched through the gates and as they turned into the roadway, Voirrey ran forward. Throwing her arms around Kurt, she clung desperately.

Stopping, he wrapped his arms tightly around her, kissing the top of her head. 'I hope your father returns soon, little one. I've had to leave my fuchsia. Look after it for me.'

A guard stood patiently for a moment, then tugged his sleeve. 'Sorry chum, but you've got to go!'

Kurt tore himself away, stumbled a few steps then, looking wretched, turned again to face her. 'Take care of our plant until I return for it.' Then he wheeled and stumbled away.

Voirrey watched through a curtain of tears until the straggle of men reached the corner.

Kurt turned, waved once, then he was gone, leaving a terrible void in her heart.

Suddenly Voirrey realised her grandfather was beside her, his arm comfortingly around her shoulder.

Glancing up, she said thickly, 'I really loved him, Daa! When he was here I always felt as if Daddy wasn't so far away.'

CHAPTER 23

Henry nodded thoughtfully. 'I know, love. I know. I saw the resemblance too.'

Hand in hand they wandered through the unguarded gates into the empty camp.

In the centre of the exercise yard, Voirrey saw a rusty tin with a healthy fuchsia growing in it. With a cry of joy, she ran to pick it up.

Looking toward where the column of men had vanished, she gently fingered the leaves of the plant.

'I shall love this as I love you, Kurt,' she whispered.

✦ THE END ✦

EPILOGUE

This has been the story of one Manx family's hardships and heartbreaks during and immediately after the 'Great War.' All the stories are as told to me, though possibly not quite in the correct chronological order.

It was told to me by my mother-in-law, Margaret Louvima (Lou) Moore Kelly, nee Quirk, who was 'Voirrey'. At the time of writing, she did not want her own name used, as she felt it would embarrass her, nor would she tell me the proper names of any of the other 'characters' in the story. Over the course of two years, I spent hundreds of hours talking to, questioning and, most of all listening in fascination as Lou's story unfolded. It was like hearing a tale of life in another world. For instance, I found it almost impossible in this day and age to imagine a little girl, from the age of four, walking a mile each way, twice a day, to take cattle to pasture, no matter what the weather. But this, Lou did every day, unless the fields were thick with snow, until the day she finally left home to go to college. Her days, from 6 a.m. to 6 p.m. were spent either travelling to and from school and at school itself. The rest of each weekday was spent either moving the cattle or doing homework.

'Voirrey' wrote to Lily for a year or two after she returned to Manchester, but as they both pursued their own lives the pen-friendship gradually tailed off and they eventually lost touch.

Kurt, unfortunately, just disappeared. Lou waited almost as anxiously to hear from him as from her father but never received a single letter. She desperately wanted to get in touch with him but had no idea at all of how to go about it. All she could do was to get on with her life, with it always in the back of her mind that when she was older she would try to trace him. However, by the time she was old enough her life was too full and she never quite got around to it.

When she finished at secondary school Lou won a scholarship to college. On what was probably one of the hardest days of her life she left home, and the heart of a very close-knit, loving family to continue her education at Hereford College. For the first few months, she was dreadfully homesick and spent much of her time in tears. Had it not been for a friend, Nancy Bridson, who went with her from Eastern Districts Secondary School and took her under her wing, she told me she did not think she would have been able to cope with the separation.

Lou graduated from college as a school teacher and returned to the Island to follow her career.

In 1931, with both grandparents then dead, Lou and her mother bought a newly built house in Crosby, a developing village about four miles west of Douglas. Two years later she married a fellow school teacher, Stanley Kelly from Peel, who had been an observer in the Royal Flying Corps during the Great War. They continued to live in the house in Crosby and had three sons.

Her mother died in 1941, still firmly believing that one day her husband would return for her.

Lou never heard from her father again until the day of her silver wedding anniversary in 1958. She and Stanley were out visiting a neighbour on that day when the second of their three sons, Mike, answered the phone. The caller was his grandfather, speaking in a loud 'American' accented voice, who wanted to be picked up from Ronaldsway airport.

When Mike asked how he would recognise him his grandfather just said, 'You'll know me, son! You'll know me!'

Mike borrowed his father's car on some pretext and shot off down to Ronaldsway, intrigued. The first person he saw was a big man wearing a large Stetson hat. Unmistakably the 'American' who had phoned.

It eventuated that 'John' had gone to Canada after leaving the Isle of Man, found himself a woman and immediately forgotten about the wife and daughter he had deserted. He had joined the Canadian police force, rising to the rank of Detective Inspector.

'John' tried to ingratiate himself with his daughter, but she had been too hurt and refused to be taken in by him. He was a likeable rogue, but completely selfish and quite dishonest. In the time he visited he tried to talk Lou into parting with an antique brass lamp, among other things, claiming it was his. However, she would not be hoodwinked because she knew with certainty that it had belonged to her grandparents. It is the lamp that is mentioned on occasions in the story and is now one of my husband's and my most treasured possessions.

Eventually, he took himself off back to Canada and never made any effort to contact Lou, (Voirrey) again. The next she heard of him was many years later when she received a letter from his lady friend telling her he had died, aged ninety-three. With the letter came a cheque for one hundred pounds, which he had left in his will to 'my friend Lou Kelly and her three sons.' It was the final rejection, the most hurtful deed he had ever done, for which his daughter never forgave him until her dying day.

Lou nursed this story all her life, apparently just waiting for someone to tell it to. When I married her middle son, Mike, in 1988 she and I became very close friends, spending a great deal of time together. As she talked to me about her childhood and the impact the camp at Knockaloe had made on her life, I realised she was telling me something of great importance and started drawing it out of her. She was telling me things that probably no else could tell, and that would be lost, should anything happen to her. The more she talked the more the memories flooded back and many times we wept together for the child she had been and the suffering she had endured.

Nor did she ever recover from her fear of the 'fairies' in Barnell glen. As an adult she dared to go into the glen if accompanied, but said she could never go alone, and not under any circumstances would she ever go there after dark. She was certain she could sense a 'presence' in the glen.

Lou had terminal cancer when she told me the secrets she had kept for over sixty-five years, but thankfully she lived long enough to read my manuscript, enjoy it and make sure I'd got it right. My greatest thrill was in knowing how much it meant to her to know that someone thought her story was important enough to want to document it.

She slipped from life on the 9th of March, 1990, seventy-five years to the day from when her father first sailed from the Island with the 1st Manx Service Company. What a tragedy it would have been if her story had gone to the grave with her!

At the time of printing, her widower, Stanley Kelly, by then ninety-four years of age, lived on, back in Peel where he was born. He finally died in 1998, at the age of ninety-nine.

The wheel had moved full circle!

www.ingramcontent.com/pod-product-compliance
Lightning Source LLC
Chambersburg PA
CBHW031409290426
44110CB00011B/310